In a Box

In a Box

Gender-Responsive Reform,
Mass Community Supervision,
and Neoliberal Policies

Merry Morash

UNIVERSITY OF CALIFORNIA PRESS

University of California Press
Oakland, California

Library of Congress Cataloging-in-Publication Data

Names: Morash, Merry, 1946- author.
Title: In a box : gender-responsive reform, mass community
    supervision, and neoliberal policies / Merry Morash.
Description: Oakland, California : University of California Press,
    [2024] | Includes bibliographical references and index.
Identifiers: LCCN 2023038215 (print) | LCCN 2023038216
    (ebook) | ISBN 9780520393509 (cloth) | ISBN 9780520393516
    (paperback) | ISBN 9780520393530 (epub)
Subjects: LCSH: Community-based corrections—Michigan. |
    Women parolees—Michigan. | Equality—Michigan. | Criminal
    justice, Administration of—Michigan.
Classification: LCC HV9279 .M58 2024 (print) | LCC HV9279
    (ebook) | DDC 364.6/809774—dc23/eng/20231107
LC record available at https://lccn.loc.gov/2023038215
LC ebook record available at https://lccn.loc.gov/2023038216

33   32   31   30   29   28   27   26   25   24
10   9   8   7   6   5   4   3   2   1

This book is dedicated to the women who shared their experiences and life stories and the probation and parole agents, their supervisors, and the Michigan Department of Corrections leadership who enabled the research and supported the confidential interview process.

Contents

Acknowledgments

The longitudinal nature of the research in this book (up to six interviews over seven years), the many women on probation and parole who participated (402 initially, and 118 in a purposive sample the book features), participation and assistance by 73 probation and parole agents and their supervisors, and the way that we collected and handled data and analysis required the efforts of many people. Much of the data collection from women on probation and parole—three of the interviews and the life story interview—was done in person, which allowed for interviewers to develop relationships with women who agreed to take part. As a result of what we did and how we did it, there are numerous people to thank. I mention a few key Michigan Department of Corrections (MDOC), project leadership, and project staff here, but every transcriber and interviewer and numerous people at the MDOC also facilitated the research. The Michigan State University Foundation and the National Science Foundation (Grant No. 1126162 and Grant No. 1430372) funded the data collection. At the National Science Foundation, Marjorie Zatz, who is now the interim vice president for research and economic development, University of California, Merced, gave invaluable advice during the development of both studies.

Three co-principal investigators for both National Science Foundation grants and the Michigan State University Foundation that funded the research contributed to the grant applications, the details of sampling, and the choice of questions to ask. They are all faculty at Michigan

State University. Professor Sandi W. Smith, Department of Communication, applied theories about communication patterns and agent-to-client memorable messages to shape, analyze, and interpret study findings. Professor Deborah A. Kashy brought expertise in psychology and skills in database management and statistical analysis to the quantitative analyses. Professor Jennifer Cobbina-Dungy conducted several life story interviews and played an important role in integrating theory on redemption from and contamination by past illegal activity as influences on identity development into the research. She also brought attention to the importance of neighborhood crime in women's lives.

Four graduate students played key roles in implementing the research. Miriam Northcutt Bohmert, currently an associate professor at Indiana University, Bloomington, and Jennifer Cornacchione Ross, now an associate professor in social sciences and health policy, Wake Forest University, managed the project during the three years when the first three interviews were conducted. Elizabeth A. Adams, now a faculty member at Temple University, oversaw transcription during that first study and during the three-year follow-up study. She read and checked every transcription against the audiotapes. She also conducted multiple life story and other interviews for the project. Marva Goodson-Miller, an assistant professor at Arizona State University, managed data collection for the period when the last three interviews took place in the project. From the first interview to the last one seven years later, she also conducted interviews, including life story interviews. Two of the many interviewers, Chelsea Wilkins and Kayla Hoskins, completed numerous interviews, including large proportions of the life story interviews. The project inspired Chelsea to complete a master's degree in social work, work as a mental health therapist, and most recently work as a lead research assistant at the University of Michigan. Kayla used data from the project for her master's thesis and PhD dissertation and is a postdoctoral fellow at the School of Medicine, Yale University.

This was a "do-it-yourself" project. We did our own transcription and managed databases not only for the qualitative data central to this book, but also for quantitative data analyzed for numerous articles and book chapters. The exemplary quality of the data shows the dedication and skill of each of the project managers, interviewers, and transcribers, including the many whom I did not mention here.

The MDOC provided open access that allowed us to recruit women on probation and parole and recruit and survey the agents who supervised them. Agents, supervisors, and the department leadership accommodated our intrusions into their busy work schedules and enabled us to recruit 402 women into the research. Doug Kosinski, retired manager of risk, classification, and program evaluation at the MDOC, acted as liaison and made this interface possible. Gregory Straub, field services director; Amanda Elliott, probation parole manager; and Teresa Chandler, communications and culture training specialist and master trainer, answered numerous questions about the history and current state of reforms that affect women on probation and parole. For many years, management and leadership let us carry out our research unhindered and gave us private space to recruit participants and conduct the interviews.

Two individuals provided information, commentary, and insight in the early stages of writing this book. Katherine O'Sullivan See, professor emerita, James Madison College, Michigan State University, read an early draft and used her sociological acumen to make invaluable suggestions. Joanne E. Belknap, professor emerita, ethnic studies at the University of Colorado Boulder, also read that early draft and pointed out key needed alterations and additions.

Abbreviations

AA	Alcoholics Anonymous
ACLU	American Civil Liberties Union
AFDC	Aid to Families with Dependent Children
CMH	Community Mental Health
CPS	Child Protective Services
MDHHS	Michigan Department of Health and Human Services
MDOC	Michigan Department of Corrections
MPRI	Michigan Prisoner Reentry Initiative
NA	Narcotics Anonymous
PPACA	Patient Protection and Affordable Care Act
PTSD	post-traumatic stress disorder
SNAP	Supplemental Nutritional Assistance Program
SSDI	Social Security Disability Insurance
TANF	Temporary Assistance to Needy Families
WIC	Women, Infants, and Children
WRNA	Women's Risk/Needs Assessment

CHAPTER I

The Research, the Context, and the Reform

The second decade of the twenty-first century was an exciting time for correctional reformers with a focus on women in Michigan. The Michigan Department of Corrections (MDOC), which oversees and delivers both probation and parole supervision statewide for individuals convicted of felonies, had just instituted women-specific caseloads. Throughout the state, agents who supervised women sentenced to probation instead of jail or prison and agents who supervised women paroled to community supervision before they completed a prison sentence received training in the special needs of women in trouble with the law and methods to meet those needs. As the only statewide shift toward gender-responsive community supervision in the nation, the reform stood out from documented county and program-level efforts to deliver gender-responsive corrections.[1] The Michigan reform grew out of MDOC staff planning and advocacy for women. Academics have paid only minimal attention to this unique reform. At the inception of the change and increasingly over time, in contrast to academics, practitioners around the country have looked to Michigan as a leader in probation and parole for women. The very large number of U.S. women on probation (718,400 in 2021) and on parole (92,700 in that same year) and the nationwide shift from mass incarceration to mass supervision warrant a close look at how the Michigan gender-responsive reforms affected women.[2]

The early stage of instituting women-specific probation and parole caseloads was also an exciting time to initiate research on Michigan women supervised in the community. The MDOC was keen on obtaining input into practices that supervising agents used with women. I jumped on the opportunity to head up an interdisciplinary team of Michigan State University faculty researchers that included Sandi W. Smith (an expert on interpersonal communication in the Department of Communication), Deborah A. Kashy (an expert in social psychology and statistics in the Department of Psychology), and Jennifer E. Cobbina-Dungy (an expert on reentry from prison in the School of Criminal Justice). Funding from the National Science Foundation and the Michigan State University Foundation made it possible to study the interactions between Michigan women and their supervising agents and the outcomes of these interactions. These grants supported research on agents' communication patterns and relationship styles with clients, how agents addressed the women's needs, and the connection of women's identities to desistance from illegal activity.

All study participants were substance involved, most as users and some as sellers. Because the war on drugs contributed heavily to many women's convictions, this is the largest group of women involved in the justice system.[3] We collected data from both supervising agents and 402 of the women they supervised in repeated interviews spread over seven years. To date, these data have informed numerous journal articles and book chapters that reveal individual-level outcomes explained by the nature of probation and parole agent communication, agents' relationship styles, women's goals and the barriers they face achieving them, and women's identity change. These publications fill a gap in the literature, but the qualitative data for the 118 women presented in this book told a more complex story about the families the women grew up in, schools they attended as youths, and interactions with child-serving agencies intended to protect and treat children. The detailed qualitative data showed that as adults, key influences on women included the communities where they lived and arrays of sometimes connected but often disconnected mental health and substance abuse treatment programs, opportunities for work, and access to social safety-net benefits. These contextual and structural influences had profound effects on how supervision affected women and on women's situations years after they started terms of probation or parole.

This book focuses on a subset of 118 of the women who started the study with at least five prior convictions. Toward the end of the series of interviews, this subset took part in an interview that elicited their life stories. Given their past histories of convictions, the women could provide insight into the process of desistance from repeated illegal be-havior, or for some of them, continuation of drug use and crime. During the entire study, which included four or five interviews plus the life story narrative, the women provided a massive amount of qualitative data in their accounts of their backgrounds, supervision, treatment, efforts to find work, applications for safety-net benefits, and steps they took to im-prove their lives. A compilation of these data and official records made it possible to examine the intertwined and sometimes contradictory effects of community supervision, residential context, income sources, agencies, programs, and broader policy and social structure on the women.

The women who took part in the research revealed how they faced sys-temic obstacles in their efforts to establish healthy and secure lives. The MDOC gender-responsive reforms positively affected individual women, but these positive effects were often diluted or even undone by employ-ment opportunities and justice and social safety-net policies and proce-dures. The ways that racism reduced access to housing, employment, and community resources compounded Black women's barriers to achieving a good life. Women took actions to improve their lives, but they often confronted two irreconcilable choices, neither of which they saw as ideal.

One participant in the research, Tina (pseudonym), made comments that reflected the contextual and structural constraints on correctional re-forms and that suggested the title for this book, *In a Box*. She talked about the help that probation and parole agents could provide and the limita-tions on what they and their clients, including her, could do. Like many women in the study, Tina was abused as a child, and the adults in her life refused to talk about the abuse. After her foster mother abandoned her, she was on her own as an adolescent. Her first husband physically abused her. She differed from other women because her first arrest occurred at age 39, later in life than most women. Her convictions were for embezzlement, home invasion, and three instances of driving under the influence. When she told her life story, she had left her husband and was living in a house that looked to be in good repair, on one of Michigan's many scenic lakes.

Tina summed up her experience on probation and explained what it meant to be "in a box" thus:

> I think that there are some really good people who are probation officers. And I think they are very limited, and they probably become extremely discour-aged because they could probably do more to help individuals. But I think they're put in a box, and we were put in the box, and the outcome I don't think was very helpful then for anybody. I mean Agent Loudell [pseudonym] I will remember because he was, he was really, you could tell he cared. I think

given the opportunity to, he could of really helped some people. But number one their caseloads were overloaded, and they didn't have the time or the resources to help people the way they wanted, he wanted to. . . . It wasn't just about me. They had limits, courts, and rules and whatever. You know they were just as much boxed in as I was.

Reflecting on the life story interview, Tina said she had moved on from the negative events in her past: "Sometimes some things you don't want to think about anymore. You just push it to the side, but it doesn't freak me out like it used to, 'cause it's part of who I am. It's part of my story, so . . . you've moved on. So it's okay."

A CRITICAL FEMINIST FRAMEWORK

This book rests on the traditions of critical feminist theory. Consistent with the feminist framework, the book is about women as decision makers and self-directed actors in contexts and social locations that influenced and constrained them as they strove to do what they wanted to do and be who they wanted to be.[4] Combined with gender, other status differentiations—social class, race, ethnicity, and disability status—influence a person's social location, and social location affects access to basic services and income. Lack of access can promote lawbreaking.[5] Thus, the research considered the intersections (that is, the combinations) of status markers, for instance women who are White, young, with limited education or women who are Black, young, with high school or more education. Early Black feminist activists and scholars directed attention to intersectionality as a correction to a prior failure to recognize that race conditions the connection of being a woman and access to opportunities and resources.[6] The women's life stories analyzed for this book illustrate profound differences between women who are similar in having multiple prior criminal convictions and being on probation or parole but differing in race.

The book is critical in its investigation of a combination of government agencies, programs, regional market conditions for people able to work, and available safety-net benefits for those unable to work. The aim is to show the processes through which women were disempowered and marginalized, or alternatively how they were empowered or empowered themselves in ways that brought them resources and life satisfaction. The attention that I pay to structural and contextual reasons for crime and well-being contradicts theories that identify individual psychological and social attributes such as mental health and antisocial friends as the sole causes of lawbreaking.[7] This emphasis on individual attributes informs widely accepted correctional practices that are based on social learning and behavioral theories that identify internal attributes and change as the key to reducing recidivism.[8] Previously published findings about the women show the importance of internal change but do not show the unimportance of social location and access to resources.[9] I ask the question, "How do women's everyday troubles and illegal activities connect to surrounding context and structures?" My hope is that information about individuals in context and in a social location will inform programs and public policy to empower women enmeshed in the institutions and agencies broadly referred to as "corrections."

Prior findings about the women's identity change as revealed by analysis of the life story interview data provided the impetus for the book. According to narrative identity theory, a life story is a construction of sequential life events that explain a person's identity at the moment the story is told.[10] Life stories connect recollections of past events to the perceived present and imagined future to convey a coherent sense of identity and purpose, and they guide a person's behavior.[11] The life stories that women constructed included chapters and events within the chapters that women saw as important enough to talk about, that reflected their identities, and that they wanted to share, usually to help other women. The story gives meaning to a person's life and explains how she or he self-identifies. Shadd Maruna's groundbreaking research on the connection of desistance from crime to making good out of past illegal behavior inspired the use of the life story interview to understand whether making good of past negative events such as trauma, addiction, and criminal activity constituted redemption and allowed women to develop prosocial identities and behavior.[12] People make good of negative past events by learning from them and by using their experiences to help other people. In contrast to redemption, if people see negative past events as contaminating the present, as spoiling or making bad the present, stagnation occurs. For the women I write about here, quantitative and qualitative analyses showed some connection of stagnation and contamination to continued lawbreaking, but a fairly weak connection between making good use of prior negative experiences and desistance from illegal activity.[13] The weak connection sparked my interest in analyzing the extensive qualitative data collected in two sequential studies for the 118 women who told their life stories. I wanted to understand how context and social location facilitated or interrupted women's shift toward seeing themselves in meaningful law-abiding roles and their actions to change their behavior to match.

METHODOLOGY

The two sequential studies of the same women used a variety of methodologies in multiple interviews with each woman. Based on prior research identifying woman-specific needs in correctional populations, Study 1 focused on gender-specific influences on lawbreaking, including abuse and trauma as children and adults, extreme poverty, mental illness, and stress from parenting.[14] Study 1 also took quantitative measures of probation and parole agent attention to these influences, communication between agents and clients, and agents' relationship styles. These data have been extensively analyzed for past publications, which are referenced when they are relevant to the qualitative findings presented in this book. Both Study 1 and Study 2 elicited women's qualitative accounts of how probation and parole agents and community-based agencies responded to their self-identified needs and how human services workers responded to their efforts to obtain safety-net benefits. The research also collected information on women's experiences in mental health and substance abuse treatment. To gather information about women's agency—their self-directed actions—at each of five interviews, interviewers asked women what they had done recently to improve their lives. Study 2 also included the life story interview during which women identified chapters of their lives and answered follow-up questions about the meaning of key episodes in these chapters.[15] During the life story interviews, the fifth in the interview sequence, most women described their childhoods and early relationships; how they started to use drugs and break the law; periods of increased illegal behavior and drug use; having and raising children; and their current situation, including parenting demands, drug use, and crime. The life story interviews ended with questions about challenges, plans, and the effects of telling the life story. The life stories highlighted a complex combination of contextual influences, barriers and opportunities, episodes and events, and outcomes that women included and that reflected their identities. I accepted the story elements that women presented as the important parts of their lives at the time the stories were told.

Although women's qualitative accounts are the primary data, I supplemented them with two types of official records. Agents' case notes supplemented women's descriptions of probation and parole agent actions. Official state crime statistics provided information on convictions and time spent in prison before, during, and after the years when interviews were conducted.

Feminist research approaches informed the collection of qualitative data and the analysis. Consistent with feminist methods and the project staff's promise to share women's stories and accounts in publications and presentations, much of this book presents women's verbatim statements.[16] Treating women's perceptions of supervising probation and parole agents, potential and actual employers, and program and agency personnel as the primary information source focused attention on not only the women who were supervised in the community but the people with power over them.[17] To establish generalizability of findings, many of the endnotes link the women's statements and stories to theory and findings from other studies. However, the text within the chapters keeps the focus on women's accounts and interpretation of their circumstances.

Also consistent with feminist methodology, interviewer selection and training promoted a nonjudgmental, supportive attitude and communication of equality, with the study participants being experts on effects of probation and parole and on their lives, and the interviewers listening and asking questions to learn.[18] The interviewers opened with statements about wanting to hear what the women had to say and the hope that this information would help to improve probation and parole. Especially for the life story interview, interviewers emphasized that women should shape the interview and share whatever they considered to be valuable information to help other women on probation and parole and to improve the supervision experience.

Women's reflections on the life story interview indicated the nature of their relationships with the interviewers and the project. Many women expressed approval or fondness for the interview team. For example, Molly commented, "They [the researchers] got some good people on here," and Eve said she could feel the "heart" of her prior interviewer. Women confirmed the nonjudgmental, respectful ways the interviewers treated them. Ariana said, "I know you not judging me at all. You care about my well-being." Freya told the interviewer, "I can tell you're compassionate, and you really listen and that means a lot." Hope's detailed reflection on how the life story interview unfolded and how it affected her matched other women's sentiments:

> It affected me to know that somebody's willing to hear my story. To want to know my story, to not see me as a different person—just see me as Hope, not see me as that number and not see me as a crack head prostitute who lost their kids. . . . [Y]our facial expressions never change. You know what I'm saying? You still kept the same [look] about you. You were never like . . .

lost their kids! . . . [Y]ou asked for the [chapter] titles of the book and you wanted to—you were interested, you really wanted to know really what was those chapters' meaning. You know, it wasn't like, "Okay, you finished now? Okay, I've got to go to the next question, I'm trying to get out of here you know?" You showed that you was really interested. So, and that helps me, you know, that helps a lot because people say they want to hear what you got to say, but soon as you get to talking and it's something uncomfortable, "Girl I just got this text [phone message]. I will get with you."

The effects and meanings that women associated with taking part in the research provided assurance of the trustworthiness of findings. Asked about the effect of telling her life story, Gabriela said, "I've shared my story probably more than the average person ever will in their life. . . . If what I am telling somebody can help them, then that's all that matters. They might remember something I said 10 years from now and it finally clicks and makes sense in their heads." Fiona expressed similar feelings, noting why she was telling her story: "Whatever I can do to try to help somebody else not feel the way that I fucking feel, so be it." Women's motivation for sharing their life stories and the meaningfulness they attached to doing so rested in part on the relationship with the interviewer and prior interviewers who worked on the research, as well as on women's perceptions of the larger project.

Of course, not every life storyteller told detailed life stories. Heidi shared the least amount of information in the interviews. She indicated that she had been arrested on an old warrant for a crime she did not commit, and she skipped or answered "don't know" to most questions. She summed up her thoughts and feelings about the life story interview: "It was okay. I don't have any more comments." Heidi's response to the interview was an anomaly, since most (94 of 118) women explicitly identified a benefit to themselves or help to another person as actual or possible interview outcomes, and those who did not usually said there was no effect of the interview or there was no negative effect.

Because justice-involved women have unique needs, over multiple interviews open-ended questions about topics discussed with probation and parole agents were based on a needs assessment tool, the Women's Risk/Needs Assessment (WRNA), developed from feminist theory and research on women's pathways to illegal behavior.[19] Also consistent with feminist theory that highlights intersectionality, the analysis informing this book examined racial, age, and residential community differences. Reflecting Michigan demographics, nearly all women identified as White, Black, both White and Black, or a mix of one of these racial identities and Hispanic ethnicity. At the start of the research, women ranged from 19 to 56 years old, and they were about equally distributed in the age categories 30 and under, 31 to 40, and 41 and older. They lived in a variety of communities that included rural areas, small towns, prosperous suburbs, distressed cities, and prosperous suburbs. Only a few identified as trans or nonbinary. The variations among the women made it possible to examine differences and similarities between Black and White women and women from different types of communities and to determine whether findings held across women varying in life stage.

The remainder of this chapter places women in three contextual and structural locations that affected what gender-responsive correctional reforms accomplished and the degree to which women could control their lives. First, to place the women in neighborhoods and communities, I report on a virtual tour of the block or the rural areas where they lived when they told their life stories. As shown in later chapters, this tour and women's descriptions of how they avoided crime and victimization in their places of residence highlight racial differences and related urban/suburban/rural differences in women's exposure to crime, opportunities for both legal and illegal work, and access to resources. Second, I describe economic conditions in Michigan and national and state neoliberal policies based on the belief that individuals could and should pull themselves out of poverty, drug use, and criminal activity.[20] These policies heavily affected the women on probation and parole by magnifying differences due to poverty. Race, community location, and financial well-being created intersections of social location that also affected the women. Third, consistent with the focus on probation and parole supervision, this introductory chapter ends with a description of supervision practices in Michigan at the time of the research. This description explains how courts influence supervision and the statewide role of the MDOC field services division in handling probation and parole for individuals convicted of a felony. It includes detail about early stages of MDOC's transition to an emphasis on responding to the unique backgrounds and needs of women.

RESIDENTIAL CONTEXT

Interviewers recruited women into the study from the caseloads of probation and parole agents in 16 of the 84 Michigan counties located within two hours' or shorter drive from the research office. The counties included 68 percent of the state's population in 2011 and all major metropolitan areas in the state. The sampling strategy enabled research staff to access women from large and small cities, small towns, and rural areas; however, it had the downside of decontextualizing women from the varied places where they lived and obscuring their opportunities (or lack thereof) to relocate. Women interviewed for this book lived in high-crime, racially segregated urban neighborhoods, better resourced and safer urban neighborhoods, high-poverty suburbs at the edge of Detroit and Grand Rapids (the two highest population cities in the state), well-to-do city suburbs, small towns, and rural communities. The criminological literature recognizes residential location as important in crime causation, and the broader sociological literature highlights residential location as a key to access to resources.[21] To imagine women in their residences, neighborhoods, and communities, I not only drew on women's descriptions of the places they lived in response to questions about how they avoided crime and victimization in their communities. I also used online resources such as Zillow.com, Realtor.com, and earth.google.com, as well as online resident reviews of apartment complexes and mobile home communities, to picture where they lived. These resources enabled me to look at each woman's residence and take a tour of the block (or for rural areas, nearby structures and land) where women lived when they told their life stories.

A large proportion of the Black women lived in poorly resourced, high-crime sections of Detroit and its outskirts, or in smaller postindustrial, economically distressed Michigan cities such as Flint, Saginaw, and Pontiac, where manufacturing jobs had declined and high income inequality prevailed. Of the 42 women who identified as Black and neither Hispanic nor multiracial, 93 percent (39) lived in these urban areas, and 2 of the remaining 3 Black women lived in Grand Rapids, the second largest city in Michigan. Grand Rapids did not suffer as much as other Michigan cities during the recession that started in 2008, but the city contained pockets of concentrated poverty. My observations from the virtual tour generated examples of the distressed areas surrounding residences of urban Black women who took part in the research:

Jill, 32, just over the Detroit boundary. This house and neighborhood show signs of deterioration and disorder. There are vacant lots, two boarded up houses with overgrown trees a few doors down, and a burned-out house four doors down.

Francesca, 35, Black and White, lived in an apartment outside a relatively large Michigan city where she had worked since adolescence as a street prostitute. The reviews of the apartment mention the smell of marijuana in the hallways, roaches in the apartments, and unresponsive management.

Janice, 36, Detroit. The front door of the house next door is boarded up. About five houses down, the house is boarded up and dilapidated. One house has the door broken open. Around the corner and on the parallel street, houses are even more dilapidated, some are open, and there are many vacant lots.

Tova, 39, Detroit. This is an 850-square-foot house in a flood zone. The house four doors away has a boarded-up front window. There are vacant lots on the street and one-story business buildings with deteriorated-looking fronts around the corner.

Eddie, 41, Detroit. This house looks like it is in good repair and is in a fenced-off yard. On this street within the block there are boarded up houses and vacant lots, trash in the yards, and graffiti.

Lena, 45, Detroit. This house is valued at $18,017 on one website. On the right side there is a high fence, and on the left a vacant house that is open. The street in back of this street has some houses that seem to be in better repair.

Women who took part in the interviews and some probation and parole agents acknowledged that in some places, crime levels varied street segment by street segment. A "good area" could be within earshot of a gun going off and a short walk to drug markets on the next block.

Many of women's descriptions of urban neighborhoods do not, however, seem like "good areas" near high-crime areas. Tova described her neighborhood and how she stayed safe in it:

Once it get dark, because I don't have a porch light, once it get dark I don't open my door. If all the kids ain't in, they better go to my momma's because they won't get in. If they don't got a key, they won't get in. And that's just me being cautious about where I stay because it's real dark around my house. Like I stay right here on this corner and it's a big lot which is my driveway, and then it's a shed which is the [housing] project's shed, and then across the street is a house and a house, and then it's vacant lots, and then it's like two houses at the corner. So, it's a fairly empty block.

The women I write about are not representative of women in Michigan or women in trouble with the law. Yet their residential locations in city neighborhoods mirror findings from other research about the connection of minoritized racial status with place of residence. In the book *The Divided City*, Alan Mallach described neighborhoods in Detroit and other cities that look similar to the urban areas where many Black women in this book lived.[22] He depicted these areas as "a lunar landscape of scattered houses, many of them empty, acres of vacant land where houses, long since demolished, once stood. . . . [O]ther neighborhoods are falling apart, hit by foreclosures, poverty, and rising crime, as vacant, abandoned houses—once unthinkable—start to appear on streets with well-maintained homes and front yards." Such deteriorated Michigan urban neighborhoods resulted from White and more generally middle-class flight away from the cities, the movement of service jobs to the suburbs, and the movement of manufacturing jobs to other states or overseas. Decades of housing discrimination contributed to the concentration of Black women in low-resource, high-crime, racially isolated urban neighborhoods.[23] Apart from these general trends, a particularly dramatic loss of population in Detroit and some loss in other Michigan cities that were economically dependent on the auto industry left houses abandoned. The city of Detroit's investment in abandoned home demolition, and sometimes desperate neighbors' burning of vacant houses to get rid of them, created empty lots throughout Detroit and other Michigan cities.

Different from the Black women in the study, 57 percent (31) of White women lived in rural, small-town, or suburban areas. They also lived in places with more housing variation: some in quite expensive housing, others in trailers or trailer-like prefabricated housing or in rural areas taken up by farms and single-family homes on large lots. Following are descriptions of some of these residences.

> Lynette, 32, a house with a large lot on a small lake in a rural area. The house looked kept up. She grew up in rural northern Michigan, and before moving back to this area she lived in an economically distressed city on a street where women prostituted.
>
> Anna, 37, small town. This area has several apartment complexes and prefabricated homes similar to upscale house trailers. The community of prefabricated homes where Anna lives has good resident reviews.
>
> Pamela, 39, economically distressed city. This is a two-story apartment complex. Pamela describes it as "a really nice apartment in a nice area. It's not the hood."
>
> Lily, 55, Detroit outskirts. This looks like a well-kept neighborhood of single-family homes.

Robert Sampson's comprehensive study of Chicago, *The Great American City*, also showed that poor Black residents tend to stay in or near census tracts characterized or surrounded by high crime and widespread poverty.[24] Likewise for the women featured in this book, most Black women stayed put or, if they moved, it was from one section of Detroit (or another city) to another similar urban neighborhood, often for the purpose of breaking ties with former collaborators in drug use or criminal activity. Marion described her move from one high-crime area to another: "I told her [supervising agent] I no longer wish to live in Wayne County. . . . Even though it's crime up here [an adjacent county], I don't know the places [to get drugs and commit crime] and don't wanna know. And it's easier to be in my own world." Hope moved from the east side of Detroit to the west side to be closer to her son's grandmother, whose vision and hearing problems impeded her travel around the city. By moving, Hope thought she could get away from the place she had worked as a prostitute and a relative who supplied her drugs. Instead, she found no change, "When I moved here on the west side I was in [an area] like a fucking west-side east-side to me. You got [a street known for prostitution], you got all the crack houses around you, so here I am, I'm— dammit the west-side don't fucking work either."

White women more often moved between markedly different locations in the state, though again breaking ties with places and people associated with crime often motivated them. Gabriela moved away from transitional housing in her prior neighborhood, where people she knew kept offering her free drugs. Later she and her fiancé moved to a "better community" that she described as "quieter," with better schools for her son and closer to her job, stores, and parks. Lana left a city and moved to a rural area not only to escape "triggers" for drug use and illegal behavior, but also to be closer to prosocial relatives and the opportunity her parents offered to cooperate in small business ventures. The capacity to move expanded women's access to resources.

ECONOMIC CONDITIONS IN MICHIGAN

At the time of the research, Michigan had experienced an economic downturn that affected the entire state, but especially the economically distressed cities where the auto industry and its suppliers had for decades provided many jobs. Michigan was in economic distress before the research began in 2011 and during the entire data collection period. Between 1993 and 2008, the top three auto makers lost 83,000 manufacturing jobs in Michigan.[25] The nationwide Great Recession of 2008 hit Michigan harder and longer than many other states.[26] Compared to other places and consistent with the virtual tour of women's residential locations, Michigan cities and towns had a higher percent of unoccupeid habitable housing due to population loss, higher unemployment and poverty rates, and greater decreases in numbers of jobs and business establishments. As a result, in the middle of the data collection, Flint, Michigan, was ranked as the ninth most economically distressed community in the United States, and Detroit as the tenth most distressed.[27] Many of the women in the study came from Flint, Detroit, and similar Michigan cities.

Adding to the effects of the failing economy on job availability, potential employers avoid hiring people, especially women, with a criminal history.[28] Employers and occupational licensing rules often prohibit individuals with felony convictions from working in jobs that bring them into contact with children or that are in the health-care field, and a high proportion of women do this type of work.[29] Women seeking work faced a difficult job market, and those unable to work or with low wages faced shrinking resources for programs and benefits designed to address individual and family poverty.[30] If they turned to social safety-net programs, women found that federal and state neoliberal policies that emphasized individual responsibility for overcoming poverty had combined with Michigan's budget shortfalls to shrink available benefits.

NEOLIBERAL POLICIES

Like other women who penetrate from courts to community supervision or incarceration nationally, a high proportion of the women interviewed for this book experienced extreme economic marginalization.[31] Of the 118 women, 98 reported annual incomes less than $10,000 at the first interview, and 94 still had incomes below $10,000 by the end of the first year of supervision.[32] This level of poverty left them reliant on social safety-net benefits. It is tedious to read about the many ways that benefits and access to them shrank at the national level, in Michigan, and especially for people with a history of criminal convictions. Yet it is important to recognize the many barriers that women confronted when they sought ways to care for themselves and often for children and other family members.

Throughout the United States, social safety-net program resources started to decrease well before the study began, and obtaining assistance grew even more arduous and discouraging during the study. This retraction of benefits grew from beliefs that individuals who sought benefits had failed to be accountable and responsible for themselves and instead depended on government resources.[33] In 1996 the federal government replaced the cash assistance program, Aid to Families with Dependent Children (AFDC), with Temporary Assistance to Needy Families (TANF), which established lifetime limits for federal aid to families living in poverty.[34] Continued eligibility for funding before reaching the lifetime limits required participation in a program called Work First, which prepared recipients for work by requiring their attendance at a 9-to-5 job readiness program during weekdays, monitored their job searches, and expected employment. TANF did not recognize women's time and effort caring for their families as work, but instead emphasized entry into the paid workforce, albeit usually as part of the insecure, low-paid workforce.[35]

Many women with children lost welfare benefits due to these changes, and if they found work, the jobs tended to be traditionally female occupations with low pay, limited stability, and few if any benefits.[36] Due to loss of welfare, women often became uninsured and had trouble accessing medical and dental care; many remained unemployed; and for those who found work, Work First's emphasis on quick engagement in the workforce tended to discourage education and to incentivize taking low-paying, often temporary jobs.[37] AFDC support had acted as a gateway for low-income mothers with substance abuse disorders to receive treatment, but the limitations on access to TANF decreased the number of women moving through this gateway.[38] Also, in 1996 the federal government eliminated alcoholism and addiction as evidence of a disability that prevents employment, thereby making individuals with substance abuse disorders ineligible for Social Security Disability Insurance (SSDI). The changes in benefits left many prior recipients in a status that is difficult to imagine—"disconnected from all means of financial support."[39]

The Michigan Department of Health and Human Services (MDHHS) administers federally supported safety-net programs such as TANF and any state supplements in offices throughout the state, and city and regional housing commissions handle public housing and rent supplements. States' flexibility in the adoption of federal program requirements and state and regional differences in economic prosperity and political orientation created between-state variation in access to assistance. Relevant to women with dependent children, between 1994 and 2010, the year before the research for this book started, the number of Michigan TANF cases decreased by 63 percent, while the number of families with children in poverty decreased by 2 just percent.[40] Also in Michigan, basic cash assistance fell from $329 million to $186 million, and childcare expenditures for welfare recipients fell from $343 million to $32 million. Funds for work-related supports, for example training and childcare, decreased from $145 million to $85 million. Moving in the opposite direction, in Michigan spending on out-of-wedlock pregnancy prevention and support of two-parent family formation and maintenance increased, from $45 million to $420 million. Without evidence that poor women were in special need of pregnancy prevention services, that expenditure had no clear benefit for the women featured in this book. Also, many of the women were improving their lives by breaking off contact with drug-involved and abusive men, so programmatic efforts to promote two-parent families did not benefit them.

The Michigan legislature banned people convicted of certain crimes from receiving TANF, State Disability Assistance (a state supplement to federal disability aid), Child Development and Care Assistance, and food assistance through the Supplemental Nutritional Assistance Program (SNAP, often referred to as "food stamps").[41] Policies that affected women during the study stipulated that a person's first conviction for use, possession, or distribution of controlled substances after August 22, 1996, adds a requirement that the welfare benefits for families with children be issued to an authorized representative, who administers the money. After a subsequent drug-related felony conviction, both welfare and food assistance are permanently denied. The legislation included probation and parole requirement violations as reasons for denial of benefits. The Michigan social welfare program policies essentially added denial of benefits to punishments the courts meted out in response to criminal convictions. This is an example of the nationwide tendency to interweave the criminal justice and welfare systems in administration of punishments of women (and others) with criminal convictions.

Simultaneous with the retraction of assistance from federal and state welfare benefits and food assistance, the Michigan state legislators reduced the state Earned Income Tax Credit by two-thirds.[42] These state tax credits had benefited all working adults who lived in poverty, especially those in families with children, and they caused people to feel less stigmatized than when they received welfare payments.[43] Further limiting resources for people living in poverty, Michigan's lack of investment in affordable housing compounded the bad effect of federal legislators' failure to fund the 2008 Housing Trust Fund to support housing vouchers and public housing nationwide. As a result, compared to other states, Michigan's low-income housing shortage was more acute. The National Low Income Housing Coalition estimated that in Michigan in 2013 there were 28 affordable available units for every 100 households with extremely low incomes and 63 affordable available units for every 100 slightly better off households.[44] Even if women obtained housing assistance, they struggled to find an affordable place to live.

A month before data collection began, Michigan tightened its already relatively short 48-month TANF lifetime limit by eliminating some reasons for exemptions; these restrictions resulted in immediate termination of benefits to over 12,000 Michigan families.[45] The changes in Michigan's Earned Income Tax credit and TANF affected many women in this study, and their accounts of their lives are replete with references to being cut off from benefits; the state running out of money for medical insurance and other types of assistance; and the unavailability of safe, affordable housing.

MICHIGAN COURTS, PROBATION, AND PAROLE

In the United States, the state-specific histories of how courts, jails, prisons, and community supervision respond to criminal convictions are characterized by shifts back and forth between treatment and punishment.[46] These shifts emanate from state legislators and appointed state agency heads with differing ideologies about whether individuals should be punished in an act of retribution; punished to deter them and others from future illegal activity; or treated, rehabilitated, and even empowered to eliminate individual-level causes of offending. At the start of the research, the MDOC and its probation and parole divisions were increasingly shifting away from punishment and prison confinement and toward assistance finding work and accessing welfare and community-based mental health and substance abuse treatment. The shift toward gender-responsive supervision was embedded in this broader, department-wide reform effort.

In a centralized state system, the MDOC hires, trains, and supervises probation and parole agents who work with individuals convicted of felonies. In what is called *felony probation*, a circuit court judge sentences people convicted of a felony to probation as an alternative to prison and specifies court costs, restitution to victims, crime victim fund payments, and fines. For parole, a parole board specifies conditions that people released from prison before their sentences are up must meet before they are free of state oversight. Common requirements are participation in substance abuse treatment, employment, and education.

Separate from circuit courts, district courts handle less serious misdemeanor charges and ordinance violations, for which the maximum punishment by incarceration is a year or less in a city or county jail rather than a state prison. Judges in the 105 Michigan district court jurisdictions also sentence people to community supervision by an agent in a probation department financed by the district court jurisdiction and separate from the MDOC. The women in this book had felony convictions and supervision by the centralized MDOC system, but district-level courts and district-level probation agents often impacted their lives. Many women had prior convictions in the district courts. Also, women could simultaneously be on some combination of MDOC felony probation, MDOC parole from prison, and district-court probation, and the supervising agents could be spread across multiple jurisdictions. Although sentencing guidelines were in place during the research, both district and circuit court judges had some discretion in setting requirements during probation and responding to violations of requirements punitively or with treatment, for example with jail time versus substance abuse treatment. The judges' influence over probation affected agent interactions with clients and, of benefit to the research though not always the study participants, introduced variations in the community supervision experience that could be studied.

When the research for this book started, Michigan had two special resources in place to fund treatment for people on probation and parole. To lower burgeoning costs of incarceration in Michigan, the state legislature passed the 1988 Community Corrections Act.[47] Administered by the MDOC, the act funds community-based programming aimed at reducing admissions to prison, improving jail utilization, and improving reentry and rehabilitative services. Community corrections advisory boards established by local county governments identify services needed by people convicted in their jurisdictions. In 2013, 73 of the 83 counties in Michigan received grants totaling $73 million to support a wide range of services.[48] Funding most often paid for cognitive behavioral treatment, supervised community service, education, employment preparation and placement, mental health treatment, and substance abuse treatment.

Creating additional practical and treatment-oriented support for individuals on parole, Michigan legislators had taken steps to shift state resources from building and maintaining prisons to parole.[49] Starting in 2003, state legislators funded the Michigan Prisoner Reentry Initiative (MPRI) to reduce returns to prison by preparing individuals for release and providing them with community services. MPRI, referred to as "Reentry" in 2012 and later developed into the current Offender Success model, required assessment of risks and needs of all imprisoned people, programs to address risks and needs during incarceration, reassessment close to the time of release, and planning for continued assistance after release. The MPRI sparked development of comprehensive services and supervision planning at the start of a prison term and continuing after release. It also assisted people leaving prison by meeting basic needs such as giving them bus tickets and transitional housing. By the time of data collection for this book, selected prisons that included the one Michigan prison for women housed people about to be paroled in facilities with in-prison parole agents who managed transition meetings, external parole agents who provided community supervision, and community service providers. For the post-release period, the MDOC contracted with community services for employment, mental health, substance use disorder treatment, and other assistance to people on parole.

After the start of MPRI, a higher proportion of eligible people was granted parole, and they received more services before and after release. Also, violations of conditions of parole were less often met with a return to prison. Instead, parole agents responded with graduated sanctions, including treatment requirements and increased length of supervision. As a result of these reforms, between 2006 and 2011 Michigan reduced the prison population by 15 percent.[50]

During the research, MDOC parole and probation agents increasingly shifted away from simply assessing whether people supervised in the community met requirements such as avoiding police contact, avoiding association with felons, and desisting from substance use; they increasingly shifted toward coaching individuals to change in a positive direction.[51] Supporting this change, statewide MDOC policy and the review process sets limits on the choice of response to each type of violation, and supervisors monitor responses and approve of any deviations. An analysis of official MDOC records for the 402 Michigan women, who included the 118 women considered in this book, documented that most of women's probation and parole violations were for substance misuse, and the most common response was to require continued, increased, or different substance abuse treatment programming.[52]

THE GENDER-RESPONSIVE REFORM

Starting in 2009, the MDOC instituted key reforms in probation and parole supervision policies and practices designed to meet women's needs. In addition to establishing woman-specific caseloads, MDOC agents who supervised the women in this book would have received three days of training that integrated collaborative case management and gender-responsive approaches to working with women and, depending on the date they started working for MDOC, an additional three to five full days of training in collaborative case management. Collaborative case management requires that interventions be supported by research evidence and go beyond reducing criminal behavior to improving the health and well-being of the individual, family, and community. In essence, this approach addresses not just risks for recidivism but a wider variety of needs. It rests on assessment tools to identify client needs and recidivism risks and case planning to address them. The training incorporated six National Institute of Corrections gender-responsive strategies: (1) acknowledge that gender makes a difference in correctional intervention; (2) create an environment based on safety, respect, and dignity; (3) recognize the importance of relationships to women and support healthy relationships; (4) recognize and attend to trauma, substance misuse, and mental health through holistic services; (5) provide women opportunities to improve their socioeconomic status; and (6) establish a network of comprehensive community services.[53] To enable implementation of collaborative case management and a focus on women's unique needs, agents also received training in motivational interviewing, which uses conversation to elicit clients' goals, values, and reasons for change and fosters agent-client agreement on appropriate methods for making change.[54]

Also unique from many other states, MDOC staff used an assessment tool that includes common recidivism risks and needs of women. In 2013, a set of questions developed as part of the WRNA was added to items that affect both women and men similarly. Especially relevant to women, this assessment collects information on self-efficacy, abuse as an adult, abuse as a child, relationship dysfunction, and parenting stress. Further complementing MDOC gender-responsive supervision, several community-based women-specific programs, including substance abuse treatment, are available in the state.[55] For people without medical insurance, either the MDOC contracted directly with these services, or the Michigan Community Corrections Act funded them.[56]

Early in the reform effort, most women perceived their relationships with supervising agents as positive on a measure of supervision style reflecting agents' caring about them, trustworthiness, and fairness.[57] Of the 118 women, 53 (44.9%) chose "always caring and trustworthy" from the choices: never, rarely, occasionally, sometimes, often, very often, and always. None of them said the agent was always punitive. Just under 70 percent saw supervising agents as never or rarely punitive and as often, very often, or always caring and trustworthy. Interviews continued over seven years as gender-responsive and supporting reforms expanded to a wider range of MDOC personnel. The resulting variation in supervision and programming during the change made it possible to compare the effects of remnants of old-style supervision with continuously expanding efforts to provide gender-responsive supervision for women.

BOOK STRUCTURE AND TOPICS

Each woman's statements during multiple interviews gave insight into the context and entities that affected her life; the reasons she broke the law or misused drugs, stopped using, and started using again; and her individual characteristics, motivations, and exercise of agency. Statements from multiple women in similar circumstances demonstrate shared experiences. At the same time, collections of statements by multiple women to support and illustrate a particular finding obscure how combined influences on one woman coalesce to alter or maintain her circumstances, well-being, drug use, or criminal activity. To present women's lives in a holistic way but also show common findings, I focus on the same 6 women at the start of each chapter, then add to their contributions by presenting analysis of the statements from all 118 women. The selection of the six women rested on the richness of the information they provided. The six women—with the pseudonyms Carmen, Bree, Carla, Raven, Mallory, and Marion— do not represent types of women, but rather constitute a diverse group whose stories act as touchstones that the reader can follow throughout the book. I selected the six women not only because of their demographic diversity from each other, but also because they provided useful information across multiple chapters of the book. The next chapter introduces the women, notes their demographic characteristics, and provides insight into how they started to use drugs and break the law.

After summarizing the situation of each of the 6 women at the start of each chapter, within the chapters I present major findings discovered in the data and develop them with the accounts and narratives of the larger group of women who told their life stories. To address the issue of whether findings for the 118 women generalize more broadly, I point out any relevant findings for the 402 women in the larger Michigan study and in other research. I refer to the material on the 6 women as the *Touchstone Stories*, the 118 women as *The Larger Group of Women*, and the 402 women as *The Full Michigan Study Sample*.

Chapter 2, "Starting Points," shows how families, schools, child welfare agencies, and juvenile justice institutions affected women's behavior and development as girls. Two chapters focus on community supervision.

Chapter 3, "Costs of Conviction," reveals the price women pay to be convicted and supervised on probation and parole. Costs include monetary fees and fines, lost opportunity, and negative consequences of some supervision practices and the label as "a felon." Chapter 4, "Agent Actions," explains how what agents say and do, which for probation depends in part on judicial actions, worsens or improves women's lives. Chapter 5, "Treatment," presents information on women's contact with an array of mental health and substance abuse services. Mental health and substance abuse treatment intertwine with community supervision when judges, probation and parole agents, and parole boards require participation. Alternatively, some women sought treatment unrelated to community supervision.

In a further step away from the focus on criminal justice agencies, chapter 6, "Marginalization," covers women's experiences working in the legitimate, informal, and illegal economies plus their efforts to access social safety-net benefits intended to assist individuals living in poverty. A few women received Social Security retirement or survivor benefits, and I describe their experiences with these sources of support. I considered separating employment from safety-net benefits as sources of income, but separate chapters failed to accurately show the interconnections. Women supplemented or substituted erratically available, limited streams of income from one source to another. The relatively long chapter on economic marginalization highlights these interconnections.

The next-to-the-last chapter, "Endpoints," shows the meaning women created in their lives, their identities, and their circumstances at the study's last contact with them. It highlights the importance of what I call *family making*, which women accomplish in different ways. Some women bore children or reestablished relationships with estranged children; some connected with parents, siblings, and other relatives; a few relied on immersion in support groups; and some who saw themselves with tenuous or no significant connections to other people did not make a family. The final chapter, "Reform," reviews the needs for policy and program changes that the women's stories and accounts brought to light. Centering this chapter on the needed changes that the women exposed elevates the voices of the those affected by programs and policies. This final chapter also considers change more broadly in and beyond Michigan and presents several promising reforms, including additional steps that the MDOC has taken.

Starting Points

Identification of initial and perpetuating childhood influences that prompted women's substance misuse and lawbreaking increases understanding of how women on probation and parole manage and fare in the array of programs, agencies, communities, policies, and political ideologies that impinge on their lives in girlhood and adulthood. It reveals prior experiences and the lasting effects that women bring into interactions with court personnel, probation and parole agents, mental health professionals, social welfare workers, and potential and eventual employers. Since the women featured in this book had multiple convictions as adults, examination of starting points also reveals ineffective or nonexistent interventions during childhood that failed to prevent their illegal behavior as adults.

Three quarters of the women (88, 74.6%) who contributed to this book located the starting point for substance misuse and crime in childhood. A high proportion lived on their own without adult material and social support and without supervision during or even before adolescence. Victimization by sexual and other abuses, family members who used illegal drugs or drank heavily, and exposure to violence between parents are well-established causes for girls' lawbreaking, and the study participants exemplified these prior findings.[1] At the first interview, over 40 percent (50 of the 118) of them said they had experienced physical abuse as a child, and over 40 percent (53 of 118) said they had experienced childhood sexual abuse. Also consistent with prior research, women identified men, often older men, as girlhood romantic partners, friends, or people they had joined with to hang out or run the streets.[2] The men encouraged and enabled girls' substance use and illegal activity. Two childhood experiences stood out as especially powerful influences on women's progression toward multiple convictions: living on their own at a young age and family members and professionals ignoring claims of childhood sexual abuse.

Women shared most of the information about childhood when they told their life stories. They were asked to identify and describe the major chapters of their lives and answer follow-up questions about positive and negative childhood recollections and general life events, such as high and low points that might have occurred at any life stage. As an additional source of information, during interviews before and after the life stories, women described early life events and circumstances when they answered questions about substance misuse and mental health treatment and about needs that they discussed with probation and parole agents.

TOUCHSTONE STORIES

A variety of reasons for starting substance misuse or illegal activity before adulthood manifested in one or more of the touchstone stories. These touchstone stories show complex interplays among several early life experiences that affected women's progression toward criminal convictions as adults.[3] The six women also identified points at which parents, guardians, schools, and childcaring institutions failed to intervene effectively.

The Criminalization of Abuse

At the life story interview, 23-year-old Carmen, one of the youngest women in the study, identified as Native American and White. Carmen lived in a rural area. During the interview she revealed exposure to violence between parents; financial exploitation by parents; lack of parental support and protection after her brother repeatedly sexually attacked her; and her mother's complicity with the police and the juvenile court judge in moving Carmen away from her family into a group home, followed by a series of foster homes. Carmen's story also shows how school personnel amplified her difficulties.

Carmen remembered her parents' constantly arguing and beating each other until she was age 10, the year they separated and the year she sustained a serious brain injury caused by a schoolmate hitting her on the head with a baseball bat. For a year and a half after they separated, Carmen's parents moved her back and forth between their homes and school districts, which were four hours apart, to alternate their receipt of the Supplemental Security Income paid to the family due to low income and needs related to Carmen's brain injury. Carmen understood why her parents had her move repeatedly, and she recognized the damaging effects:

> All this jumping every month back and forth, back and forth, it was hard on school. You know it was just a really stressful time. Every 30 days I'd switch. . . . I failed two years actually, the same grade. . . . They were only switching back and forth because each third of the month I would get a check, so one wanted it and then the other wanted it and then the other one wanted it. . . . I kind of felt like the odd one out because, it's not enough time to get situated and havin' to pack your stuff to go down there and then a month later havin' to pack it all again.

Surely school personnel noticed Carmen's sporadic enrollment, but she did not mention any intervention by personnel at either school to stabilize her attendance, and the constant moving went on for well over a year.

Carmen's family situation led to her expulsion from school for violence against schoolmates and staff: "I got kicked out of school for fighting because I took all of my frustration and anger out at people at school." In one incident, when a school friend admired Carmen's self-fashioned pierced nose and asked her to do the same for her, Carmen refused, and the friend threatened to beat Carmen's seven-year-old sister, so Carmen hit the friend. This is what Carmen remembered the school principal saying: "I wasn't gonna go nowhere in life, and all this mean stuff, you know? Like, I'm just gonna be in prison my whole life and no one loves me, and no one cares about me because I'm just a rude person, and I don't care what I do to other people." Carmen called the statement that she did not care what she did to other people a lie, and she thought her 13-year-old schoolmate deserved to be hit for threatening her 7-year-old sister. Carmen reacted to the principal: "So I ended up grabbin' her [the principal's] coffee cup and whipping it at her. It bounced off her face and broke the window, so I ended up doin' juvi time [juvenile detention] for that." The school personnel's pushing Carmen into the juvenile justice system exemplifies a national problem, the school-to-prison pipeline as it affects girls, especially girls of color.[4]

Showing how little support she received from family, Carmen said she felt more cared for in juvenile detention than at home:

My whole life I've been in and out of juvi cause, to be honest like, sometimes I do stuff just to go there because I felt more loved in there because, you know, we have friends—well, they're not your friends, but like you go there, you meet people. You kind of have a friend relationship, something I didn't have when I was at home. I hardly ever talked to anyone [at home] and, I just kept to myself in my room.

Carmen's relationship with her mother further deteriorated after she and her sister told the police that their older brother had sexually assaulted Carmen from ages 10 to 13. Carmen said the police dropped the case after an investigation for two reasons: she did not report the abuse until she was 15, and her brother passed a lie detector test during which he denied the assaults. Carmen's mother pursued a charge of a false report to the police in juvenile court, according to Carmen because she resented the time it took to handle the allegations. After issuing a finding of a false report, the juvenile court judge ordered placement in a group home. Carmen felt betrayed by her mother and the judge:

[The judge] ended up makin' him [my brother] not guilty and I ended up doin' eight months in juvi [a group home] because my mom tried to say I filed a false police report. Ever since then, I was jumpin' from foster home to foster home 'cause she was mad 'cause she went through all the court stuff for like a year. You know, you should be there for your daughter. I just don't understand.

The sequence of events Carmen described mirrors a historically documented pattern of a girl being victimized by a family member, followed by the juvenile court's criminalization and confinement of the girl.[5] Juvenile courts have most often criminalized victimized girls from minoritized groups, so they most often follow a sexual-abuse-to-prison pipeline.[6] Even though group homes have the formal goal of providing support and treatment, Carmen saw the placement as punishment. Just as she called juvenile detention "juvi," she referred to the group home as "juvi." She saw the judge's finding as criminalizing her, with her mother's support.

Shortly after she returned home, her mother kicked 16-year-old Carmen out because she was pregnant. At seven months pregnant, to protect the fetus Carmen refused to go out with the expectant father to drink and smoke weed. In response, the man dragged Carmen up a flight of stairs face down, and Carmen miscarried. Distraught over losing the baby, Carmen stole a car so she could go see her grandmother. After the gas ran out just over the county line, Carmen broke into another car and stole a wallet in hopes of finding gas money. At that time, Michigan's cutoff age to be treated as a juvenile was 16, and Carmen was 17. After being convicted in two different courts as an adult, she began probation supervision in one county for the auto theft and in another county for breaking into and entering the second car to steal gas money. In a sequence of actions, her family, the school, the police who investigated the sexual attack, the juvenile court judge, and the judges who presided over the courts handling adults' felony cases transformed 17-year-old Carmen from being a girl with a serious brain injury due to a schoolmate's attack, who was sexually victimized by her brother, was financially exploited by her parents, and was physically abused by the expected baby's father, and who broke the law in an impulsive reaction to the abuse that caused the miscarriage, into an adult on probation for felony convictions.

Living on Her Own

Bree completed the life story interview at age 29. She described herself as Black and White, and she lived in an economically depressed city that had experienced a massive loss of auto manufacturing jobs. When she was 11, her parents split up, and Bree lived with her father in another state. After running away because he was "too strict," she moved to Michigan and lived with her mother, who started using drugs and "kind of didn't care anymore." Bree described the family's living situation: "She kept food in the house, but other than that it wasn't anything else other than food, you know, basic needs, tissue." Her mother did not realize that Bree had stopped attending school: "She had a job. All she used to do was go to work and come home and go straight to her room. So, I never really seen her. . . . [I]t was kind of like passing by." Bree spent her time "hanging with friends, trying to steal cars, stealing clothes." Then she realized the potential profit from selling drugs:

> My mom lived in a trailer, so—well, at that point in time when I started selling drugs—the guy that I was going with, he used to sell her [Bree's mom] drugs. And I kind of thought to myself, "If he can do it then I can do it. And she [mom] can spend, you know, 500, 600 dollars a week in credit on drugs, then, you know, I can get it myself." So, I started selling my mom drugs, and it wasn't just her, it was, kind of whoever needed it.

Like Carmen, Bree first moved away from her family at age 16. Bree rented her own trailer in the same trailer park where her mother lived. She initially relied on drug-sales earnings, which she later supplemented as a strip club dancer.

From Violent Parents to Violent Intimate Partner

Mallory, a Black Detroit woman and one of the oldest women in the study, told her life story at age 55, just after she completed a residential substance abuse treatment program and moved into transitional housing supported by MDOC. Showing parallel early life experiences across the age cohorts, like the younger women, Carmen and Bree, Mallory had lived on her own early in life. One incident led to permanent separation from her parents, who had previously repeatedly attacked each other and her. After a holiday family gathering, Mallory's father refused to help clean up, so her mother dumped a pot of spaghetti on his head. Mallory continued, "I had never seen him fight my mother like he was that particular time. It was getting really, really bad." Mallory grabbed a knife from the kitchen "to like avert their attention over to me where they would stop." She remembered that her father passed out from drinking, and her mother set the house on fire:

> He was in his Lay-Z-Boy [recliner] chair and he passed out. And she took his cigarette lighter and lit the Christmas cards up one by one. There was about 20, 25 cards or more and she lit 'em up and the whole wall just went up in flames. And the house, it was paneling on the walls too. Yeah, that paneling it just, it went up real fast and she was going out to the car. But then the car wouldn't start so that gave me a little time. I'm tryin' to, like, "You gon' leave him in here?" She's like, "To hell with him. Yeah, I'm going. Are you coming or not?" And I was like, "Don't leave him in here like that." So, he's dead weight to me, you know, and I'm little. So, I'm trying to drag him out. I finally did get him out on the front porch, propped him up on a bush and was covered in smoke and I guess the neighbors called the fire department.

Mallory's mom drove herself and Mallory to the local police precinct. "So she led them to believe that I set the fire and they were trying to lock me up for being a rebellious teenager and my mother just sat there like a stone statue and was gonna let me take the fall for what she had done." Mallory described her decision to leave her family:

> When I went back to the house I could see the damage from the fire, people, they're worried the house was messed up. It was destroyed. And my father was walking through there trying to salvage whatever he could salvage but I didn't stay. I wanted to take advantage of this moment to spend the night at my girlfriend's house, and I hung out right there and I never went back home. I went back to school after the winter break or whatever and I got into a fight, and they kicked me out of [the district's] public schools. . . . So I just never went back to school, never went back home. To this day [at age 55] I have not stayed overnight in my mother's house.

Like Carmen, Mallory expressed disbelief at her mother's actions and a sense of betrayal, saying she could not figure out "why she was gonna feed me to the wolves for something that she did." The life-threatening level of family violence in Mallory's story is extreme. Not only did Mallory witness violence between her parents, but she acted to prevent each of them from killing the other. Living on her own, Mallory stopped attending school and stole to meet her needs. A juvenile court judge placed Mallory in a group home, but that intervention did not prevent Mallory's eventual drug addiction and the crimes she committed to support her use of heroin.

Mallory's complete story shows missed opportunities for intervention by school personnel. Before the house fire, when Mallory was in the seventh grade, her father used a belt to beat her in the school lunchroom in front of teachers, staff, and students. He whipped her "from one end of the dining room thing, in the gymnasium to the other end" because, without permission, she had taken her bagged lunch from home to eat at a friend's house instead of in the school lunchroom. When the interviewer asked about the school response, in Mallory's recollection, nobody intervened. Normalizing the physical violence by her father at the same time she described the harm to herself, Mallory said this beating was not abuse because it left no welts, but she was "so humiliated, so embarrassed, so hurt." This incident occurred in the early 1970s, which may explain the school's tolerance for Mallory's dad's beating her in the school. However, the multiple problems with school behavior and attendance should have alerted school personnel to the need for interventions with the family rather than district-wide expulsion of Mallory.

After aging out of the juvenile justice system, Mallory lived with an abusive man who introduced her to drugs. He tried to force her to eat what he liked and do what he liked to do, and she tried to appease him by going along. She explained how she came to use heroin:

> I asked him. I said, you know, "Give me some." 'Cause I'm thinking that if I'm doing what he's doing maybe this will stop the beating. If he like apples, I'm a learn to love 'em and if he liked baseball, I'm a love baseball. So he's shooting this dope, I wanna shoot some too and I begged him. He didn't wanna do it, but he did it anyways and it still didn't matter.

When the beatings continued, recalling the 33 years that her mother had spent with her abusive father, Mallory said she thought, "History will not repeat itself." She believed she or her husband would kill the other one, so she left him in her twenties. From that point until a few months before the life story interview, Mallory accumulated numerous convictions for crimes committed to support her heroin addiction. Starting in 1978, the courts convicted her for cashing a check without an account, 11 counts of larceny (most from a building), 5 counts of retail fraud, possession of drug paraphernalia, possession of marijuana, and several charges for being a habitual offender.

Death as a Trigger

Carla, age 32, self-identified as White and came from a small Michigan city populated by a mix of young professionals and people living in poverty. After her stepfather died when she was nine, Carla, her mom, and her siblings lived in extreme poverty. Largely unsupervised during adolescence, Carla spent her time hanging out with older peers, smoking cigarettes and marijuana, and drinking alcohol. At 17, she spent three months in the hospital with liver damage from a recently diagnosed autoimmune disease. After her discharge, Carla believed she was about to die. Figuring she might as well do anything she wanted, she joined peers in using acid, cocaine, and crack. She had a baby that the father accidentally smothered by rolling onto the child while he was asleep, after which Carla escalated her use of methamphetamine because she "wanted to die." She explained, "So I was pretty much self-medicating myself and I didn't realize that until I was actually sitting in a jail cell going to prison. But I was in and out of jail the last couple years before that." Carla concluded her comments about childhood: "I was doomed from the beginning." Although Carla did not live away from home, she spent adolescence unsupervised and with peers who provided easy access to drugs. The deaths of her stepfather and baby and the expectation of her own imminent death resulted in Carla's early use of illegal drugs. The trauma of her child's death precipitated her increased use of methamphetamines to cope. Time in jail, which could have been a point of programmatic intervention, did not stop her continued use of drugs.

The Downward Spiral

Fifty-five-year-old Marion lived in metropolitan Detroit and described herself as Black and Hispanic. She saw the most positive aspect of childhood as living with her father and relatives from his side of the family in a large, economically thriving city on the East Coast. At age nine she moved to Michigan to live with her mother and her father's brother, who had married her mother. This stepfather/uncle abused her mom, who shot him (nonfatally) in the stomach in what the court deemed to be self-defense. Marion traced her drug use to when she was 16 and her dad, who still lived outside of Michigan, "drank himself to death at 33 years old." She described the effect: "I shut down, shut away. That's when I began, cause I had intentions of going to college, but I regressed. . . . I went all the way off the track and never seemed to make it back." Marion's drug use escalated in her twenties. She worked at a Michigan auto manufacturing company earning a good salary that, combined with her live-in partner's income and money from a lawsuit after a car hit her while she was walking, enabled the couple to buy cocaine for themselves and their drug-using friends. She ended up jobless and penniless. "And it just went as fast as it came, and just woke up one morning, no job, and then lost the house, and, I mean, it just went and then I went to prison so it's crazy." Marion's retail theft and sales had supported her addiction for more than three decades. Before the prison sentence that brought her into the study, Marion had been convicted of 12 counts of retail fraud, assault with a dangerous weapon, running out on a bond, and disturbing the peace. Marion described the trauma of her father's death; early exposure to high levels of family violence; and in her twenties, the lure of using cocaine with peers, as precursors to repeated offenses to support years of addiction. She did not connect the different negative events to each other, but regardless of how much each of these precursors affected Marion's long record of convictions, they remained a part of her past and sense of self.

Childhood Sexual Abuse and Drug Use

Raven, a 38-year-old Black woman, lived in an economically distressed Michigan city. She followed yet another route from family troubles into being on her own and using drugs in adolescence. She grew up in a neighborhood she called "the hood" in an economically thriving but racially segregated midwestern city located outside of Michigan. She turned to drugs in adolescence in response to repeated sexual assaults by a stepfather and his son. At first she kept the abuse to herself to avoid destroying her mother's happiness with the marriage. When Raven revealed the attacks, her mother stabbed her husband, and Child Protective Services (CPS) placed Raven with her aunt, a truck driver who spent most of her time away from home and, according to Raven, "didn't know the first thing about raisin' a teenager." Raven explicitly attributed her illegal activity during adolescence to the sexual assaults: "I got in trouble because I was high. . . . People don't understand. I was raped from 10 till I was 15, so of course I got high. . . . I did heroin. I've did coke. I've did a lot of drugs." When Raven told a high school counselor about the sexual assaults, the counselor told other teachers, and the information spread to students. Raven said the knowledge "over the whole school" that she was "screwin' my daddy" precipitated her leaving school. After Raven, her mother, and her four younger brothers moved to Michigan, her convictions as an adult were for cashing fraudulent checks and on another occasion, cashing stolen checks. Raven viewed these convictions as wrongful, saying she either did not know the checks were fraudulent or that another person stole the checks. Raven's story of her youth shows an inappropriate CPS placement with her aunt and the school counselor's harmful handling of Raven's revelation of being sexually abused, as well as drug use in response to sexual abuse. The recent convictions for financial crimes do not seem to be related to childhood sexual abuse, and as noted in chapter 6, "Marginalization," may have been a response to her lack of any income to support herself and five children, or alternatively as she claimed, may have been a miscarriage of justice.

Childhood Starting Points

The six women's accounts of the start of substance misuse and law-breaking show how families that provide little or no material or social support and supervision, violence between parents, adults' failure to protect girls from sexual abuse, and profits from selling drugs promoted girls' living on their own. Girls saw men abusing their mothers, mothers abusing men, and mothers responding violently to men who abused them and their daughters. When parents did not believe girls' claims of abuse, this broke the relationship and gave the girls reason to leave the home. Abusive and older men also promoted the girls' (and later the women's) drug use and crime. Schools amplified girls' troubles by expelling them and sending them into the juvenile courts for punishment. Time spent in juvenile institutions and jails did not interrupt the connection of childhood problems to adult criminality for these women.[7] Not all harm that the women described had a clear causative connection to use of drugs and alcohol and other lawbreaking, and sometimes women identified just one of a series of childhood adversities as their reason for being in trouble with the law. Whether or not they were just an accumulation of adversities or many different causes, the women highlighted multiple negative childhood events and lasting bad effects in their life stories.

Girls on Their Own

A large proportion of the women (49.2%, or 58 of 118) said they lived on their own as girls. Some resided with or moved away from what Laurie Schaffner calls empty families, with parents and guardians characterized by "divorce, overwork, substance dependence, incarceration, mental illness, ill health, homelessness, and death."[8] Schaffner's research showed how the adult family members' myriad difficulties prevented them from adequately meeting the needs of their children or themselves. Even if girls stayed with empty families, they were left to their own devices. Abusive family members—be they fathers, mothers, stepbrothers, stepfathers, stepmothers, or foster parents—provided reasons for girls to move out. In *Complicated Lives*, Vera Lopez showed the complex family situations that led girls to use drugs and break the law.[9] I also found complex ways that girls' families promoted their initial steps toward multiple convictions as adults, including different forms of empty families, different forms of abuse and resulting damage to girls, and combinations of these with each other and with other influences. To convey this finding of multiple forces affecting girls, I present the childhood circumstances of several women besides those who told the touchstone stories.

Like Bree, Mary, Francesca, and Jolene presented life stories that show how empty families affected the women early in life. As noted, after Bree's mother stopped caring for Bree, Bree moved into her own trailer and sold drugs to support herself. Mary also sold drugs to support herself, but under different circumstances. Mary's family members' drug production and distribution, her mother's acceptance of income from Mary's drug sales, the family's lack of income from other sources, and community opportunity for drug dealing worked together to promote Mary's early entry into drug production and distribution. As a young teenager, she financially supported herself, her mother, and two younger siblings, "I've been getting us money, paying these bills, paying that light bill, that gas bill, that water bill, that rent that was $350 a month." Mary started out working at a fast-food restaurant, but "it just wasn't enough. . . . If the lights got cut off, I want to get this shit to come back on." Just as Bree saw the potential income from selling illegal drugs in the trailer park where she lived, Mary realized that selling drugs was an accessible opportunity to earn a high income in her Detroit neighborhood, which she referred to as "the redzone," "the hood," and "bad."

Mary's uncle facilitated her illegal activities. Not only did she support her natal family by selling drugs, but she raised the enrollment fee to attend a private high school by "cooking dope" for her uncle. To pay the monthly tuition, she took over her uncle's drug-dealing business while he was in prison. Mary explained that once she started covering all household expenses, she could come and go from the house whenever she wanted. She saw herself as the "man of the house" and resented that nobody was watching out for her even while she was in dangerous situations dealing drugs in a high crime neighborhood late at night. After moving into her own residence and graduating from high school (in that order), Mary continued to support herself and her mother and siblings with earnings from drug dealing until she was apprehended and imprisoned.

Francesca's story shows how a man filled the void left by an empty family and how he promoted her drug use and prostitution. She remembered that around the age of three, she repeatedly heard her mom crying while her dad beat her, until her mom shot and killed him. She said her mom hated her because she looked like her dad, and when the interviewer asked about a positive childhood memory, she could not recall one. Francesca left home at 13 to live with a 20-year-old drug dealer because her mother, who was addicted to drugs, did not have enough food in the house. This man, whom she met when he paid her for sex, took her to get crack, as Francesca saw it, to "lure" her in to drug use, and he encouraged her to earn money by prostituting:

> He's just like, "You're a little promiscuous, why don't you go get money?" And he just took me on a corner and dropped me off, and then I stood there for about 20 minutes, and somebody picked me up and gave me 60 dollars. And I was never really into him [the man she dated], so . . . I gave him and his brother 20 bucks and told them that I didn't need . . . them to watch me anymore because I wasn't trying to have a pimp.

Showing the impermanence of living apart from her mother and the related effects of her mother's drug addiction, after she moved back home at 14, Francesca started snorting coke with her mom, and she alternated between living at her mom's and her boyfriend's residence. Francesca continued to stand on the corner and prostitute for over a decade. She saw her need to be numb as the reason for taking drugs: "I was self-medicating on drugs 'cause I've never dealt with any emotions. . . . I started using at 13 and when you're high you're numb." Although Francesca said she did not work with a pimp, she gave her boyfriend, who had encouraged her to prostitute, a small amount of money so he would spend time with her, and she was living with him years later at the time of the life story interview.

Unlike the women who moved out as girls, Jolene did not initiate living apart from family; instead, her mother moved out of state and left Jolene without a means of support or a permanent place to live. Jolene knew her mother engaged in prostitution: "I seen her selling herself for drugs. I seen just a lot of stuff growing up." At age 13, Jolene's mom introduced her to crack, which Jolene saw as the start of her problems: "I think it ruined my life." When Jolene was 15, her mother sold the family's belongings and then, on her way out of town, she dropped Jolene off at her boyfriend's house. The boyfriend's mother could not financially support Jolene long term, so Jolene stole to support herself. In jail at 17, Jolene learned about methods of cooking meth and about shooting up:

> When I was in jail for drinking, I learned how to cook meth and got out and cooked methamphetamines and got strung out on meth just from 90 days of being in jail. I didn't even have a clue about meth before I went there. . . . I sat there. I wrote it all down. I was 17 years old, and when I was in jail she [a woman in jail] taught me how to cook meth right at the table in jail. And I got out and couldn't wait to do it. And then the next time I went to jail, I learned, you know, that people were talking about shooting up and how good it was, and I never shot up before I went to jail, and I got out and couldn't wait to get out and shoot up and try it. Yeah. I learned all the stuff and did the stuff by being in jail, when I could have been sitting in a group and learning how to change my way of thinking.

By the time Jolene was 19, she was serving time in prison for a conviction for cooking methamphetamines.

Sexual Abuse Ignored and Doubted

Carmen's mother either did not believe Carmen or did not act to protect Carmen when her brother sexually attacked her. A number of women similarly described adults ignoring childhood sexual abuse or claiming it never happened. This type of betrayal often occurred in a mix of other toxic family experiences, which together with the betrayal motivated girls to leave home.

Candace's story shows how myriad events—her mother's drug use and neglect, sexual assault by her biological father, and her mother's lack of response to the sexual assault—led her to live separately from her parents at a very young age. She described how after her stepfather died when she was six, her family felt empty:

> After I lost him, it's like I lost my entire family, because that's when drugs and alcohol started to become a part of our lives, my mom's life. And, you know, it affected us as children. So, the family was going through a lot of turmoil. I mean, my mom struggled really hard. She's a very good mom. She worked plenty of jobs to try to make everything work for us. But I guess in her time of need she got lonely, and she got caught up in the wrong crowd, and they introduced her to the drugs and alcohol.

Candace said that after her mom partnered with the man who "brought drugs [cocaine] into her life, everything went down. It's like I wasn't even in existence to them anymore." Candace stopped going to school, there was no food in the house, and "there was a lot of people in the house . . . getting high in every room." In the fourth grade, Candace started staying overnight and then living with her best friend's family. In her words, that family lacked "structure," so she "ran the streets and started having sex early and started smoking marijuana and drinking." She stopped attending school because her friend's family lacked the legal documentation to register her, and her mom could not provide documentation because she "was somewhere where you probably couldn't find her." Candace missed most of the fifth and sixth grades, and she stopped attending school in the seventh grade.

When Candace was 11, her mom took her to stay with her biological father and the woman he lived with. Candace explained, "My mom needed somewhere for me to go. She was too busy getting high and she just didn't have time to deal with me." Candace's biological father molested her the first night she stayed with him and continued to do so for "a few years." When Candace told her mom, she "blew it off and sent me back." After her dad split up with his partner, he forced Candace to have intercourse with him. Candace slit her wrists, and her father found her passed out in the bathroom and took her to the hospital. Candace knew that the hospital staff suspected abuse:

> They had me all in the psych ward for a minute or whatever. . . . They was talking to me and asked me [about abuse]. I was just too afraid to tell them. I told my mom. She didn't believe me. Why would I tell you people? You guys are just going to tell me I'm a liar too, so I never tell anything to anybody.

After attempting suicide, Candace moved back in with her best friend's family. She and her friend associated with men from Detroit who regularly visited the smaller, economically distressed city where Candace lived. "We sold drugs [crack] and we got in . . . all kinds of trouble with the law, breaking the law, stealing, and stuff like that. I used to shop-lift with them and everything." Sexual abuse prompted Candace to live with her friend's family again, which due to the lack of any adult super-vision meant she really lived on her own, vulnerable to the influences of older men who gave her access to drugs and opportunity to bring in il-legal income.

One of the men laced marijuana with cocaine and encouraged Can-dace to try the "different high." She liked the high and escalated to snort-ing cocaine. In the chapter of her life that she entitled "When I Was Lost," Candace described her feelings at the end of adolescence:

> I felt like nobody loved me. I didn't have any family. I'm with my best friend and they showing me as much love as they knew how because of I'm pretty sure they didn't know any love of their own because you know, the life-style that they were living in, nobody was on them. And they [best friend's parents] would just let us run loose and they didn't care anything about it. We'd be out in the middle of the night. Her mom would never come look for us. . . . It was rough because I felt like I was alone. I was always questioning God, like, "Why would you even create me to be out here in the world by myself?" I literally had no one to turn to, no one.

Candace reflected back on telling the story of her childhood: "I skipped around [in the life story]. It's hard to just put it all together in one time. It's overwhelming."

Lynette's repeated claims of early childhood sexual abuse that her parents ignored, rape by a stepbrother that her parents said did not hap-pen, childhood marriage and childbearing, limited education, and an abusive older husband all before she turned 17 stand out as an extreme example of the connections of childhood sexual abuse with other forms of victimization and betrayal by adults. Even though she told them about repeated rapes over two years starting when she was eight, Lynette's par-ents sent her to spend time with her dad's friend, who had done this. Later when she was in foster care due to neglect and her mother's re-fusal to care for her, her parents did not believe Lynette's claim that her stepbrother had raped her during a home visit. To avoid another home visit, Lynette left foster care and moved in with the man she would soon marry. Even though Lynette was just 13, her mother signed over custody to the future husband's older 18-year-old brother. According to Lynette, her mother also signed for her to marry when she was pregnant at 16 to protect the then 18-year-old future husband and father of her child from being charged for having sex with a minor. This husband was violently abusive; for example, he threw Lynette out a window when she was pregnant. Lynette's parents, the foster care system, and the courts allowed transfer of custody of a 13-year-old girl to an 18-year-old man and then allowed her early marriage to his younger brother.

Lynette's efforts to escape from her husband led to her drug use as an adult. She traveled with him to a state in the south-central region, where they lived in a motel. He made her sleep on the floor and had another woman, who brought in income prostituting, sleep with him in the bed. When he and the woman went out to buy drugs, Lynette escaped with her baby and returned to Michigan. In Michigan, with no means to support herself or her child, she partnered with a man who talked her into trying heroin, and after that her life revolved around getting high. "Yeah, I was 87 pounds, and stripping for money for dope. . . . Like, I danced and would maybe make 50 dollars a day, then I started making 1,000 dollars a day, and all I had to do was enough to get my fix, and that's . . . all that mattered." Lynette described her greatest regret: "Using needles is my biggest regret, 'cause that would have stopped . . . all the chain of events that happened in my life from happening. . . . I wouldn't have lost my kids because I wouldn't be a drug addict." The outcomes for Lynette match the negative results that the World Health Organization and UNICEF warn against as reasons for considering marriage under the age of 18 a human rights violation.[10] These negative outcomes, combined with a history of childhood neglect and disbelieved sexual assaults, left Lynette vulnerable to the influences of men who encouraged drug use that resulted in dependence on illegally earned income to support her addiction.

Considerable literature establishes that justice-involved girls and women have high rates of childhood sexual abuse.[11] What is striking is the women's recollections of being ignored or not believed and seen as liars when they revealed abuse. Covering up, ignoring, and denying childhood abuse magnified the harm to these women. Nina directly attributed drug use and addiction to the unspeakability of sexual abuse in her family. She knew that her father abused her stepsister, and she first suspected and later believed that he knew his brother (Nina's uncle) sexually abused Nina. To deal with feelings of betrayal and disgust, Nina took her mother's prescribed pain pills, and the resulting addiction led to her use of heroin. Nina explained why discovering that her father molested his new wife's daughter affected her "tremendously": "I was being molested by my uncle, and I used to think that my father knew that, but I thought, you know, that couldn't be right. I must be imagining it wrong, but then I started questioning it, yeah, I think that he allowed that to happen." The stepmother's mistreatment of Nina's younger brother caused Nina further distress, to the point that she had an "it doesn't matter anymore" kind of attitude. She thought, "I really was on my own and that my family wasn't perfect, that there were a lot of secrets. There was no family anymore." Coping with the emptiness of her family, Nina asked a cousin with shoplifting skills to show her how to steal. Another cousin showed her how to get and use heroin. For years, Nina supported herself and her addiction by working at retail fraud "like a job."

Pushed and Pulled into Trouble

For the women just described, parents and guardians either pushed girls out of their homes, did not meet basic needs so the girls moved out, or denied or ignored girls' claims of sexual abuse. Girls' early separation from parents and guardians differs from depictions of running away as an incident followed by return to the family or placement in a juvenile justice or child protection agency program or foster home. Nobody made efforts to keep track of the girls living on their own or return them to their families. Moving away seemed more like a drift out of the household, or in Jolene's case, being "dropped off" at a new temporary residence, than the typical conceptualization of one or more runaway incidents. Creating further distress, denial of girls' sexual abuse or blaming them for it and the failure to discuss the abuse limit victimized individuals' resilience after the violations.[12] The combination of empty families and ignored and denied childhood sexual abuse put women at high risk for long-lasting post-traumatic stress disorder (PTSD), anxiety, and depression.[13]

Childcaring and Protecting Institutions

The women's accounts show how personnel in societal institutions—schools, CPS and foster care, police, juvenile courts and juvenile justice programs, and jails—that ideally should educate, nurture, and protect girls either ignored them or made bad situations in their lives worse. Their action and lack of action show missed opportunities to interrupt the connection of childhood adversities to eventual conviction as adults. Like parents or other guardians, schools and agencies seem to have let girls live on their own without investigation or opposition; agency personnel did not believe girls' reports of abuse; and no one took effective action when girls fought in school, attended school sporadically, or stopped attending altogether.

Candace's story not only shows how she progressed from being neglected by her mother and sexually abused by her father to running the streets with older men who promoted and enabled drug use, selling drugs, and stealing. It also shows the lack of effective response by the school and hospital staff. There did not seem to be any effort by school personnel to reengage with Candace when she attended sporadically and then stopped attending at all. Because she moved to a neighborhood served by a different school when she lived with a friend, only a district-level tracking system and response could have been effective, but no such system helped Candace. Because Candace's mother ignored Candace's statement that her biological father sexually abused her, Candace believed there was no point in telling anyone, including the staff at a hospital's psychiatric unit, about the abuse. I do not know whether the hospital staff had adequate screening methods or tried to follow up. Candace's experience makes it clear that medical contact could have been a point of effective intervention into her repeated sexual abuse, but it was not an effective point of intervention for her.

Schools pushed girls out when they displayed signs of trauma and distress as reactions to chaotic or damaging family contexts, and this practice most heavily affects Black and Hispanic girls.[14] The school pushed Raven out when a counselor broke confidentiality regarding her stepfather sexually assaulting her, and the school expelled Carmen when family troubles manifested themselves in fights at the school. Similarly, after Sally's brother sexually assaulted her at age 12 and her mother did not believe her, she said she was "angry all the time . . . 'cause I was exposed to somethin' that I never experienced before. I was very, very angry. I fought all the time. I was getting expelled, you know, kicked out of school all the time." During a period when Daphne's parents argued and after they split up, she frequently skipped school. When she attended, she fought with other students, with the result that she was "kicked out." Not only did family crises and the sexual abuse of girls in families spill over into girls' fighting in school and then being expelled, school personnel's and schoolmates' attacks on girls' character—like the verbal attack the principal directed at Carmen or the schoolmates' talk about Raven having sex with her stepfather—made their time in school unbearable.

Some women thought CPS workers, who have the job of protecting children, turned a blind eye to their victimization. Toya said that from age 9 to 11, her mother sold her and her sister to a group of men for money in exchange for sex with the girls. Toya told school staff, and they called CPS. She answered the interviewer's question about what CPS did: "They didn't react at all, to be honest. They didn't react until my sister was pregnant. And they were like, 'Oh, why is she 12 and this dad is like 40?'" When CPS took action, Toya's dad was incarcerated for an offense unrelated to trafficking the sisters, and her mom "signed off" on transferring custody of the sisters to the state, whose caseworkers placed them with foster parents who adopted them.

Foster home placement that resulted in adoption brought its own abuses for the sisters. At 16, Toya followed her older sister when she ran away from the adoptive home. She explained why her sister left: "She thought my adoption mom was abusive. She would bite the kids, the younger ones. She would make them look in the mirror and tell them how ugly they are. She was very—just not a good mom. And my sister said, 'Screw it,' and she just left." With her mother and adoptive family eliminated as feasible options for a place to live, Toya moved in with her biological father, who introduced her to drugs. "I hung out with my dad. My dad's like, 'Oh this is what we do.' So that's how I found out about alcohol and drugs and what all that was. It's led to all my problems, why I've had so many to be honest." One abusive family can negatively impact a child for life. Toya endured a series of abusive families while in the care of CPS.[15]

Maya stands out from other women because of the radical action she took at age 12 to get help from CPS. Maya lived with her mother, who belonged to motorcycle clubs that took her away from home much of the time. Maya tried to stay with five younger siblings to avoid leaving them in a bad situation: "Our life was really hell because we had a lot of different peoples in our life, you know? Different men's trying to do stuff to me and my sister and stuff. Yeah, and when I was younger, she [mom] just used to leave us in the house all the time and we didn't have any food and didn't really go to school." To improve the living situation, Maya "burned down the house so somebody would come and take us. Yeah, I got tired of taking care of five kids that I couldn't really take care of." When the interviewer asked about a positive childhood memory, Maya said, "I guess when I got tooken. That was a good change in my life. . . . We was able to eat every day, able to you know, have clothes to wear, and it was a positive change . . . instead of being in a house with no food, no lights and gas and stuff." Maya spent time in a girls' group home, but for the most part she stayed with her siblings and looked out for them in foster care settings. Looking back, Maya assessed the way she and her siblings lived in foster homes: "It was still abusive and everything so it ain't really turn out good. But it was better than what we was in, but it still wasn't good."

In an example of inadequate police response to girls' sexual abuse, parallel to Carmen's experience of police dropping the case against her brother, the police doubted Anna's reports of her stepfather's abuse between ages 6 and 12:

> I went to tell the police. They did an investigation and removed me from the home for like two days, and then my mom told me she was going to put me in foster care, I'll never see her and my brother again, and I need to go back and tell them it was all lies, so that's what I did. . . . The cops believed that I made up this whole, like, really specific detailed story.

Anna said that after the abuse stopped, "I attempted suicide twice. I just didn't want to be alive. I couldn't deal with what had happened to me." Continued contact with her stepfather weighed on Anna. "Yeah. I started acting out at school and at home and, my doctor, when I was 14 put me on like, a tranquilizer because I would just flip out. So, I was in the mental hospital a lot, in and out." She saw her childhood as a "big lie" because family members ignored the abuse. "We always just had to pretend that we were normal, that nothing was happening, 'Don't tell anybody ever.' You know, and it was just the huge secret that I had to keep, and it was awful." Anna did not attribute addiction to heroin in her twenties to the childhood sexual abuse. She explained that she lived with a man who introduced her to drugs, and the first arrest at age 20 was for larceny committed with this boyfriend to support their drug use. However, she carried the experience of abuse unacknowledged by the police and either undetected or inappropriately treated by the family physician into her interactions with criminal justice personnel.

The detailed excerpts already presented provide information about the interventions of juvenile courts in the girls' lives. For Carmen, the juvenile court supported her mother's desire to punish her for reporting that her brother raped her, and at other times school fights landed her in juvenile detention. One might conclude that the court and related placements and programs were fundamentally punitive, but Carmen said that she sometimes wanted to return to juvenile facilities, where she had someone to talk with. It is plausible that the juvenile court staff and the judge assessed Carmen's family environment as requiring a group home placement that would keep her from the aversive family setting.

Marilyn, however, made clear the negative effects of the juvenile court and placements on herself and her family. Her mother had taken prescription medication for as long as Marilyn could remember. When Marilyn was 12, she and a friend took the pills prescribed for her mother ("eight different kinds of pills, like Kronospan, Vicodin, all types"), and adults in the household found the girls passed out. Based on their observations of Marilyn's mother, the two girls thought they would get pleasantly high from the drugs. Marilyn said the charge against her was "delivering and manufacturing," and when the interviewer questioned this, she explained, "She was already at my house. We both had took 'em at the same time and they just charged me because I'm the one that gave them to her, you know, and her parents were upset." It remains unclear why the charge included manufacturing or whether it actually did. However, the charge of distribution for a girl who shares her mother's medication with another girl is like "charging up" girls for assaults rather than status offenses when they fight with a parent.[16] This pattern, a part of the "get tough on crime" movement, led to increased use of out-of-home placement for girls during the period when many women in the research were juveniles.

Marilyn said she had never been in trouble before, but the judge sent her to a training school:

> And I met a whole bunch of people in there that, stealing cars and doing this, doing that, stuff I had never heard of, you know. So, I ended up graduating from there when I was 14. That's when I went home. That's when the second [attack] had took place as far as him [older brother] molesting me when I was 14. I had only been out for a short period of time before I had . . . joyrided in my dad's car. . . . And he [dad] pressed charges on me so I got locked back up for that.

Marilyn and the girls she met in training school took the car together. The courts placed 15-year-old Marilyn in another training school, where she attempted suicide:

> So, I was there for two years. And I wasn't making any progress whatsoever there. Like we had a big riot in there where all the kids from all the different areas, you know, went and was hitting staff and running, and, it just went from there to, I went and hung myself in the bathroom. . . . They said my whole face and everything was purple, cuz I had a line on my neck for like, forever, like a long, long time.

She gave the reason for her suicide attempt:

> You grow up like that, you go and you go through you know all these people, you don't have no mom and dad. You just got staff. And it's, 12 to 17 that's the years that make you who you are. Those are the years that you develop everything, and you learn about everything, and that's all I learned was being there and being there. . . . As soon as you meet a staff member all they see is that charge that you're there for. . . . [S]o if somebody seen you as a home invasion charge, they're automatically gonna go and assume that I would steal something from them. Or, you know, that I'm that type that's gunna go into somebody's house or just takes stuff from people. Just like assault, if somebody sees an assault on your record, they're gonna automatically think that you're violent and that you're a angry person. It's just how it is.

Marilyn's time in the training schools not only affected how she saw herself reflected in staff members' eyes, it also affected her relationship with her father, who was paying off $10,000 in costs of her institutionalization, assessed at $100 a month based on his low earnings. Due to this debt, he repeatedly told her, "You're always a loss." Marilyn's long stay in Michigan's training schools harmed her by teaching her how to break the law and by exposing her to staff members' and her father's labels of her as a criminal and a "loss."

Detached from families and school and managing their neglect, rejection, and trauma, the women described here seemed to be largely ignored and invisible to the agencies intended to educate, nurture, and protect them during childhood. Exceptions occurred in response to especially shocking events, such as Toya's 12-year-old sister's baby being born to a 40-year-old father or Maya burning down the house to get help from CPS. Still, after brief interventions following these shocking events, the women who crossed the divide from adolescence to repeated convictions as adults continued to experience abuse at the hands of guardians, foster families, and adoptive families.

The absence of women's comments about positive things that happened to them in schools and in interaction with police, CPS, and courts was just as striking as their negative accounts of school rejection, harmful CPS interventions, and damaging or ineffective juvenile justice system contacts and placements. A few women remembered getting help from child-serving and child-protecting institutions and agencies. Vivian's positive childhood memory was that her eighth-grade teacher encouraged her and even bought her a graduation dress when she finished middle school: "I had a teacher that really I looked at as like a mother figure almost and for my whole eighth grade year she kind of encouraged me so much that I went to camp my first year of high school." School support ended abruptly when family disruption had more influence than a teacher could have. At 15, Vivian ran away to escape her father's abuse of her mother and her mother's addiction, and she dropped out of school. Blaming herself for the bad result, Vivian identified running away and getting involved with an older man as the greatest failure of her life: "I was dropped out of school, pregnant, and started living life on my own, working as a girl. I feel like a failure right now. I had all of it. I went to Emerson High School, I was smart, I was too—I could do it. I just gave up." Vivian trivialized the effect of living with her drug-addicted mother. "But it still was on me. I still gave up on life at the moment when I decided to be grown." One teacher's attention during one year could not overcome the influence of family violence and Vivian's mother's addiction.

Also identifying a bright spot during time in a foster home, while she was in prison, where she told her life story, Wendy spoke about the psychiatric foster home worker who taught her to play chess, swim, and bowl. She lived in a psychiatric foster home after the discovery of her sexual abuse since age four. She said that the worker's efforts showed that he "must have seen something in me to take time to show me these talents." Sugar similarly positively assessed being in a foster family for six months while her dad was securing custody of her: "It was a really nice couple. He was a police officer. Actually, out here, his name was [Foster Dad L]—really sweet old man. And he still remembers us to this day even though I was this age." Sugar's positive foster care experience ended when CPS returned Sugar to her family. For the sample of substance-involved women with multiple convictions, positive experiences with intervention were short lived, but negative experiences with child-serving institutions tended to be repeated and have bad effects that continued for years.

The Burden of Racism

Latrelle, a Black woman who attended a predominantly White school, described the lasting effects of racism during early adolescence. As an adult, she summed up the effects of racially motivated bullying as a girl and the lasting awareness of racism as an adult:

> Everything is all everywhere . . . police brutality; racism is always number one, Black on Black crime, I could go on. It's all important, but what people really need to realize is that a lot of people still teach their children to hate. . . . It's obvious. You know, just like I said, we moved to [a suburb

of Detroit]. I was in the seventh grade, so I was just like I said 12, 13 maybe years old and I, you know, I learned a lot. You would be amazed, yeah.

Latrelle's racial victimization influenced her to gravitate away from the community where it occurred and toward peers where her family previously lived. In that context Latrelle began using and selling drugs. Many scholars have described the burden and stress from constant exposure to racist actions.[17] The effects of racial violence added their own burden to girls' and eventually women's day-to-day experience, either as a key influence on involvement in drugs as happened for Latrelle, or in combination with other harmful events in girls' and women's lives.

Lasting Effects

The effects of childhood adversities continued into adulthood and stayed with the women. During the life story interview, May repeatedly said that she did not understand how her mother could not know an uncle molested her nightly when she was three or four and how her relatives could think May was responsible for the sexual behavior at that age. She overheard her relatives talking about this and saying, "She fast." May remained angry at her mother at least up to the point of the life story interview, when she was 28, and she described herself as very protective of her own daughter as a result of her sexual abuse. Sally's mother accused her of breaking up the family by lying about her stepbrother's raping her when she was 12. Her parents sent Sally to live with a nearby neighbor after the brother's court hearing, and they reimbursed that family with food stamps, by Sally's account, so she would have enough to eat. When Sally ran into the stepbrother in her thirties in a local store, she reacted with fear: "I froze, like, like I, my heart went to beatin' real fast, and I'm thinkin', 'Damn, I thought I was over this fear part of him.'" Renee, age 37, continued to have bad dreams about sexual attacks she had endured in multiple foster homes: "And some of them I remember and some of them I don't remember . . . [M]y mind is blocked out." A man in his late twenties or early thirties followed Lydia, then age 7 or 8 and now 49, in his car while she was biking home from school. She pretended she lived at another house, but he outsmarted her, resumed following her, pulled her off her bike, and molested her. After her parents called the police and she talked to them, her mother said Lydia was at fault because of the way she was dressed. At 49, Lydia expressed continuing outrage: "Blaming me! And I'm thinking, 'First of all, we weren't even allowed to pick out our own clothes.' You know, she blamed me for what I had on." The women's statements reflect widespread tendencies throughout society and in families to discount girls' claims of sexual victimization and to blame them for it.[18] Blaming girls for being sexually victimized compounds the negative effects of the victimization by leading to self-blame, which in turn reduces victimized individuals' capacity to cope.[19] Considerable research shows that adverse childhood experiences increase women's risk for suicide during adolescence and adulthood and result in substance misuse, low self-esteem, anxiety, depression, sexual revictimization, high-risk sexual behavior, and recidivism.[20]

CONCLUSION

Women in this chapter started adult probation and parole supervision with a combination of damaged relationships with the mothers, fathers, and stepparents who raised them; limited education in schools that ignored their absence or pushed them out; persisting trauma from childhood sexual abuse and exposure to violence; and histories of early drug and alcohol use. Childhood exposure to parental substance misuse, intimate partner violence, poverty, and heavy responsibilities for siblings and household chores lead to negative social and emotional outcomes.[21] As noted previously, prior research documents differing prevalence of these childhood adversities and damaging school and court responses to girls' reactions for girls differentiated by community norms and by race. The analysis here provided some evidence of these differences, for example, race-based bullying and tolerance of violence against women in some rural areas, and race-based bullying. At the same time, it showed that across all groups, including those differentiated by age, many women grew up experiencing negative childhood events, heavy household responsibilities, and punitive responses to their resulting reactions.

Perhaps some girls with challenges growing up had better experiences with child-serving institutions than the women included in this book, and as a result they avoided convictions as adults. For the women who told their life stories, experiences with child-serving agencies tended to be punitive, short lived, or ineffective in protecting them from childhood neglect and abuse. Because Michigan's cutoff age for the juvenile justice system at the time of the research was 16, by age 17 women had spent time in jails with older women who were seasoned in using drugs and breaking the law and who encouraged them to follow their example. The few women who talked about police investigation into their childhood abuse described how their cases were dropped, or even how they were criminalized, and their abusers were exonerated. Lynette, Carmen, and Toya grew up in rural communities. Their reports of child abuse and steps to get out of abusive situations came to naught, perhaps because of a culture of tolerance of abuse found in some rural areas.[22] Holding victimized girls and emerging adults responsible for drug use and crime as though they had alternative opportunities to manage and survive flies in the face of knowledge about adolescents' decision-making and coping capability, the negative influence of childhood maltreatment on emotional regulation, and the constraints on agency that many of the women faced in adolescence and early adulthood.[23]

Women brought their backgrounds and their experiences with helping, correcting, or punishing agencies into their dealings with probation and parole agents, mental health providers, and substance abuse treatment. Their backgrounds shaped their emotional states and their financial poverty, and thus their need for social safety-net benefits such as food and housing assistance, medical care, and mental health treatment. The remaining chapters show how women with the histories highlighted in this chapter fared on probation and parole, in mental health and substance abuse treatment settings, in the workforce, and with social welfare agencies.

CHAPTER 3

Costs of Conviction

In most jurisdictions in the United States, individuals pay to be processed through the courts, spend time in jail, and receive supervision on probation and parole.[1] Women who contributed to this research incurred these sorts of legal financial obligations. For their circuit court felony convictions, they could be on parole after release from prison or on probation instead of in prison. Their legal financial obligations included fees for supervision and, for some women, electronic monitoring, paid to the MDOC. Judges could order other types of fines, restitution, and payments to the state's victim compensation fund. Women on probation after convictions for less serious misdemeanors paid fees for supervision in probation departments attached to lower-level district courts. Depending on the type of court (district or circuit), the geographic location of the court (rural, suburban, or urban), and the personal proclivities of judges, judge-ordered payments varied. In addition to supervision fees, some district courts required payments for drug and alcohol tests and substance abuse treatment. Regardless of the type of court, women incurred additional debts for child support ordered by family courts. Magnifying the burden created by these costs, during the entire study period, Michigan drivers' licenses were automatically suspended for an indefinite period for failing to pay fines, costs, fees, and assessments ordered by the court for offenses unrelated to driving.[2] Suspensions occurred regardless of financial ability to pay the debt. Losing the right to drive had especially serious consequences in Michigan, where the limited public transportation in many areas and the distances people had to travel to work or for other essential activities made access to a vehicle essential.

Michigan judges had discretion in assessing a person's ability to pay, setting requirements for level and timing of payments, and responding to failure to pay.[3] By law, presentence reports prepared by probation agents for judges to use in setting the parameters for payments had to include an estimate of a convicted person's ability to pay.[4] If a judge determined that the amount a person on probation owes would create a hardship for the individual or that individual's family, she or he could lower payments or excuse them completely, give women a longer time to complete payments, or allow community service to substitute for payments. Since neither Michigan laws nor guidelines provided a precise way to determine how much an individual can afford, judges have considerable discretion in orders for payment and responses to nonpayment.[5]

Several parts of the six interviews conducted with the women yielded information about costs levied and how costs affected women. At the first interview, and for any new convictions before the second and third interviews, women described their treatment by judges and noted how the sentence (including fines, fees, and restitution) affected them. During those first three interviews, structured questions about women's conversations with the supervising agent about education, employment, financial stressors, safe and stable housing, mental illness, and substance misuse generated additional information about costs. For each topic the woman and agent discussed, the interviewer asked about the content of the discussion, referrals, and whether the discussion and the agent's actions made things better or worse or had no effect. Providing additional opportunities to describe the results of money being owed, at the final interview about a year after they told their life stories, women responded to the question, "Looking back, how has your experience with supervision affected you?" Finally, at all but the life story interview, interviewers asked, "Are there things that you have done to make your life better?" In response to this question, some women identified paying legal financial obligations as an accomplishment, and others noted how these costs blocked their efforts to improve their lives.

Just before the research began, the American Civil Liberties Union (ACLU) published a report on Michigan (and four other states) that showed how monetary costs of criminal justice processing drained low income people's financial resources and how nonpayment resulted in lockup in jails and prisons.[6] The ACLU case analysis for Michigan discovered instances of charges up to $95 a week for supervision, additional jail entry and exit fees, daily jail room-and-board charges, and one woman who owed nearly $10,000 for tether (electronic monitoring) fees. The ACLU report concluded that the 2008 nationwide recession, which impacted Michigan more than other states, resulted in increased reliance by the district court and its probation department on money from people charged and convicted for misdemeanors. Judges in rural district courts that most needed streams of revenue required especially high payments and directed court staff, including probation agents, to aggressively pursue monetary payments from convicted individuals. In many states and criminal justice jurisdictions, these types of payments provide a critical stream of revenue flowing from people who had broken the law to courts and probation departments that rely on the income to support operations.[7]

A profile of the financial situation of women at the start of the study shows that the monetary costs of conviction could consume a high proportion of women's limited income. Of the 115 women who provided information, 98 (85.2%) reported annual incomes of less than $10,000, and 94 of 116 (81.0%) still had incomes below $10,000 by the end of the first year of supervision. At the start of the research, over half (66, 55.9%) of the women indicated that they were able to work but were unemployed, 23.7 percent (28) worked part time or could not work due to disability or demands of caring for children or other family members, and just 20.3 percent (24) worked full time. Nearly half of the women (50, 42.4%) lived in a household where no member had full-time employment, and close to half (63, 46.6%,) answered "yes" to a question about whether they had recent severe financial problems "like eviction, bankruptcy, calls from collection agencies, cut-off utilities, problems getting child support payments, repossessions of property, and things like that." Indicating the strain resulting from their financial situations, 66.0 percent (79) of the women worried about how they would make ends meet. A few years later, by the time of the life story interview, women on average continued to live on little or no income, and almost the same proportion agreed that they worried about making ends meet.

During the study, high MDOC supervision fees were in effect, for example up to $15 a day for tether. District court fees could be even higher or could be in addition to MDOC fees for women sentenced to probation and parole in multiple court jurisdictions. The injustice in this system is that for individuals who could not pay court, supervision, and jail costs, these debts resulted in more costs for extended supervision or jail time, so they ended up owing more than better resourced women who could more easily meet their legal financial obligations.

When they could not cover conviction costs but met other requirements, women on parole and those on probation for felonies (the women supervised by MDOC agents) sometimes fared better than those sentenced to probation for the lesser offenses handled by district courts.[8] Once the stipulated supervision period ended, if women met all other requirements, MDOC agents usually terminated probation or parole. Although this ended supervision and its related new costs, nonpayment could result in the debt being turned over to the state collection agency, which would establish a payment plan or, if the debt was not paid, take the money from tax returns. Alternatively, for individuals who did not resist paying but who lacked income or other resources, MDOC supervision debt could be forgiven. Forgiving debt conformed to MDOC policy and staff training intended to shift the focus of supervision toward meeting women's needs and away from sending people to jail or prison for violations of supervision requirements. Yet due to involvement of judges in probation cases, the possibility of being simultaneously supervised in both circuit and district courts, and variation within the ranks of probation and parole agents, MDOC-supervised women still might go through rounds of nonpayment, jail, new costs, nonpayment, and more jail.

The remainder of this chapter takes a broad and deep look at the costs of supervision as they played out in women's lives. These costs extend beyond monetary fees, fines, and other expenses to disruption in education and employment, emotional strain, and spillover effects on women's families, most often the children they cared for. Some women with means to pay off debts enjoyed a privilege discount that allowed them to avoid these collateral costs.

TOUCHSTONE STORIES

Most of the six women highlighted at the start of each chapter described a considerable burden from the cost of being supervised in the community. Raven stood as a partial exception because her supervising agent acted to reduce the monetary costs.

Convictions in Multiple Courts

Carmen's situation illustrates the financial demands created by supervision in two court jurisdictions, one where she stole a car and the other where she broke into another car to steal gas money. Carmen saw insurmountable obstacles to paying what she owed two court jurisdictions for fees, restitution, and a required GED program. Since sustaining a brain injury in elementary school, she had had 35 to 45 seizures at a time, five or six times a week. Her disability insurance for the seizure disorder was terminated because her mother cashed the disability checks and spent the money while Carmen was in jail. Carmen saw no possibility of finding a job because potential employers would view her unpredictable seizures as a liability. Creating additional barriers to employment, after her father destroyed her belongings in a fit of anger sparked by her complaint about having the sole responsibility for caring for her dying grandmother, Carmen needed $10 for a social security card, $25 for a birth certificate, and $15 for a new ID to even apply for jobs. Her lack of income made the cost of school to earn the court-required GED ($50 a trimester) plus her $50-a-month supervision fees prohibitive. She explained how dual-county supervision led to her being in and out of jail: "I just kept on getting arrested for violations, 'cause I didn't have the money to pay my fines, you know? So, every time you're late on your fines, they make you do time in jail. It was like a never-ending circle." While Carmen was in jail in one county, the agent in the other county violated her for not paying fees there. The threat of jail time if she failed to pay court-ordered costs, replacement costs of documents necessary to find a job, and the cost of required GED classes left Carmen feeling stressed: "If I don't get in school soon, she's gonna violate me, so like it's kind of stressful." In addition to Carmen, other women's statements presented later in this chapter show their stress, angst, and despair when they thought about the high costs of supervision and their low or nonexistent income. Research on limited and no-income people outside of Michigan confirms the connection between a "piling on" of multiple legal financial obligations that left people in fear of incarceration and resulting stress and anxiety that affected their mental and physical health.[9]

After release from jail for an assault unrelated to her initial convictions, Carmen faced violations for not paying fees and restitution ordered by both courts. She set forth her reasons for opting for prison: "So finally I just told them to send me to prison so I can get it done and over with, and they ended up sending me for two and a half years." Carmen's decision extracted her from what she called the "circle" of violations for nonpayment and jail time, but she paid with a lengthy prison sentence.

Extension of Supervision

Following a conviction at age 21 for selling drugs, Bree could not keep up payments for court fees, so the agent extended probation. Bree reacted by absconding from supervision: "I didn't have my fees paid off, so she extended it, and I felt like that was just not right so I just said, 'forget probation,' and just didn't go back." Bree viewed the extension as unfair, because it kept her on probation for longer than specified by the plea bargain she had made in court. Unable to find work because of a record of convictions for possession of guns and possession of narcotics with intent to sell, and ineligible for safety-net benefits because of a prior felony conviction, Bree made a living dancing in a strip club and selling drugs. While absconded, the police arrested her while making a drug delivery. She had a gun on her hip, a backpack stuffed with a pound of weed, more weed in the car, a scale, and bullets. She had bought the gun "from the streets" to protect herself from being robbed of her substantial nightly earnings from drug sales and dancing. The new convictions, coupled with having absconded from probation, resulted in her getting prison time followed by time on parole that brought her into the study. Although their reasons for going to prison were different, difficulties paying the costs of supervision were links in the chain of events leading to both Carmen's and Bree's incarceration.

Lost Opportunity

During the first year of supervision, Carla put her energies toward paying court-related costs. Just before the life story interview, she answered the question about whether she had done anything to improve her life:

> Well, not that I think of, just been paying off all my fines and all my stuff and to where I'm getting out completely. This month I'll be completely off owing anybody at all—no money to the Secretary of State [for driving infractions and license renewal], won't owe no money to the courthouses no more 'cause I almost got that paid off. I been paying that for the past two years now.

Carla met her monetary obligations to the courts and the secretary of state, which left her without money to pay off student loans. As a result, she could not return to college, where in the early months of supervision she had signed up for coursework in general studies to prepare for further study in business management. By diverting her monetary resources away from paying student loans, she paid a different type of cost: limited education and reduced potential for future better-paying employment. For the Michigan women and in other studies, this type of trade-off by people with low incomes who have financial obligations due to citations or convictions solidifies their position at or below the poverty line.[10]

Simultaneous Supervision

At age 55, Mallory faced a longer sentence and more requirements than she had expected based on past experiences with probation and parole: "I never got it stacked up like this—probation, drug treatment, community service, fines, and costs." Being on both probation and parole simultaneously contributed to the multiple requirements and obligations:

> So I got a probation officer and a parole officer. You know, I don't know who's going to be what. I gotta see both of them, I guess. Well, I know I gotta see Ms. Harold. But I always thought the parole superseded the probation, but it doesn't. In this case here [the jurisdiction where she agreed to take part in the study] I'm under probation status. You know, and I call in once every month to the parole office and leave a message with Ms. Winter that I'm still here.

Early during supervision, Mallory's limited income amounted to $24.50 in public assistance every two weeks, and she lived in transitional housing for people leaving prison. She said her supervising agent gave her envelopes and told her to bring some of the restitution money she owed every time she reported. When the interviewer asked how receiving the envelopes affected her, she said it made things worse: "Cuz I didn't have no job with no income at that point, you know. Nothing, I didn't have nothing coming in of my own." The combination of lack of income and repeated reminders that she should pay created an emotional cost: "I'm drained, emotionally, I'm drained."

Accumulation of Burdens

Marion summed up the burden she felt because of conviction costs in the advice she gave to other women, which was to "stay out of the way." She explained what she meant:

> Stay out of the way means when you're in trouble you make it worse by continuing to engage in trouble. It just becomes a nightmare and then, like now, I can't pay these lawyer costs and court costs and fees. You know, the system it really sucks. It makes it where you lose your job, then they charge

you—have the nerve to charge you sixty dollars a day just to be in county [jail]. And then I filed for my taxes and then you tell me you take every dime, and they'll need the remaining balance. So yeah, just stay out the way. Just don't go there, stay out the way.

Marion's comments show a spiral into increasing debt that lands people in jail, leads to job loss and housing instability, and increases financial precarity, which research in other settings with other populations confirms.[11] Carmen, Bree, Mallory, and Marion all described a sense of hopelessness about meeting financial obligations when they saw no possibility of getting legitimate work or securing enough money to live on. They reacted to their despair differently. Carmen gave up and went to prison, Bree absconded from supervision and made money illegally, and Mallory and Marion just felt overwhelmed and hopeless. Reinforcing the potential for these sorts of negative outcomes, research in other settings shows how legal financial obligations can leave people feeling they must break the law to survive and can result not just in hopelessness, but in fear, frustration, anxiety, despair, and illness.[12]

Agent Advocacy

In contrast to supervision experiences that seemed to intensify the negative effects of high costs of conviction and low income, Raven's probation agent reduced her burden. Like the other women, Raven struggled with supervision and court-related debts, especially after welfare support for herself and her five children was cut off when Michigan's financial crisis led to the state's reducing the length of time a family could receive assistance. She remembered how the agent advocated for her with the judge to help her avoid penalties for nonpayment:

[The agent said,] "Well I'm just gunna go down to the judge and tell them that you don't have no income." I had to bring her a couple papers in from DHHS [Department of Health and Human Services] but that was cool because it said that I don't get anything and then once I found that job . . . she was calling me at work like, "How you doing? You working good? How many hours you getting this week?" and stuff like that. Then, I bring her my check stub and she like uh-uh. . . . My checks was like, we got paid every week and I swear 18, 30, 22 dollars. Like, . . . the biggest check I got was 147 dollars, and I gave her 60 dollars out of that for my fines and costs. When she took it to the judge, she like, "Judge, the girl ain't working that many hours but she has gave us well over half of what she done made. I feel like we should give her, you know, a little more time or whatever," and he was okay with it. I feel like she really worked it in my favor.

The agent's efforts to get precise details about Raven's financial situation and her advocacy, combined with the judge's willingness to take the agent's advice, reduced the immediate negative impacts of conviction costs.

So far, the six women identified the stress of monetary costs, which took a high proportion of very limited incomes; diversion of money from education to funding court and supervision operations; and perceptions of supervision and the related costs as a nightmare worse than going to prison. A close examination of the statements of other women contending with costs of supervision that far exceeded their financial means reinforced these findings and expanded understanding of the range of common and unique difficulties they faced in paying their conviction-related debts.

THE LARGER GROUP OF WOMEN

Similar to Carmen's description of repeated violations for nonpayment in one court because another court had her in jail for nonpayment, Renee explained how jail time put her in "double jeopardy" after a conviction for using a stolen credit card: "I sat eighty-two days in jail, which I don't think was fair because it's kind of a take-take situation. . . . They want me to pay to stay in jail, and they also want me to pay this money back." Renee had paid her light bill with the credit card, and after discovering it was stolen, she left the state for four years before returning and turning herself in. She described the aftermath: "I went to jail and have been going through crazy stuff ever since then." Renee appreciated that the probation agent coached her on how to handle court appearances for nonpayment of restitution and jail costs, but in the end, "the money part, she really can't help me with." For Renee, judicial orders of jail time began a vicious cycle of "room-and-board" costs to stay in the jail, failure to pay because of being locked up, release with more debt than before going to jail, and more jail time due to inability to pay off these debts.[13]

For Elsie, the cost of random drug testing, which many district court probation departments required women to cover, created more than financial problems. Elsie struggled with a relapse to drug use after being cut off from mental health services during her transition from a residential substance abuse treatment program to the community. She paid $9 for each required drop to test for drug use, but she never knew how many times in a month she would wake up and make the phone call that let her know it was her day to test. She lived on monthly disability checks, which totaled just over $700 a month, and tried to save enough to cover the unpredictable number of drops during a month:

> Back in May, I dropped more than probably seven or eight times. And I was like, I really did not have that money. . . . I save up money for what I think, you know, just how many times I'm going to drop. So, I'll save up maybe fifty or sixty dollars. But you know, to do that every morning and, you know, sometimes, once—it was only one time that I only dropped once that month. But I have to get up every morning, call, see if my color came up, make sure I have nine dollars.

The system of paying for random drug tests went beyond monetary cost. It created stress over meeting both day-to-day expenses and the unpredictable monthly cost of drug testing during a period of being cut off from mental health care. A multistate study found that this pattern of constantly calculating the level of debt and balancing paying it off against family members' needs created extreme stress.[14]

Like Elsie, Molly struggled with the costs of drug testing. Molly had no income because she had just left a 90-day treatment program, so she had not found work. She set forth her dilemma of deciding whether to pay for testing or use her money to meet her children's basic needs:

> Shoot I mean with me having to go through everything and do everything it's sad that we put yourself in a position where any money you get has to go to dropping [drug testing] and bus fare, because you know I needed a pack of diapers a couple years ago. . . . I had to put that aside and say well if I get called to go have to blow [breathalyzer test] today, that's my TBT [breath test for alcohol] money. I have to put that first before anything with my kids, and that's really sad, like I mean serious sad.

Transportation problems increased Molly's monetary costs and created physical and emotional costs:

> I've got to take buses over there. . . . I'd have to load up somehow two kids, two infant kids almost—one crazy one year old and an infant—load them whether it's winter, dead winter, or summer, take them on the bus. They want you to take the stroller down, pick up your kids. I've got two kids in my arms, a stroller, loading on the bus that's already moving by the time you step on it, pretty much. Get off, walk, go drop, two kids, come back. It's very difficult. It's possible but that's so much stress on you, physical stress and emotional stress.

When the agent recommended another year of supervision and the judge agreed, Molly thought about the cost for each additional year:

"Another 700 to 900 dollars supervision fees. It was adding up to a lot, another thousand dollars plus fines, plus 700-dollar late fees, and then not to mention the drops and all that." Looking back at her entire time on probation, Molly said that supervision made her "feel inadequate" and was "very stressful . . . cuz it you know, so many obligations with probation that you have to do . . . and then you gotta meet obligations for your family and it's like, if you can't, things could weigh on people." Molly's statements are especially relevant to women, who more often than men on probation and parole have responsibility for the day-to-day care of children, and thus they face the choice of paying for necessities for children or paying conviction-related costs.[15]

Francesca also shared details about her shrinking income and supervision-related financial responsibilities. Her expectation that her debts would last for years intensified when she was cut off from food assistance and medical insurance. She hoped to regain medical insurance after a diagnosis for attention deficit disorder so she could get medication to help her concentrate in school. She had $20 per month deducted from her checking account for a $300 debt for child support, which she had almost paid off. She owed $4,000 in court supervision fees from prior felony convictions. She also owed $4,100 for driving with improper plates, and she could not regain her driver's license until she paid that debt. Francesca was on the brink of homelessness during several interviews. The court had been taking $6 a week from her earnings at a job, but during periods of unemployment the deductions stopped. She knew that she was at risk of arrest if she stopped paying for a substantial period. At age 35, she estimated, "I'll probably be paying on it until I'm 50." The costs of court and regaining a driver's license left Francesca feeling hopeless, and like Carmen and Marion, thinking she would never complete supervision, because she had no way to pay the costs.

A Narrow Focus on Payment

Conviction-related costs could skew interactions with supervising agents such that communication exclusively focused on payment. Fiona described serious mental health problems that started in childhood and were compounded by severe child and intimate partner abuse. During each of the first three interviews, Fiona repeatedly said that the primary message from the probation agent was "make your payments." Her meetings were brief: "I'm in there for maybe, at most, three or four minutes." Asked whether the agent's comments were helpful, Fiona answered,

"I don't understand. Like that's not who I would go to for help with something like that. [What you do is] just come in, do what you're supposed to do, get out." Three-and-a-half years after supervision started, as part of her life story Fiona explained why the criminal justice system was "wrong": "I've had probation on my ass for the past four years. It is not a motivator for me. . . . I have completely rehabilitated at this point. I'm not using drugs anymore. I'm fully functioning, and I'm still on supervision for all kind of money. . . . They did not put me in rehab. . . . I did it all on my own." The sole focus on making payments not only cost Fiona financially, but it undermined the MDOC's reform efforts to reduce recidivism and generally improve women's lives by focusing on their needs.

Shannon also remembered that the agent she saw for a year and a half emphasized paying off legal financial obligations by repeatedly asking, "Did you pay this? And do you have your fines?" Shannon shared her thoughts about the debts:

> No. I can't afford to pay anything on my fines. I only get 600 dollars a month [disability] . . . and that's my rent. My [adult] granddaughter pays . . . electric and the gas and . . . we struggle to pay the phone and the cable and . . . I mean, but we do it. And then my son and with his little bit of help on the side doing side jobs, that helps, but it's a struggle.

Over multiple interviews, Shannon consistently described conversations with the agent as restricted to questions about payment, but omitting other topics. "When we meet, it's quick and simple, 'Have I been in contact with the law?' 'No.' 'Do I have any concerns or issues?' 'No.' We're done." Shannon's life story was full of references to her drug use since her mother introduced her to crack at age 13, selling drugs most of her life, and prostitution since age 15 when her sister told her to sell herself if she wanted to eat. Yet across four interviews, Shannon specifically noted that the agent did not discuss substance abuse or mental health needs. Shannon shared her thoughts about the agent: "You have no consideration for me being clean. You have no consideration for me trying to do the right thing. I don't get 'You're doing good Shannon' or nothing." Shannon assessed the supervision experience: "I think her caseload was too big to care about what a person was going through. I don't know—it just made me feel like there was no purpose for the parole." Different from Fiona, who propelled herself into a network of mental health services, Shannon expressed a desire to obtain these services with the help of the parole agent. This did not happen because, like Fiona's agent, Shannon's agent's sole focus on payment contradicted the

MDOC's official policy of emphasis on supporting clients and getting them into needed treatment.

Fiona's and Shannon's experiences with conviction-related costs re-occurs in other courts. A study of judges in multiple Illinois courts documented how social problems of poverty and crime were transformed into individual financial problems of convicted individuals paying court costs under threat of extended supervision and jail.[16] The researchers observed numerous hearings that focused on paying costs and ignored the initial offenses and rehabilitation.

Conviction Costs Extended and Multiplied

The memorable message Lily, age 55, took from court and supervision was that she likely had a life sentence to probation: "And they told me I could be paying the rest of it. . . . I could be on it the rest of my life until I pay." Lilly found it "frustrating" that the judge did not listen when she told him she had no income and that a disability prevented her from off-setting costs with community service. Facing an anticipated lifetime of court payments, she absconded from supervision. In absconded status, Lily could be arrested on an outstanding warrant and returned to correctional supervision and be sanctioned with additional penalties, including incarceration. In the end, Lily paid for supervision by giving up freedom and equanimity to avoid court and supervision costs:

> I don't leave my house, and then anytime I come in contact, if I'm with a friend and they get pulled over, it, it's nerve wracking. I'm always wondering if today is going to be the day. Because, I mean, they don't want to hear nothing you have to say until you get back in front of that judge and I've been talking with some women, and it took one a while to get back from that spot [absconded status]. So, I don't know, they need to come out with a better system than that. . . . [Court personnel say] just come in here. But I know if I just come in there, what's gonna happen?

Lily worried intensely about being arrested and jailed, because she knew from experience that in jail, she would lose access to medications crucial for her physical health.

While absconded from supervision, Lily had made positive changes in her life. Addicted to drugs since age 22, except for the years when her children were very young, she had pictured herself as "90 years old run-nin' out tryin' to get me some drugs." A year before the life story inter-view, her four adult children gave her an ultimatum—it's the drugs or us—and helped her stop using. A daughter who was a nurse let her move into her home in a suburb where she lacked access to drugs and arranged for medication to lessen withdrawal symptoms. Two-and-a-half years later, Lily felt purpose in her life in her role as mother and grandmother to a total of 20 individuals. Yet at the last check of official records, unfinished business with the court for absconding had been on Lily's official records for at least a decade. Lily avoided monetary costs of supervision by absconding, but she restricted her own freedoms out of fear of the result of apprehension if she turned herself in. She reasoned that she had no money to hire a lawyer to tell her what to do, so all she could do was "take my chances" in front of a judge. She decided not to take a chance.

Rural women's lawbreaking across multiple counties likely reflects the absence of local "drug money" or other illegal opportunities closer to home. Like Carmen, two other women from rural areas had court and supervision costs in multiple counties. Sugar talked about how being on probation in three counties resulted in her expectation of years of probation supervision: "I think I got thirty-two months out here, and I still owe over 2,481 dollars out here and I'm on probation in County 1 for County 2, but it's all transferred out here to County 3, and I owe over 2,000 dollars out there. So, they're not going to let me off anytime soon."[17] Amy also experienced simultaneous multicounty supervision. While addicted to heroin, she and her friends specialized in stealing copper off phone towers in the rural areas of four contiguous counties. The financial arrangements for supervision were as follows: "Yes, and like this is paying to County 1, but they're supervising me for County 2, so I pay supervision fees to County 1 and court fines to County 2. And then I pay fines for County 3, and I pay fines for County 4." MDOC agents transferred supervision to the office that served the location of a woman's residence, but that did not eliminate or coordinate required payments across multiple jurisdictions. When district court probation simultaneously handled some of the cases, not only was the coordination of payments a problem, but depending on the relationships between agents in different jurisdictions, women might report to multiple agents at the same time.

Lengthy terms of probation brought nonmonetary costs in the form of spillover effects. As noted, Carla might have increased her chances for a good future job by completing payments on student loans and then attending college if she had not used her money for conviction costs. Even though she had a supportive, motivating probation agent, Ariana also gave up on her dream of being a pharmacy technician, in part because it took her three years to pay court costs. At first the agent helped Ariana feel less discouraged that the felony conviction would stand in the way of her doing the type of work she wanted:

> She's the one kind of make me feel better. Like, well, I could change things around. All I got to do is being motivated and, you know what I'm saying, try to strive for the best, so. I thought about it, I said "you know what, you right." I'm not going to let this hinder me, you know. Because staying out of trouble shouldn't be hard, and I go to school and get my degree, I get it expunged, it be A-1! I'm good.

Ariana's inability to find a job that she could reach without a car and that would hire her with a felony conviction, and the three years it took her to pay her fines, fees, and restitution, erased the benefits of the agent's motivating communication.

During the life story interview, Ariana identified the low point in her life as realizing the felony conviction made it impossible for her to continue her studies at a community college and find a job in a pharmacy. She identified becoming a mother as a major positive turning point in her life, but in the next sentence she highlighted the persistent barrier to studying to be a pharmacy technician. "Like I said, I still can't go to school for what I want to go to school for, and it's just, like, I don't know, I'm, like, stuck right now." An agent's encouragement can only go so far in helping women change their social standing through education and prospects for future employment. The combination of court and supervision costs, lack of transportation, employers' hesitance to hire a person with a felony conviction, and later the birth of a child coalesced to keep Ariana in a factory job. "I needed health insurance, my baby needed health insurance, and they had a good package, a 401K [retirement investment], a lot of things, so you know, I just had to keep my eye on the prize, I guess." Spending years paying for court fines and fees, supervision, and jail room and board could eat up a person's time and money and prevent her from getting an education that would increase the chances of a desired, good-paying job.

Tammy's supervision experiences also illustrate the limitations on a supportive agent's help within the constraints of probation and parole supervision. There were negative effects of lengthening supervision to allow time to pay the costs of supervision, which would increase the total costs in the end, but Tammy saw the extension as a good thing. The agent arranged an extension of supervision to four years for a larceny conviction, so Tammy did not "get violated and put in jail." Just as women's options were limited, agents' options were limited. In Tammy's case, the agent saw two less-than-ideal options for Tammy: going to jail or extending the period of probation and the related costs. This is an example of a finding that reoccurs in the next chapter: agents doing what they could to help women, but the context of corrections, community, and access to income limiting the positive effect agents could produce.

The Privilege Discount

For the women discussed so far in this chapter, the difference between monetary conviction-related costs and capacity to pay was large. For women with more resources, this difference decreased substantially, and they avoided other types of costs that come with conviction. In contrast to Lily, who could not afford a lawyer to help her end her status as absconded without risking her health and freedom, women with privilege noted how having a private lawyer rather than a public defender represent them in court reduced monetary costs and stigmatization. There was an especially pronounced difference in public and retained defense in Michigan, because at the start of the study the state had no centralized public defense funding for training and to set standards; instead judges developed their own systems.[18] Whitney, a Black woman who grew up in a family with financial resources, had a bachelor's degree from a state university. During her second marriage, she and her husband made a good income in real estate. When he started to free base cocaine and became addicted, she joined him in using, their real estate ventures failed, and they depleted their financial resources. After they split up, Whitney turned to stealing high-end goods and selling them to support herself and pay for cocaine. Her education and money positioned her to hire an attorney to represent her and to present herself in a way that elicited a favorable response in court after she was charged with theft:

> When I say I was treated with dignity and respect, I mean I was talked to and not degraded because of what I was doing, but I know that if you are represented by an attorney, a paid for attorney, your sentence is lighter. I've experienced having a court-appointed and also having an attorney that's been paid for. So, you are treated differently when you pay for your attorney.

As evidenced in the accounts of poor women, the monetary costs of supervision multiply and create emotional costs when they become unpaid debts or payment stretches out over time. Whitney summed up the importance of ending her time on probation quickly by describing her reaction to the agent's remarks: "'Keep up the good work. You can be off of this in September.' And I'm like, 'Wow! September!' Because I cannot wait! I just, you know—not that I can't wait because I'm going to go into the criminal life, I just . . . not having something over my shoulder."

Women with a well-resourced parent, especially one with status in the community, could avoid monetary costs, jail and prison time, and a permanent record of felony convictions. Two White women, Linsey and Sonya, grew up in families with financial means and spent childhood and adolescence in prospering suburbs outside of small cities. Both women experienced adversities during childhood. After her stepfather "beat the crap" out of Linsey for not receiving a high school varsity letter, Linsey stopped attending high school a few weeks before graduation. In response, her parents told her to leave home. She moved to a university town, where she stayed with acquaintances or slept in cars, and she fell in with a drug-using crowd; took part in "raves" at which crowds of people got high and partied; and used cocaine, heroin, and other narcotics. She described her attitude by citing a popular song lyric: "Freedom is just another word for nothing left to lose." Toward the end of seven years of drug use, Linsey lived with a man who abused her and, after her prior boyfriend returned from prison, she frequented a "dope house" with him to, as she put it, "get all this crap out of my mind and just escape." To support their addictions, Linsey cracked a safe at her workplace and faced charges for that and stealing money as well as possession of narcotics. Linsey's mother and stepfather helped her avoid a prison sentence by paying for a private attorney rather than leaving her dependent on an appointed public defender. She said her attorney "actually worked miracles, and he got me to where I am right now. . . . If I complete probation, my felony drug possession will be dropped. The misdemeanor retail fraud will always be there, but all I ended up getting was the two years [probation] for prostitution." Linsey's childhood adversities—early childhood exposure to her mother and birth father arguing before they divorced, her birth father's reneging on promises to maintain contact with her, her stepfather's physical abuse, and being ejected from living at home when she did not complete high school—marred her childhood and adolescence, but resources from her parents kept her out of prison and wiped out a permanent record of felony convictions. Also, although Linsey's family problems were not trivial, they were fewer and less persistent than many of the problems that other women experienced.

Sonya benefited from her mother's financial help and capacity to advocate for her with the judge and probation agent. After high school graduation, she lived on her own and supported herself working as a waitress. Sonya let her heroin-addicted boyfriend, whom she had dated since adolescence, move in with her, and she became addicted herself. They ended up selling all their belongings, unable to pay rent, and living in their car. At age 26, during the period of her drug use, the courts convicted Sonya on two counts of larceny, two for domestic violence, one for misuse of a credit card, two for driving under the influence, and one for possession of a narcotic. Sonya's mother turned her in to the police when she could not stop her daughter's drug use but then arranged with the judge and the probation agent that Sonya would not go to jail, but would stay in a halfway house, and after a period back with her family, would go to a 90-day residential treatment program. Sonya could always find waitressing jobs, and she used her earnings and a gift from her mother and stepfather to pay her court and supervision costs. Sonya correctly anticipated that her felony charges would be expunged after she completed two years of probation. By the life story interview, Sonya's mother had arranged for Sonya to learn to be an assistant to a lawyer by interning with a family friend. For both Linsey and Sonya, the costs of court and supervision did not become a never-ending cycle of payments and punishments. Through the process of expungement, they avoided damage to future employment prospects. They also spent a relatively short time living with the limitations set by the courts. As scholars have pointed out, privileged women avoided the "layaway plan" to maintain their future freedom by paying continuing costs spread over extended time.[19]

CONCLUSION

Some women spent years, hundreds or thousands of dollars, and hours of community service feeling trapped by conviction-related costs. One solution was to cease reporting, but absconded status brought its own costs in the form of living in hiding to avoid detection, possible incarceration, or extended community supervision with new costs. Especially for poor women, paying for supervision was not a good investment in the future, because it limited resources for education and training that would enable future employment at good jobs. A singular focus on paying led some agents to disregard other needs that had major effects on women's drug use and future crime. The narrow focus added to substantial stress that most women felt and put them in a "catch-22" situation in which their alternatives—going to jail for nonpayment, paying costs at the expense of getting an education, or what could be years longer on supervision—created the nightmare of more debt and less ability to pay.

Compared to better resourced people who come into the justice system as defendants, poor people pay a greater proportion of their incomes for conviction costs. Regardless of race and ethnicity, women who live in poverty are especially likely to be stressed by the need to divert money from their children's basic needs. They feel the physical and emotional stress of meeting supervision requirements at the very moments that they are taking care of children or, like Molly, holding children in their arms while boarding a bus to take them to the drug testing site. Nationally the negative effects of conviction costs fall most heavily on Black and other marginalized groups, who are increasingly overrepresented among the poorest U.S. citizens.[20] The higher concentration of poverty among women of color means that a higher proportion of them pay a large proportion of their income to cover conviction costs, confront the system without privately retained lawyers, and give up opportunities for using their resources to support their children's and their own advancement.

This chapter noted gaps in access to mental health treatment when women left substance abuse programs, jails, or prisons. Similarly, it showed how being cut off from medical insurance or welfare added to the burden of conviction costs. These examples foreshadow the more in-depth coverage of inaccessible treatment and cutoffs and denial of monetary assistance in chapter 5, "Treatment," and chapter 6, "Marginalization." First, however, the book turns to examples of agent actions that, consistent with MDOC probation and parole reforms, helped and empowered women, or that broke with reformed policy and harmed the women on probation and parole.

CHAPTER 4

Agent Actions

This chapter presents women's depictions of their interactions with supervising probation and parole agents and their assessments of how different types of agent actions helped or hindered them in avoiding substance misuse and crime and achieving aspirations for a good life. The MDOC had begun its shift toward widespread use of gender-responsive assessment and supervision and motivational interviewing, but agents still varied in their implementation of these approaches, and district court probation was not part of these reforms. For MDOC agents, external pressures such as large caseloads and agents' personal differences in education and correctional philosophy also affected the application of the new approaches to working with women. As a result, in the context of a substantial ongoing shift in MDOC supervision, women described a variety of supervision practices.

Sections of four different interviews conducted with each woman produced most of the information about agents' actions. Three interviews conducted in the first year of supervision elicited detailed accounts of women's conversations with agents about a mix of needs previously found to be common among justice-involved women. Prior research identified these needs and established their connection to recidivism. They include education, employment, financial well-being, safe and stable housing, mental illness and substance misuse, and avoidance of criminal peers and abusive partners.[1] For each topic discussed with agents, women gave their recollections of agents' comments and actions and the effects of what agents said and did. Providing more information on what women heard from supervising agents, the four interviews included questions about agents' messages that women used as a standard to judge their own behavior, and in some cases as a reason to change their behavior. Finally, the last interview, conducted about a year after the women told their life stories, asked for a retrospective look at the nature and effects of supervision.

Official case notes covering 18 months of supervision contained additional information about agent actions. For each woman, agents maintained a running record of meetings, phone calls, checks with people who knew the woman, home visits, drug and alcohol test results, referrals to programs, violations of supervision conditions, new offenses, extensions of supervision, orders for more or different treatment, and new incarceration. I used the case notes to confirm and supplement information from women, for example, reports of new convictions and statements that the agent did or did not make referrals to programs. The few instances of conflicting information are either noted or excluded in the examples of supervision experiences in this chapter.

Many women wove comments about the importance they attached to agents' caring about them and listening to what they had to say into examples of helpful supervision. When they only recalled the agents' directives and punitive responses for not following directives, they did not value the relationships positively, and they typically viewed supervision as burdensome and purposeless. Prior research with the full Michigan study sample and in other states confirms positive outcomes when agents combine a caring and fair relationship style with nonpunitive controls in a dual-role relationship.[2] The six touchstone accounts that start this chapter and the examination of statements by the larger group of women in the study that follows echo these findings. They also identify specific agent actions that showed women that the agents cared about them and were trustworthy and nonpunitive. Agents acted to facilitate access to resources; advocated for women in courts and treatment settings; and coached them in their interactions with court, treatment, and child protection workers. Some agents who emphasized the consequences of failure to abide by regulations had what I call split-role relationships. They encouraged and helped women to obtain mental health and substance abuse treatment, but they primarily focused on women's compliance with the conditions of supervision and the likely consequences if they did not comply.

Directives and Threats

Over the course of data collection, five probation agents in two counties supervised Carmen. Chapter 3, "Costs of Conviction," showed the challenges of simultaneous supervision in multiple counties that emphasized paying costs under threat of jail. Carmen characterized her interactions with her first agent in one of the counties, an agent who supervised Carmen for 18 months, as a series of orders to attend programs and warnings that she would go to jail unless she met not just monetary but all other requirements. She described limited discussion: "[S]he asks me if I stay out of trouble, if I moved, and if I can pass a drug test. That's all we talk about. I'm in and out in five minutes." When questioned about discussion of each of several typical needs of justice-involved women (for example, education, safe housing), Carmen repeatedly gave the same answer to these questions in all three interviews: "She just tells me not to get in trouble or she'll throw me in jail." In a deviation from this pattern, on the topic of mental health, Carmen noted, "She said it wasn't mandatory . . . and I took it upon myself to go to mental health so I can kind of like fix my anger problems." Even though Carmen did not recall much discussion of mental health, the official case notes showed that the agent monitored Carmen's participation in treatment. Still, the primary message that Carmen took from this agent was to stay out of trouble, report her address if she moved, and avoid positive drug tests or she would go to jail. At the follow-up about a year after the life story interview, looking back at several years of supervision by multiple agents, Carmen felt the experience gave her "more sense of control now" because she realized that following other people into illegal activity was not "worth it." In a classic example of deterrence, the pains of supervision and related jail and prison time motivated Carmen to stay out of trouble.

During supervision, Carmen wanted the probation agent to recognize the conflict between the probation requirement that she search for employment and her father's requirement that, reflecting society-wide expectations about girls' and women's responsibilities in families, she take care of her ailing grandmother. Her father enforced his expectation by responding violently to Carmen's request for help caring for her grandmother:

> I take care of my grandma, like she has to be fed, changed, clothed, bathed and I was tired of doing it myself, so I kind of blew up. . . . [My father] kicked me out without my dog, sold my dog, burnt all my clothes, my social

security card, everything. And ever since then I'm the only one at the hospital with my grandma. So, like she [the agent] doesn't understand why my dad did that. I really don't understand. If it's just me helping out and there's five other people in the house, why isn't anyone helping me? I'm more stressed to do good [on probation], but just thinking about my other family, you know, my grandma's on a ventilator right now. She's not doing good, so instead of going to see her at the hospital, I have to be out looking for a job. Like the last two weeks, I've been living at the hospital with her. So, it's like kind of hard to leave because every time I leave, I'm scared that she's gunna pass.

Showing the seriousness of what Carmen referred to as her "anger problems," while on probation she was in a jail holding cell after an arrest for physically fighting with police who stopped her walking from the next-door neighbor's house to her home in possession of alcohol as a minor. Another girl at the party had called the police to report her use of alcohol because she was angry at Carmen. Carmen admitted that in the holding cell, she "broke a girl's nose" and tried to drown her in the toilet. She linked her prior victimization to her violent behavior:

> I was sleepin' and I was irritated already because I was sittin' in jail again, you know? Fifth time in like two years, and I'm tired of it, and she [the other woman in the cell] was drunk, and she just kept on talkin' a lot and I'm like "Will you please be quiet?" So, I try to fall back to sleep, and she kicked me on purpose, so I got up and I hit her. I don't like people beatin' on me. I've been through it enough with abusive relationships, so I finally just learned how to stick up for myself, and I guess I stick up for myself way too much now.

The judge dismissed the charges for fighting with the police because they did not declare themselves as police, and the police report documented this omission. He sentenced Carmen to a year in jail for the assault on the woman in the jail cell.

After release, Carmen avoided more supervision by opting for prison time to complete the initial sentence. Again showing the seriousness of her inability to control her anger, she said she spent the lengthy two-and-a-half years in prison because she told the parole board members, "fuck off" and walked out of the room when she heard one of them say that she was not going anywhere in life, and she deserved to have a stillborn baby when she first came to prison. Carmen's victimization in her family, abuse by the man who got her pregnant and then caused the miscarriage, and the stillborn baby born in prison indicate her risk for trauma, which prior research has connected to women's anger and violence.[3] The agent's emphasis on staying out of trouble, paying costs of supervision, jail time, and then prison time all sidestepped the serious issue of trauma and anger.

Attention to Women's Insights and Circumstances

The agent did not respond to Carmen's feelings of being torn between spending time with her dying grandmother and probation requirements to search for work. Carla compared an agent who similarly did not take her context and insight into account to another agent who did. As revealed in the prior chapter, during supervision Carla concentrated her energies on paying court and supervision costs. When she returned to her hometown after release from prison, contrary to what Carla thought would help her stay away from drugs, the agent placed her in housing for people on parole:

> They put me in this house with another drug user that I used to use with. And at that time, she wasn't doing good. So I'm fresh out of prison, they put me in a home and like, I go to go see my agent. She said you're going to be going to this house and this girl's living there and right when I found out I'm like, "You got to be kidding me. Like seriously?" Like they pretty much just set me up. . . . Within a couple months I'm using again.

To avoid readdiction to methamphetamine, Carla thought she could "party here a little bit" with heroin. Consistent with the larger Michigan study of 402 women that showed women did not discuss their problems when they believed the agent would incarcerate them, once she was addicted to heroin, fear of a parole violation and return to prison kept Carla from asking the agent for help.[4] The agent discovered Carla's drug use through routine testing and sent her to a 90-day secure program that MDOC operated as an alternative to returning to prison.[5] Carla said that while she was there, "I just really looked at what made me do a lot of the stuff that I do."

Back on parole, but with a different agent in a small city about an hour from her hometown, Carla listed several immediate needs—lack of money, clothing, and knowledge of the city—plus she struggled to, as she put it, learn to live sober:

> I was so fresh to sobriety, you know. That's one thing you have to learn, how to live clean, how to handle things because now—you know before I used to go chase and run for drugs, so I didn't feel nothing or have to deal with anything. So I had to like re-teach myself how to handle situations and how to deal with things. . . . It's really hard when you're starting to actually

deal with your emotions and you've never done that, like, in a while because you've been just so, you know, messed up.

Carla appreciated the new agent's efforts to meet specific needs as they arose: "Agent Belview was awesome. When I went to Agent Belview, I'm like, 'You really helped me a lot.' She actually cared and wanted me to do good and stuff and she got me into a lot of different programs that were very effective."

After Carla's expulsion from one required substance abuse treatment program for swearing at a counselor who told her she was not taking the program seriously, the new agent referred her to another program that Carla found more convenient and helpful:

> I have a hard time getting around because I don't have a driver's license. So, they make the times convenient and the place convenient for me to get there. It makes it easier because it's a women's group that she put me in. And they do it right here at the parole office. So, it's real easy to get up here. And then she set it up to where we report right after we go to drug class, our drug group.

Carla said the program was effective because the counselor was not a "jerk," by which she meant that he listened to what she wanted to say. "[Jerks] wanna hear what they wanna hear, and they don't like it when you really tell 'em what's really going on." With this counselor, Carla told the truth: "Yeah 'cause I was bein' honest, you know. I wasn't lyin' and sugar coating, like, 'Oh, I don't wanna go get high.' 'Naw [no], today . . . I wanna go get high, fool, you know, I'm havin' a hard time today.'" The agent successfully matched Carla to a substance abuse treatment program she could easily get to and take part in and that had a counselor whose approach fit Carla's idea of effectiveness.

The new parole agent also scheduled the first appointment with a mental health counselor after Carla said she needed counseling for depression. Later during the year, Carla arranged for the baby she was carrying to be adopted by a couple in another state. When the agent suggested additional counseling to deal with feelings about the adoption, Carla let her know that the adoption agency already provided counseling. She told the interviewer that her agent's suggestion showed her that the agent cared.

The agent's pattern of repeatedly responding to Carla's changing needs for substance abuse treatment and mental health counseling helped Carla complete a substance abuse treatment program for the first time and convinced Carla that the agent cared about her. The agent's approach also helped Carla desist from substance misuse and related illegal behavior. Supervision with the new agent and the treatment referral influenced Carla to stop assuming that people in authority were "all bad" and out to get her. "I always thought that everybody was against me and just out to get me, and . . . I used to butt heads more. . . . Now I don't have to."

Raven described her agent as understanding and responsive to her need for counseling, but not understanding about why she ignored supervision requirements and lived with a man who had committed a felony. After sensing Raven's emotional distress over watching four younger brothers grow increasingly disabled, the agent referred Raven to mental health counseling. This referral, coupled with advocacy with the judge to reduce the costs of supervision, epitomized a dual-role relationship that emphasized caring and that deemphasized punishment. By advocating with the judge to reduce Raven's supervision cost, the agent shifted attention away from paying fees and toward the counseling that Raven said ended her drug use. "I don't get high no more. Like that's not part of me no more. I've did counseling." The agent referred Raven to counseling after Raven shared "thoughts and stuff I was having" about helping her mom raise her developmentally challenged younger brothers. As the brothers matured, Raven watched their health deteriorate to the point that one of them, who was 34, became incontinent and blind. Raven described the agent's response and then her response after she revealed her family situation:

> I left here [the reporting center], went and talked to the lady [counselor], and I've been okay ever since. I wouldn't have went if she [the agent] wouldn't have said, like "you really hurting. You really need to talk to somebody. I see it all in your face that you need some help. . . ." If she wouldn't have said that like that, I probably would still be talking to myself in a room or writing letters to myself, writing back and all type of stuff. I was a Looney Tune [cartoon]. I wrote myself letters and I answered them, literally, but that was my way of having somebody to talk to, you know what I mean?

Raven had reasons to avoid counseling. When she told a high school counselor about her stepfather molesting her, that counselor violated her confidentiality, with the result that rumors spread to her schoolmates. A second experience reinforced her fears about sharing her past:

> Yeah, when I was with my stepdad and his son molested me or whatever, I went to see a counselor. It's like after I seen him for almost a year, he ended

up killing his self about another case that he had. That did something to me in a sense of how do I know that the stuff I'm telling you not gunna make you crack to the point where you want to do something to yourself, you know what I mean? Like, because . . . and that case wasn't as severe as mine. It wasn't somebody whose dad and stepbrother was molesting them.

The agent's attention and immediate response to Raven's emotional state reduced the barriers to Raven's seeking counseling and met Raven's need for someone to talk with about continuing symptoms of trauma.

As an exception to the overall positive relationship, Raven believed the agent ignored her circumstances and related needs when she directed her to live apart from a man with a past felony conviction. Raven presented an understanding of her situation that the agent did not consider:

> Every guy pretty much has had a run in with the law. They got caught in a drug house or something and he plead to everything that was in the house because he's not a snitch. . . . I mean, he got out of prison once, stayed out for a few months, went back because he dropped dirty, stayed in there for a few months, and then he got back out. I mean, it's okay. He ain't abusive. He pays the bills. He do the bulk of everything because I haven't had no income. So, he takes care of everything, so he got my vote (*laughs*).

Raven's assessment of the unavailability of men without a criminal record in a predominantly Black community in a distressed city is consistent with the documented high rate of Black men's incarceration.[6]

Raven knew from personal experience about her high risk for intimate partner victimization as a Black woman, whose vulnerability has been attributed to historical and contemporary barriers to Black men's economic success and the legacy of slavery.[7] She explained, "She [the agent] can tell me all these things [about associating with a man with prior felony convictions], but the only thing I really see is the abuse." Raven based her concern about abuse on her history with her oldest children's father:

> I had a miscarriage because he beat me so bad. We in the bed and literally my baby laying next to us, and I get up to go to the bathroom and come back and this little baby laying here. . . . I done passed the baby and didn't know it just because he beat me that bad. He done jumped on me to the point where I don't have but a little feeling in my front tooth and I got a gash in my head from where he busted me on the top of my head with a crate. Abuse is not for me.

Raven further explained how past experience and immediate context justified her decision to stay with a partner who had a criminal record,

"Like if you find somebody who hitting you, no, that's not good. But somebody with a record, . . . like some stuff you just can't change. I mean, that's how I look at it." Raven prioritized having a nonabusive partner who covered essential household expenses over complying with supervision requirements to avoid associating with a man with a felony record. The limited local availability of men without a past felony conviction and Raven's prior victimization by a partner justified her prioritization.

Split-Role Relationships

Bree said the agent's message that stuck out for her was, "If you drop dirty, I'm going to lock your ass up." She said she thought of this "every day, every second of the day, every time I wanted to pick up a blunt." In two different interviews, Bree described the same incident that annoyed and angered her: the agent telling her a test showed marijuana use when she had not used for months. These recollections of supervision emphasized control and the threat of punishment, though like Raven, Bree saw a good outcome from the agent's successful efforts to connect her with mental health counseling.

At the start of supervision, Bree attended a substance abuse treatment group, which she said had neither a good nor a bad effect since her drug use was limited to smoking marijuana. Bree explained why the agent changed the requirement to individual mental health counseling with the same therapist who led the substance abuse treatment group: "I had an accident. One of my guns went off in my ear. And it was kind of like a—I guess they would call it a suicide attempt or whatever. So since then, she [the agent] had just wanted a therapist." Although she signed a consent form that allowed the agent to monitor her progress in therapy, Bree did not want the agent to share information with the therapist:

> She called my therapist and just get to talking about it with her like, "Did you know this?" and "Did you know that?" and "Did you know this?" I really didn't appreciate that. Like, you know if I want my therapist to know that, you know that that's not your job [to give information to the therapist].

Although Bree wanted a greater separation between supervision and counseling, when she looked back at six years of supervision with the same agent, she said that because of the referral to treatment, the agent was "a good agent all the way around." Prior research has not considered the possibility of this type of split-role relationship with a supervising agent focusing on control and consequences but requiring individual therapy that would provide caring and trusted support. For Bree, this split had a positive outcome, and in fact she wanted an even greater split that would limit the agent's communications to the therapist.

Lengthy Criminal Histories, Multiple Programs

Both Mallory and Marion were 55 years old, had long histories of criminal convictions, started supervision using drugs, and took part in multiple treatment programs while under supervision. However, their experience of supervision differed. After Mallory left prison and started parole, she participated in outpatient substance abuse treatment and separate mental health treatment for schizophrenia, but she still relapsed on heroin within a few months. The parole agent could not find an open bed at a dual-diagnosis residential program, and then Mallory's new conviction for retail theft resulted in a probation sentence. The presiding judge ordered participation in a specific 90-day residential substance abuse treatment program. Mallory tested positive for heroin and other opiates numerous times during two years of supervision, including twice when she returned to the residential treatment facility after being away for mental health appointments and multiple times after she completed residential treatment.

Mallory described conversations with the agent as a series of warnings and reviews of requirements. She said that when she talked about "things from my past," the agent did not care, so Mallory dropped the topic. "She would rush me and that makes me feel that it's not caring coming from her part." At the follow-up to the life story interview, Mallory said simultaneous and lengthy supervision on probation and parole left her "drained emotionally." The agent and a judge made numerous referrals, but Mallory's relationship to the agent seemed to lack the positive connection that other women attributed to the agent's caring about them. It is not clear whether this resulted from too much supervision and related requirements and fees, Mallory's decisions, or the agents' and Mallory's relationship.

Marion also painted a complex picture of supervision, the agent, and referrals. She started supervision with positive drug tests for THC (tetrahydrocannabinol, the chemical responsible for most of marijuana's psychological effects) and cocaine, admissions of daily use, and repeated failures to report for supervision appointments and return the agent's phone calls. She acknowledged that she was in a "tug-of-war" with the agent because the way she was used to living conflicted with the agent's requirements and directives. In the next sentence, she said the agent gave her "initiative," so she thought,

> If I can just stay crime free, case free, drug free, incident free, all these I got to work on. . . . The closer I get to August [the end date for parole], the harder the temptations. They pop up. They come and go. But she told me, you know, just walk a straight line 'cause she can issue [a revocation that results in prison]. She informed me that she will, so that's enough for me.

Different from Mallory, Marion saw the agent in a positive light. "The supervision helped me knowing that I didn't know what to do with my life. . . . I was running my life into a ground, a vicious cycle." She expressed gratitude for the parole agent who encouraged her to take part in numerous groups and services: "Better that I had somebody to talk to, and that she was really concerned, not just, you know goin' through the motions. She . . . she cares." In the last interview, she talked about a point in supervision when she "got myself straight" before discharge. Once Marion stopped testing positive for drug use and complied with requirements, the agent discharged her within the first year of parole. The agent's actions to communicate that she cared about Marion differentiated the two women's experiences with supervision.

Complexities of Agent Relationships

The six women provided information about a range of agent actions. Carmen shed light on the negative effects of the agent's emphasis on directives and threats. She also explained that the agent ignored conflicting demands for Carmen to care for her dying grandmother and simultaneously job search. Raven similarly felt the agent ignored circumstances that led her to live with a man with a prior felony conviction. However, like Bree and Carla, she appreciated the agent's sensitivity to her need for counseling. Two women, Mallory and Marion, with long records of convictions and multiple requirements to attend programs, differed in whether they believed their agents cared about them and thus in their related levels of satisfaction with supervision. Prior research documents positive results of caring relationships, and the touchstone stories underscore this finding and go further to show how the agents' full understanding and consideration of women's circumstances enhanced their relationships with women. The examination of the full group of women with multiple convictions confirms and develops these findings, identifies additional actions that agents took, and expands on the effects on women.

THE LARGER GROUP OF WOMEN

Directives and Threats

Women besides Carmen and Carla confirmed that agents who empha-sized detecting and punishing violations of requirements had a chill-ing effect on conversation. Rosa, the youngest woman who told her life story, had a history of childhood abuse and a series of violent confron-tations "on the streets." Although she started out on probation, at the time of the life story interview 22-year-old Rosa was in prison for burn-ing down a friend's house, physical conflict with the police who arrested her, and destruction of police property. She explained why she set the house afire: "I also got into a huge fight with this friend because of some-thing dumb that I don't remember, so my friend came to my house and bashed my window in. So, I retaliated and set her house on fire, and the State charged me with arson and now I'm in prison." Before her first in-terview, Rosa had one of the most extensive criminal histories of any study participant, and she had multiple convictions between the time of her first interview and this incarceration for arson. Her official record of convictions included several instances of retail fraud, one instance of home invasion, several assaults (sometimes with battery or a dangerous weapon), armed robbery and larceny, and destruction of police property.

A few months after starting supervision, Rosa described the super-vising agent as quick to issue a violation, so Rosa avoided talking about her home life, she said "because many of the things going on were pro-hibited and would result in a violation." The probation agent's threats to issue violations did not curtail Rosa's lawbreaking, but they signaled to Rosa that she should not share details of her home life. Rosa's reluctance to disclose information about her family blocked the agent from offer-ing social support, including referrals to services that might have helped Rosa deal with her past and present circumstances in ways that would reduce her lawbreaking.

Elsie provided another example of the negative fallout of supervision interactions devoid of meaningful discussion. She depicted communica-tion from the probation agent: "Okay, you doing this? You doing this and this? Okay, see you next time." During supervision, Elsie had seri-ous problems. She struggled with a relapse on crack cocaine. Time in jail followed by time in a residential substance abuse treatment program left her disenrolled from mental health care, out of the medication previ-ously prescribed for mood swings, and tempted to "self-medicate" with illegal drugs. Elsie described the communication that she sought from the agent: "I'm like, 'Okay, well dang, you going to, like, you know, talk to me or something? Ask me, you know, how I'm feeling— if I'm depressed?' Anything could be going on." Elsie absconded from probation for two and a half years. Then she decided to let the probation be revoked and did jail time to avoid further supervision. She and Carmen, who also opted for prison time rather than probation, saw more harm than help resulting from supervision.

Attention to Women's Insights

As the touchstone stories revealed, the degree of women's openness in discussions with agents, specifically whether women believed they could offer their thoughts and opinions during conversations, often determined whether agents understood the reasons for women's actions. The realities of women's lives and their knowledge of themselves and their circumstances informed their beliefs about how best to complete supervision and avoid drugs and crime. Like Carla's agent, Rhiannon's agent ignored her insights about the best place to live. After being on parole for less than a year, Rhiannon's relapse on heroin led to a conviction for home invasion, specifically for going into her dad's home to sleep, eat, and shower. Her agent wanted her to go to a transitional housing program for substance abusers. Rhiannon gave her reasons for rejecting the idea:

> There's drugs everywhere in the facility . . . everywhere. . . . I feel like you're putting me right back in an environment with drugs. It's right in the hood. My dope dealer's house is right down the street. There's drugs everywhere. There wasn't really a discussion. She just told me this is how it's gunna be . . . more or less in an e-mail and didn't ask me how I felt about it.

Rhiannon gave a detailed explanation of why she thought agents need to "take the initiative to hear what their probationers and parolees have to say before making life changing decisions for them:"

> They don't know what we have been through as far as prison, living on the streets, what might trigger us to go back out there. Because for me personally, even at this point, my agent made a life changing decision for me and doesn't even know how I am. I'm a runner. She doesn't know my feelings on that. Maybe I might actually be triggered by going there [the residential facility]. We might know more about the streets than they think we do. Or that we have more knowledge about how things are ran in the streets than they do and the judges, because they have a perception from the law side. Now people who are using in those types of facilities, or in those areas aren't

gunna walk up to an agent or a cop and say, "Hey, by the way, we're using in this facility." So, I think they need to take the initiative and listen instead of saying, "This is how it's gunna be done." Because a lot of times when . . . especially when you're dealing with people that have been incarcerated, they have issues with authority. So, when you come at them like, "This is how it's got to be done," their first instinct is to either A: run; B: retaliate; and we react on it.

Research on the larger Michigan sample showed that an authoritarian pattern of communication predicts this type of reactance to avoid agent restrictions on women's freedom.[8]

Rhiannon reacted by running. She said she absconded from supervision when she considered her options: go to the transition house and "abide by the law and die" or stop reporting so she could "live another 20 years." She said she "got pregnant along the way," and after being on the run for a year, when the baby was two months old, after a month in jail the judge discharged her from parole. Rhiannon thought that the negative drug tests during pregnancy and her daughter's being drug free and in good health at birth proved to the judge that she stopped using drugs. She remembered the agent's exact words, "I wouldn't recommend what you did for anybody else, but what you did seemed to have worked for you and I wish you the best of luck in the future." Rhiannon had no official record of recidivism. A close look at Rhiannon's statements shows that she engaged in a deliberative decision-making process of taking her "street knowledge" into account and making a reasonable choice to not follow the agent's directive. Rhiannon reflected on her decision to run: "I honestly can't even tell you if I would be alive or not right now if I would have made a different decision."

Focus on Felt Need and Support

Given the myriad needs women brought to the supervision experience and the MDOC's emphasis on identifying and meeting those needs, probation and parole agents devoted considerable time, usually with good results, to implementing judge and parole board requirements for programming, arranging admissions to programs, and responding to program shortages or women's failure to successfully complete programs. Apart from formal assessments of needs, agents drew on their understanding of women's backgrounds and lives to figure out what would most assist them. They devoted energy to matching services, resources, programs, and their own support to women's needs. When referrals and placements failed to help or women did not use them, agents made a "rematch" or substitution, sometimes repeatedly. Agents referred women to programs for substance abuse and mental health treatment, homelessness, lack of income, and job training and readiness. Drug and alcohol relapse and women's rejection of programming or violations of program rules complicated referrals and placements. Some programs accommodated relapses back onto substance misuse, for example by setting increased restrictions on what women could do, but others terminated women's participation, which left agents searching for alternatives. It was common for agents to refer women to a series of programs to find alternatives after relapses or to meet needs that unfolded over time, for instance initial outpatient substance abuse treatment, followed by inpatient treatment after a relapse, followed by an outpatient program combined with job training.

In an example of how agents steered women through multiple programs, after her release from prison, Jasmine's new conviction resulted in a probation sentence. Jasmine initially became "strung out" on crack cocaine to deal with multiple negative events—her mom's early death, her dad's suicide, and her husband and sister having a child together—and since then she had struggled with addiction and was in and out of prison. During the most recent time on probation, she had completed inpatient substance abuse treatment and left with a staff recommendation to attend a life skills program. When Jasmine had a dirty urine, the agent pointed out that the life skills program did not provide any substance abuse treatment, so she should attend a different program. Jasmine valued the agent's response: "What I've seen in the past, when you make one little mistake like that, they immediately throw you in jail or something like that. And so she's taken the time out to deal with the issue, instead of just throwing me in jail, which is not going to deal with it." The program the agent chose helped Jasmine form a support group of former participants who stayed in contact.

In addition to referral to the appropriate program, Jasmine's motivations and her related exercise of agency played a big part in her desistance. She chose to continue substance abuse treatment several months longer than required. At the start of supervision, recognizing the need to change, she thought to herself, "Well back when you got into all that trouble starting all that stuff, then you got on the drugs, then you went to prison, and here you are doing the same thing that got you, you know, that took part of your life away in the first beginning. What is wrong with you? You need to wake up." After completing residential treatment,

Jasmine attended outpatient treatment sessions "way over, probably about a year and a half over" the usual time.

The agent also helped Jasmine access a comprehensive housing program for people who were homeless or at imminent risk of becoming homeless. This program assisted with the search for housing, education for renting or buying housing, tenant-landlord mediation, and a financial subsidy. Given the shortage of low income housing and some housing authorities' prohibitions against serving individuals with a felony record, the program gave Jasmine unusually good access to a place to live. The agent's actions revised the initial referral to a life skills program to include multiple continuing social, educational, and financial supports. The agent's actions took the emphasis off just repairing Jasmine's life skills deficits and instead helped her build networks and relationships that gave her access to support and resources.

A probation agent also gave Maura, age 53, support that enabled her to leave an abusive man and obtain mental health treatment and disability insurance. After her husband unexpectedly divorced her when she was in her forties, Maura partnered with a man who forced her into prostitution and introduced her to drugs. Maura pointed out the result of her agent's focus on building her courage to apply for needed services:

> I'm getting my own place, I'm drug free, I see a psychiatrist, I see a therapist; these are things that I needed since I was little . . . I always got told by everybody, or people that I was with, ex-husband and that, that I didn't need help. [They said] "just take vitamins, or smoke weed and that'll help."

Maura summed up her optimism about her future:

> My therapist, my psychiatrist and Miss Brown [the agent], yeah, they're the ones that make me feel good about myself. I get up every morning and I say there's a purpose in life, I'm trying to get my own place, I'm drug free, alcohol free, and I see there's a light at the end of the tunnel, instead of it being dark.

Molly's third arrest for driving under the influence of alcohol resulted in a three-year sentence to probation that the court extended to four years due to her initial inability to pay court costs, and then again to five years because she relapsed. She said the third arrest occurred when she drank so much alcohol that the police pulled her over for driving the wrong way *after* the airbags deployed, an experience that Molly described as like driving in a fog. Molly's probation agent in the county where the police arrested her oversaw her supervision, but a series of four other agents supervised her in the county where she lived. For all but the final year, Molly described herself as "stuck" and supervision as failing to meet her needs. "There was never any options for nothing. It was like, OK, you're doing this or you're not doing this, . . . not even looking at your circumstances or options or anything." She said she "fought against the treatment" the judge offered and "relapsed for a couple years, like really stupidly hard." Molly saw the final two years of supervision as a "blessing," when a new agent recognized that she had changed, or as Molly told the judge, "I'm fighting for my life." According to Molly, the agent met her critical needs:

> She went above and beyond to just make sure I had everything I like possibly could need if there was anything within the community that could help me. Like she really, really tried and she even found that she's the one who even saved me misery the past year, like in August I had to go and figure out something 'cuz, I still didn't have a home for me and the kids and we were living with family and they were about to start school and I wanted them to be more stable, so I just ended up saying forget it, I'll go with the program that ensures them being in a stable environment and school. So, she really actually found the program for me and called and went above and beyond to make sure they heard her and put me on the list and got me in as soon as possible.

A year later, Molly noted that this program "opened up like a whole community for you" and it "made sure to have every one thing you could possibly need to get back on your feet, . . . to give you all the tools that you can need to get your life back together." She listed the daycare center, the after-school care program, the one-year life skills program, and nutritious food and adequate clothing as parts of the program. After she had been a year in residence, the program continued to provide transportation to a "better school district" for her children, assistance with housing and furniture after she left the residential setting, and a continuing support group. Molly ended her comments thus: "This program is insanely great."

The stories of how agents arranged and enabled desistance-promoting matches between women's needs and a variety of supports, services, and programs show the combined effects of the agents' efforts, available programs and resources, and women's motivation and drive. Jasmine's time on probation epitomized wraparound programming that addresses multiple needs as they surfaced over time. Maura's agent and mental health professionals the agent connected her with gave Maura the "courage" to leave an abusive man, participate in mental health treatment, and apply for disability insurance and subsidized housing. Molly explained why the agent wanted her to go to a one-year residential program with a continuing after-care program: "It's because I don't have a lot of family support. I just don't have people available, like there's no babysitters. We [she and her husband] do everything on our own, and there's no transportation so, it's been really rough." The combined impact of linking women to appropriate resources and empowering women to use them plus women's desire to build a crime-free life promoted desistance from substance misuse and illegal activities and improved women's lives.

Desired Control by Agents Who Care

Psychologists who developed the concept of dual-role relationships and applied it to community supervision brought attention to the expectation that probation and parole agents simultaneously exert controls over the people they supervise and provide support and assistance in a way that shows they care and they can be trusted.[9] Consistent with the idea of dual-role relationships, some women noted how agents tried to promote their self-control by pointing out consequences of their behavior for achieving the goals the women valued and telling them to think through the results of actions before acting. Agents pointed to the consequences of violations and new arrests for women's children, safety at the hands of a partner, quality of relationships, and future well-being. As an example, Isabel welcomed the agent's directive to keep her hands off her 21-year-old daughter when they argued:

> Stipulations, guidelines, you know, things. I know if I cross this, what's going to happen. And I'm terrified. I don't want to be away from my kids. I don't want to go to jail. I don't want to ever, ever, ever re-track that. So having that in my head and knowing that if I cross this line that she means business made it better.

This type of control, by pointing out negative consequences that mattered to women, like being separated from their children, differed from threats of jail that women saw as unfair and punitive.

In her eyes, the way that the agent who supervised Sugar enforced the directive that she earn a high school diploma signified that he cared about her. She remembered that when she said she was taking the online courses to complete the diploma for her children's sake, he countered, "Your kid, no. You're doing this for you so you can better yourself and your future." She saw him as caring about her: "You know, he wanted the proof. He wanted to see my work. He wanted to see my grades." Sugar summed up the effect of the agent's saying she was working on earning the diploma for herself, "I got my high school diploma because he pushed me. I did it." She compared her interactions with him to those with a previously assigned agent: "She didn't really care. Like, it didn't matter, so I told her what she wanted to hear. She was fine with it." Earning the diploma had so much meaning to Sugar that she attended the graduation ceremony in Pennsylvania.

Notable in making sense of Sugar's positive assessment of the agent's "pushing" her to obtain a diploma is that she did not always portray him as accepting and kind. She described him as "mean" and herself as very stressed when they first met, and he set forth his concerns about her children and what she would need to do to avoid his calling CPS. He also set forth expectations about what she would need to do to avoid his sending her to jail and prison. She mentioned that he would "yell" at her when she brought her cell phone to meetings. In contrast, in addition to his interest in her education, he asked to see a picture of the baby she gave birth to during supervision, and she said, "We, I got really close." Was this agent bullying and paternalistic, or was he combining fair controls and caring? Without data from alternate perspectives, I cannot provide a definitive answer to this question. From Sugar's perspective, his saying more than once, "You're not doing it for nobody but yourself" served as a memorable message that she said affected her efforts to earn a diploma. People recall memorable messages for a long time and use them to judge and sometimes correct their behavior, which appears to be the pattern Sugar followed.[10] Sugar described the relationship as changing for the better as she became close to the agent, and after he retired, she kept in touch with him.

Thinking they would fall back to using drugs without the control provided by supervision, Penelope and Kirsten acted to extend supervision. Expecting a baby around the time her jail term would end, Penelope worried she could not stay away from drugs, and thus she would harm the fetus after leaving jail. The agent sought judicial approval for Penelope's jail release before the baby's birth and arranged for admission to a residential substance abuse treatment program that allowed children to live with their mothers. Describing a similar action to extend controls, Kirsten told the interviewer how she prolonged parole even though she had money to pay all costs and be discharged:

> I want to tell you the truth. . . . I had the money to pay it, and my husband says, "Did you go?" I went to the building to pay it and everything, and I walked back out and my girlfriend said, "That was quick." I said, "Yeah just take me home." And my husband said, "Well did you pay it?" I said, "No."

He said, "What?!" I said, "I don't want to get off parole right now, I'm afraid." So, I didn't pay it. I want to be off, I want to be done with it, but the thought of doing it was like, okay now that's gunna give me a leeway, . . . if I have a bad day, what will I do? So, I thought, well just a few more months, you know, and then I'll pay it, you know, and then it's been a few more months, and I've been making little payments.

These examples show how a combined caring and control style of supervision positively affects women's thinking and actions.

Working the System to Women's Advantage

Women who talked about supportive supervision described how agents worked probation, parole, and the wider array of programs and resources for their benefit. Agents used their expertise in the operations of courts, correctional agencies, and the MDHHS to advocate for women and coach them in their dealings with these entities.

Agents modified judge's directives for programming to ensure that it addressed women's needs. Lydia's story of how she and her probation agent sorted out whether treatment for alcoholism or mental health would be most effective illustrates this process. Lydia's adoptive parents beat, criticized, and degraded her as a young child, then blamed her when a stranger molested her. Decades later, talking about these childhood incidents to a therapist distressed her, so she drank alcohol while driving home, and the police stopped and arrested her. Responding to the arrest and conviction for driving under the influence, the judge ordered participation in an alcohol treatment program and Alcoholics Anonymous (AA) meetings. Lydia knew the alcohol treatment program did not address her needs:

> I got dismissed from the program twice and they called it maximum utilization—that they couldn't help me anymore. . . . Well the major health problem has been my depression. I mean, that's been it. I remember being in so much pain that as a little kid taking a whole bottle of baby aspirin. Yeah, just because I thought it would make me feel better, you know. It wasn't an addiction thing. It was the advertisements on TV, "This is going to make you feel better."

Lydia felt relief that the agent realized she needed mental health counseling not AA meetings. Looking back after supervision ended, Lydia tempered her positive assessment of the agent by pointing to the lack of referrals to classes that would help her better herself. She said, "You know, I wish there would have been more guidance [about employment], instead of just posting, like they would post things on the wall, like, a list of who hired people with felonies." The agent compensated for the judge's limited focus on alcoholism rather than mental health services in deciding what help Lydia needed, but Lydia wanted help with employment, too. Women like Lydia wanted wraparound services that met multiple needs as they came to light over time.

Recognizing the lure of "fast money" available in Marie's neighborhood, an agent who took the lead in supervision ran interference with another agent who threatened jail if Marie did not pay fees for being on tether. Marie's poverty, which intensified during her supervision, made it difficult for her to pay:

> I think because I have the felony, I'm not going to be able to get Section 8 or low income housing or none of that. And I'm low income, believe me. . . . I'm struggling with three kids and no help from their father. It's hard. It's very hard. Like [working] at the Salvation Army, checks and stuff, after gas and rent and lights and water and . . . all of that stuff, I'm broke. I don't have no extra money and I don't sell drugs so I can't go to their dad and be like, "Well, I did this [brought in drug money] so you can do this." So it's just like, I'm just hit. Don't nobody give me no money.

Seeing the chance to make "fast money" and Marie's poverty affected the lead agent's actions. After the "tether agent" threatened to tell the lead probation agent about skipped payments, according to Marie, the lead agent said, "Pay what you can and don't stress about it. Because I don't want you to feel like you got to go sell drugs to get this money to pay off this tether and then you get into trouble to do this. . . . And I'm not going to violate you for that once they call me."

Marie's perceptions of the help her agent gave her by working the system in her favor affected her thinking about breaking the law. She wanted to show her agent "respect," because the agent gave her "leeway" by not issuing her a violation for outstanding tether costs:

> I think like, "Oh, I can make this quick money right quick. I did it before. And then I ain't going to go to jail. It's only going to be one time." Knowing in the back of my head if I go make this couple of dollars right quick and it was that quick a second time is going to be like, "Oh, it ain't going to hurt this time too." So, then I think about, like I said, all the stuff Ms. Delacross [the agent] has done for me and all the leeway she's given me and, you know, enabled for me to do what I got to do and not get in trouble. I can at least give her that much respect to try to . . . at least try to do it, you know?

Marie knew the agent wanted her to improve future job opportunities: "She want me to get my GED, and she want me to get back in hair school because she don't want me working at the Salvation Army for the rest of my life. That's what she told me exactly." The agent promised instrumental help with GED education by offering to write a letter supporting Marie's readmission to school after she had dropped out three times, first because she could not handle raising two children and school at the same time, then because she was homeless and had no transportation or babysitter, and the third time because she was living with an abusive man. In addition to clarifying that she was not going to issue a violation for nonpayment of tether fees, the agent understood the pull of "fast money" that came with selling drugs. She also accepted Marie's reasons for dropping out of classes and encouraged continued education so Marie could eventually improve her financial standing. The way the agent worked supervision turned out well for Marie in the short run. A few months after the start of probation, Marie was expanding her hair business, but eventually she fell back into selling drugs in a pattern analyzed in chapter 7, "Endpoints."

For women supervised in multiple jurisdictions, the agent in one place sometimes helped women by running interference with the other agent. On probation and parole simultaneously, Lynette reported regularly to the parole agent in the jurisdiction where she lived, and she updated the probation agent in a distant part of the state by phone. The probation agent threatened jail for violating the stipulation that she obtain her GED. Lynette expressed her outrage:

> She really wanted to lock me up and throw away the key because I didn't get my GED. They had no other reason to violate me but that. And I was way pregnant. Like, you're going to take me to the doctor's every week this pregnant? You guys are ridiculous—for not getting my GED?

The parole agent advocated against issuing a violation and jailing Lynette for not obtaining a GED. Lynette restated the parole agent's communication to the probation agent: "The woman has done everything she can possibly do. She's, you know, high risk pregnancy. She can't even get out of bed. And you're trying to put her in jail?"

Like Lynette, Linsey had felony probation supervision at the same time she was on supervision in district court for a misdemeanor prostitution charge. Linsey felt disrespected by the first question the district court probation agent asked, "Do you know who the father of your child is?" Linsey reacted, "I just wanted to reach across the table and smack him. How can you talk to me that way? You know, I don't care what my charges were." The MDOC agent validated Lindsey's anger about the inference that because she had a conviction for prostitution, she slept with various men without knowing which of them might get her pregnant, and she arranged for Linsey to stop reporting to the other agent. For Lynette and Linsey, MDOC agents acted to protect the women from jail and insult, respectively. In the process, Lynette felt the agent understood the reality of the limitations imposed by her pregnancy, and Linsey felt validated in her reaction to the question, "Do you know who the father is?"

Agents helped women navigate CPS and other divisions in the MDHHS. Penelope, whose agent arranged residential substance abuse treatment so she would not be tempted to use drugs while she was pregnant and as a new mother, relapsed into drug use after leaving treatment and lost custody of her child. Penelope said that when she interacted with the agent, custody was "a big part of our discussions," and the agent's actions enabled her to regain custody: "Well, she knows the whole story about me losing my daughter a couple months ago, and she knows that it's everything that she requires me to do is the reason I got her home. . . . She reminds me of where I went wrong and that makes it a good thing." Penelope was certain that her fulfilling the requirements the agent set convinced the judge to grant custody.

Linsey also relied on her agent to ensure that she kept custody of her child. When she applied for food assistance, the MDHHS worker pressured her to also accept public assistance and participate in Work First, a job readiness and placement program. The worker said this would help Linsey better provide for her child. Linsey countered that the MDHHS worker could call the probation agent, who knew that she took good care of her daughter. Knowledge of Linsey's conviction triggered the MDHHS worker to question whether Linsey was a fit parent. Very upset and worried that she might lose child custody, Linsey called the agent, who reassured her: "Nothing was going to happen, and if they had a problem, she would talk to them." Given the prevalence of broken relationships with parents and the often transitory and abusive relationships with men, maintaining child custody served as the most accessible way for women to form families, which was a very important goal for most women. Penelope welcomed the agent's advice about how to regain custody, and Linsey felt reassured that the agent would help her should the MDHHS worker investigate her fitness as a mother.

Cierra's agent gave advice about how to obtain medical insurance. For the short run, the agent referred her to the MDHHS, where Cierra qualified for insurance for herself and her children. For the long run, the agent advised Cierra to seek employment at a workplace that offered health insurance. "The job I'm in right now doesn't have health insurance. . . . I should always be looking to kind of improve on that to work for something that would help me be able to afford that, or get a company that would offer that." Like the advice Marie received to focus on paying for education rather than paying court fines and fees, Cierra's agent gave empowering advice to find a job that provided benefits. This future-oriented advice could build Cierra's potential for having sustainable medical insurance that did not depend on eligibility for public assistance, a source of money that chapter 6, "Marginalization," shows could be cut off or reduced with little or no warning or reason.

First because she took a long time to pay court fees, and second because toward the end of the period of probation she had a new charge for driving under the influence and without a valid license, Francesca spent five years on probation. She shared Penelope and Kirsten's sentiment that control was a positive feature of supervision. She noted that while she was on "a short leash," the agent held her accountable for her actions and got her "out of two circumstances." In the first circumstance, the police wanted her to work undercover, but the agent told them that since she no longer used, she should not be put in jeopardy by buying or selling drugs. In the second circumstance, after an arrest on a year-old warrant, the agent's court testimony resulted in the case being dismissed. Francesca thought the penalty would have been jail, which would have a bad effect: "And being in jail really does no good for me. That's just a place for me to go find new addicts and people. There's no recovery and sobriety over there. I just learn where to get more drugs from and more people to get high with."

During the first year of supervision, Francesca used drugs, failed to report for drug tests, refused to start and complete drug treatment programs, and worked sporadically. She remembered the agent meeting with her in the jail and saying, "You don't belong here." Even when she was breaking the law by prostituting, she thought about the agent's statement, looked around her at other people using drugs and buying and selling sex, and because she didn't "belong here," she headed home. The agent made referrals to a series of inpatient and outpatient substance abuse treatment programs, most of which Francesca took part in sporadically or not at all. Francesca did follow up on a referral for depression at a center that provided substance abuse and mental health treatment along with disability assessment. As a result, Francesca learned she had bipolar and attention deficit disorders, and she started to take medication. Even though Francesca violated supervision multiple times, the agent used the caring and control approach, with control in the form of warnings rather than jail.

Short-Lived Desistance after Wraparound Programming

Despite receiving wraparound services and individualized programming to meet their needs, women of different ages, social class backgrounds, and racial and ethnic identifications relapsed into drug addiction or had new convictions. They lived in places that ranged from deteriorated inner-city neighborhoods to wealthy suburbs to rural areas. No one factor explained why they fell back into old patterns of illegal activity. Some refused to participate in the services offered or ordered. Others relapsed on drugs because of urges to use or barriers to obtaining continuing mental health and substance abuse treatment and medications. Persistent extreme poverty, a rejecting job market, the ease of making "fast money," and skills in shoplifting and distribution of stolen goods pushed and pulled women to continue or resume illegal activity.

Pamela's story illustrates the benefits of a combination of agent advocacy and individualized referrals to access resources, programs, and housing followed by a new conviction. The parole agent advocated for Pamela to receive resources and special services through parole and other agencies. After seeing the low amount of disability payments that Pamela received for a "brain trauma" and "severe depression," the agent successfully helped Pamela apply for and receive the maximum amount allowed. The first time that Pamela dropped dirty, the agent sent her to substance abuse treatment and then had her held in jail for evaluation so that she could be referred to "mental health reentry," which meant she would be on a specialized caseload of an agent trained to work with people who had severe mental illness. Looking back at supervision, Pamela described the good results of the agent's arranging help with both substance abuse and mental health: "It made me offer the best to live in society. She helped me . . . as far as getting housing and counseling and getting on the right track. I moved away from negative people. . . . I started going back to church. . . . I started focusing more on my daughter and me and my grandkids."

When Pamela could not secure a safe place to live, the agent used personal connections so Pamela could rent a house from a police officer in the community. Pamela's new residence deterred people who used drugs from reconnecting with her: "Like if I'm sitting on my porch, people will say, 'Oh can I come over?' and I was like, 'No, I rent from the police.' Kind of keeps bad people away from me." By the time of the life story interview, Pamela was no longer receiving disability insurance because she worked cleaning houses. Although she praised the agent for getting her "back on the right track," three years after telling her life story she was arrested for receiving and concealing a stolen automobile and resisting and obstructing the police. She spent another 18 months in prison and started a new term of parole.

Offering another example of considerable programming and a vision of a bright future during the first year of parole followed by new convictions, by the time she told her life story, Janelle lived in a cheap motel in a high-crime area on the outskirts of Detroit. She told the interviewer that she was feeling the bad effects of crack cocaine, and the motel gave her "comfort" because she had stayed there before going to prison. In fact, an arrest for prostitution and drug possession at the same motel led to the prison sentence followed by parole that brought her into the study. In the early months of parole, Janelle secured the first job she ever had, working 24 hours a week, midnight to 8:00 a.m., at a fast-food restaurant. The work was irregular, and sometimes she would get there only to be told that she was not needed that day. The parole agent connected her to substance abuse treatment, mental health treatment, an anger management class, and a homeless shelter. The MDOC reentry program helped with essentials such as obtaining identification, paying traffic tickets so she could reinstate her driver's license, and giving her bus tickets. Toward the end of the first year of supervision, Janelle looked forward to doing "new things" like going to movies, seeing a play about the musician Marvin Gay, and going to the gym.

At the same time that she made positive changes in her life, Janelle had serious financial problems. Her income was insufficient to sign a lease, so she moved in with a man she met in a homeless shelter. He abused her, they used drugs together, and they both relapsed. Food assistance would have substantially improved Janelle's financial situation, but she was ineligible. Janelle could not understand why drug-related felony convictions made her ineligible for food assistance, "but you let some guy who raped six little girls get it." She could not afford her parole fees, and she made a vague reference to needing to start paying "forty dollars here and forty dollars there." Despite the substantial and varied services and some hope for the future, Janelle had new convictions for receiving

and concealing two stolen vehicles, and at last check, she was on probation for these auto thefts.

In response to the life story question about how she saw her future,
contradicting her positive views at the start of supervision, Janelle answered "death" and explained:

> Drugs, drugs, drugs—and that's the struggle of my life. And I know it ain't no
> good, and I just do it because. And . . . like, everybody sayin, "You so pretty,
> you so pretty." But I'm ugly to me because I know what I look like when I'm
> on drugs. . . . I got scars. I got scars on my body and stuff. . . . I know that
> either [I need to be] killin all the negativity around me and getting out of it
> or I'm going to die. It's so many girls getting killed out here and so much bad
> stuff happening that it's inevitable if that's the life you choose.

Janelle did not see any options for improving her life. The parole agent
had used best practices to surround Janelle with programs and resources,
but without an income and wanting to live outside a homeless shelter,
Janelle took the risk of living with a stranger who turned out to be abusive, and together they relapsed on drugs.

IN A BOX

Even when agents took enabling and empowering actions, some of
women's needs for help and resources could not be met because agents
had little or no access to or influence over consistently available employment or safety-net program benefits that provided a livable income,
long-term or lifelong access to mental health and substance abuse treatment, and lasting personal networks that gave social support and encouraged legal behavior. Also, even with support and resources from
agents, some women lacked or lost motivation to avoid drugs and stop
relying on illegal income.

In part because of the availability of MDOC reentry resources for
people on parole, even though many women on probation had needs
as great as those of women on parole and in some cases had previously
been on parole or had spent considerable time in jails and prisons, in general, probation agents had fewer resources to offer than parole agents.
Still, to some extent both probation and parole agents were "in a box"
with the women they supervised. They had to manage within the system of supervision fees; judge-ordered probation requirements or parole
board conditions; available community programs; available and accessible educational and employment opportunities; and the sporadically
available, reduced, or eliminated resources for Medicaid, housing, public

assistance, and food assistance. Potential employer rejection of people based on their criminal history added to the limitations embedded in public policies and community programs. The ramifications of being "in a box" become more apparent in the next chapter, chapter 5, "Treatment," and even more apparent in chapter 6, "Marginalization."

Treatment

Michigan women on probation and parole had relatively good access to mental health services, including substance abuse treatment. When asked whether they needed and received mental health treatment at the start of supervision, two-thirds of the 78 women who indicated a need said they received treatment. Toward the end of the first year of supervision, all 62 women who reported a need said they had received services. Access resulted in part from treatment availability statewide, since the state ranked in the second best quartile (eighteenth from the top) in a comparison of the number of people in mental health treatment per 100,000 population in one day in 2011, the year data collection began.[1] Access also resulted from availability of services specifically for women, justice-involved individuals, and those with mental health or substance-related needs or both.[2] Just under half of Michigan mental health facilities specialized in substance abuse treatment, a common need among the women, and a similar proportion provided a mix of mental health and substance abuse treatment. One-third of facilities offered specialized programming for adult women, and almost a third had programming designed for justice-involved individuals. Of course, once the various combinations of characteristics and need are considered—for example, justice-involved women needing treatment for substance abuse and other mental health problems—a specific type of help might not be available.

In light of possible combinations of characteristics and needs and in a state with good but not top-notch access to mental health care, supplemental funding was important to the women in the study. For the many women without insurance or personal resources to cover treatment costs, funding for mental health treatment came through one or more sources. Support came through legislated funding of the state's community mental health centers and, starting in 2014, the state-supported Medicaid expansion to cover mental health care for an increased number of people who lived in poverty. The state Community Corrections Act also funded a variety of services that included mental health treatment for people on probation and parole, and the Michigan Prisoner Reentry Act allocated money to the MDOC to contract for mental health and substance abuse treatment (and other services) for people on parole. Although Michigan was not in the top of states for availability of mental health care, women on probation and parole had access to treatment through these additional sources.

Women shared their treatment experiences in response to questions about discussions with agents about mental health and drug and alcohol use. Treatment also came up in women's answers to questions in five of the six interviews that asked about availability of financial support for treatment and about how women had improved their lives. At the end of the first year of supervision, interviewers asked women who had been in substance abuse treatment about the quality of treatment and the part the agent played in connecting them to treatment. Some women volunteered additional information about treatment providers and programs in answers to questions about behavior-influencing messages they recalled over a long period and general questions about the nature and effects of interactions with the agent.

Even with the relatively good availability of mental health and substance abuse treatment for Michigan justice-involved women, barriers prevented timely, continuing treatment well matched to needs and circumstances. Women post-supervision lost special access to treatment resources, so there were gaps and voids in care. More generally, due to the nationwide opioid crisis, Michigan's community mental health funding could not keep up with demand during the research period.[3] Showing this shortfall in treatment availability, a 2014 study of a Michigan sample found that low income women had strong motivation to improve their mental health, but unreliable and changing health insurance coverage and fluctuating low-wage employment limited access.[4] This pattern is documented for women in this book toward the end of this chapter and in chapter 6, "Marginalization." Many women in the study received mental health and substance abuse treatment, but appropriate and continuous care was not always in reach.

Treatment from community mental health agencies followed the MDHHS practice guideline for intervention, specifically the use of person-centered planning, which is "a process for planning and supporting the individual receiving services that builds upon the individual's capacity to engage in activities that promote community life and honors the individual's preferences, choices, and abilities."[5] Perhaps because of these guidelines, women's accounts of treatment revealed markedly more positive experiences than studies in other states that show ineffective or destructive treatment in U.S. prisons and for justice-involved women in the community.[6] To some extent, mental health services were walled off from community supervision to maintain confidentiality within the therapeutic relationship, though to abide by supervision requirements, many women signed waivers so agents could check on participation.

TOUCHSTONE STORIES

As part of MDOC's push toward matching interventions to assessed needs and consistent with justice-involved women's high prevalence of mental illness and substance misuse, MDOC probation and parole agents often referred women for treatment.[7] Sometimes judges and the parole board mandated treatment that the agent monitored, though treatment also might be voluntary and unrelated to supervision requirements. The six women who open each chapter showed a key difference in how the agents related to them and to treatment providers. Three of them described agents with a caring, nonpunitive dual-role relationship style. These agents supplemented the support women received from therapists and counselors. The other three women described agents who made referrals to treatment or implemented directives to obtain treatment but tended toward a limit-setting style of relating to the women, creating a split-role relationship in which the agent focused more on control and monitoring, and the treatment professionals provided support.

Dual-Role Relationships

Like many women in the study, Carla started supervision with lingering symptoms of PTSD, which she attributed to finding her baby daughter smothered after the child's sleeping father rolled onto her. Carla said that when something reminded her of her daughter's death, she went "right back to that same night, like it's so vivid. It's just like yesterday. I can picture every little pinpoint, the color of the comforter. . . . I'll never forget like the doctor's coming in and telling us that she died, you know, or holding her, none of that stuff." Carla blamed herself for being at work instead of watching over her daughter when she was smothered. The baby's death triggered the escalation of Carla's drug use to numb her feelings, and she started parole still having flashbacks to the night the baby died. The agent's referrals, the diagnosis of PTSD, and subsequent treatment helped Carla. "When they told me what was wrong with me and stuff, I finally like came to terms with everything. . . . I just started thinking different about how everything went down, my life, like I started looking at things differently."

Talking about the agent's referring her to counseling, Raven praised the "triage" that led to individual counseling and weekly, home-delivered family counseling for her and the children. The family counseling convinced the children that they could talk to Raven about anything, an outcome of importance to Raven, because as a teenager "being molested, being on drugs, being on the streets, and stuff like that," her mother was unavailable for discussions. Family counseling dovetailed with Raven's view that raising her children was the central purpose of her life. Matching women's common need for holistic assessment and intervention, Raven's counseling extended beyond substance misuse to reasons for her emotional distress, and it improved Raven's and her children's interactions.[8]

Like Carla and Raven, with encouragement from the supervising agent, whom she described as very caring, Marion took part in several programs in a package of wraparound services that included residential and intensive outpatient substance abuse treatment and medical care for depression. Marion described one of the programs, "It talked about cognitive thinkin', it talked about resources, it talked about changing your life and your pattern. It was interesting. Each week had a different thing. And the man that runs it, he was interesting . . . he wasn't boring." Marion had an extensive record of retail fraud before, during, and after the research. Different from Carla, Raven, and other women who stopped breaking the law and using drugs, Marion did not describe any change, growth, or insights gained in treatment. Instead, she saw time spent in programs as a means to avoid prison when she violated conditions of supervision, and she described the program as a series of interesting presentations rather than a setting for reflection and change. Without engagement in self-change and a legitimate source of income, substance abuse and mental health treatment and a caring parole agent were not enough to produce desistance.

Control-Oriented Agents and Treatment Referrals

Women could experience mental health and substance abuse treatment unrelated to their relationships with agents. The outpatient substance abuse treatment program the agent required Carmen to attend expelled her after she tested dirty for "pills," and Carmen ignored the agent's directive to take part in an alternate program. Carmen saw "fixing" what she referred to as her "anger problem" as her greatest need, and she independently located the mental health treatment she thought would help. Interviews with Carmen confirmed the seriousness of the "anger problem." As previously noted, she described being expelled from school for fighting and violence, breaking a jail cellmate's nose and trying to drown her in a toilet, and swearing at members of the parole board. Carmen said that the mental health counseling she found initially made her angry because staff kept bringing up her past instead of judging her for who she was now. A year into counseling, she assessed the program positively:

> Yeah, I've learned how to control my anger and I learned how to do things on my own. It's better when I learn how to do things on my own, because I don't gotta worry about what other people are telling me. I like figuring stuff out on my own—the mental health, . . . trying to get back in school, getting jobs on my own.

Consistent with Carmen's take on treatment and also with the methods of motivational interviewing, considerable research shows that client-therapist agreement on the goals of therapy promotes achievement of those goals.[9] Carmen's recognition of her inability to regulate her anger and her independent effort to locate the program that addressed this problem promoted a positive counseling experience that enabled her to take control of planning her own life.

As presented in the chapter on agent action, Bree had a split-role relationship with the supervising agent and the therapist that the agent insisted she see for individual sessions after a suicide attempt. Bree wanted to determine what the therapist knew about her, but the agent repeatedly called the therapist to give her information. The therapist returned some control to Bree: "She'll be like, your agent called me, and she said this, and she said that. I didn't want you to feel like you were left in the dark." Each month Bree and the therapist prepared the monthly progress report for the agent together, a process that again gave Bree control over the information the therapist shared about her. Asked to identify a message that she thought about frequently, Bree remembered something the therapist had said: "If you can put your mind to it, you can do it." Bree said the therapist "really cared" about her. "You get some people, some groups that the counselor's just there just to be there, and you get some that really actually care and want to help them." Bree thought that therapy changed her way of thinking and her outlook on things that happened to her. Therapy empowered Bree, and except for the referral to treatment, supervision focused on control and, according to Bree, at times intruded into the relationship with the therapist.

In another example of a split-role relationship, Mallory saw the parole agent as more controlling than caring, but she found support in a residential substance abuse treatment program a judge ordered her to attend after she committed a new offense while on parole. The gender-responsive residential substance abuse treatment program gave Mallory an opportunity to finally discuss abuse as a child and later by her husband:

> It did help me in more ways than I thought or what I was looking for. It helped me open up. It helped me to kind of grow up. It helped me to look at things differently and to look at people differently and not be so hard on myself or not to give myself up. It helped me with a lot of guilt.

Different than prior counselors, those at the treatment program did not respond to her like "just another drug addict." The constant presence of counselors in a residential treatment setting was conducive to the formation of this type of individualized and supportive relationship.

Unique Effects of Treatment

Each of the six women identified at least one treatment experience characterized by contemporary standards for practice that matched clients' perceptions of their needs to the treatment interventions and promoted clients' taking control of their lives. Some agents built similar alliances with the women, whereas others emphasized the control aspect of their jobs and left the support and empowerment to the mental health professionals. In both situations, women described mental health providers who offered a degree of tolerance and freedom that probation and parole agents could not offer because of the expectation that they would monitor behavior and respond to violations and new offenses. As a result, mental health treatment made a unique contribution by supporting women and giving them tools to cope with trauma, addiction, and other negative experiences. The remainder of this chapter further examines findings about the women's interface with mental health and substance abuse treatment, beneficial features of treatment, and barriers to effective treatment. It also shows how some women exited from court and correctional contact by immersing themselves in ongoing mental health or substance abuse treatment.

THE LARGER GROUP OF WOMEN

Opportunity to Talk about Traumatic Events

As might be expected of women with histories of trauma, several women valued the opportunity to talk about these experiences with treatment providers. Kiara provided a good example of how treatment helped her move beyond negative events that she had not disclosed for years. Weekly counseling groups and monthly individual sessions through community mental health services gave her an opportunity to talk about at least two past events. One stemmed from her and her siblings' being the only Black children in their elementary school, where White students harassed and bullied them. For example, before Kiara and her brothers left the school bus, a group of students would take their backpacks and empty the contents outside of the bus: "You know and like we'd come out there and our backpacks be thrown, stuff everywhere, like they just . . .just cruel, just things like that." Additionally, when she was 12, a cousin raped her; her parents pressed for prosecution, she begged them not to proceed, and she never talked to them or anyone else about the assault. Kiara linked these ignored traumatic events to drug use in high school: "I didn't want to like remember or think, so you know no matter who it was or what it was, like that's when I started trying to find things [drugs] to like not to deal with it." During supervision, Kiara sought treatment to deal with the resulting depression and anxiety:

> Through the years and all the experiences, it's definitely done a lot of damage inside so that's my other things is like working on myself as far as like my confidence. You know dealing with different things in life, you know as far as like pain, hurt, everything. . . . Just learning how to deal with my feelings, and that's what I'm doing by like therapy and, you know, counseling and stuff like that.

Kiara learned to write down her feelings and to "feel, deal, and heal." Talking about these gains in relation to being raped by her cousin, she said, "Like for today, it makes me stronger now because I talked about it and like I'm dealing with it." Before she had "pushed everything down" and "covered everything up."

Getting the Complete Picture

Just like they appreciated supervising agents who understood their past and current circumstances, women appreciated treatment professionals' efforts to get a complete picture of them, what they valued, and their lives. In the midst of a mental health crisis, Lana planned to kill herself but changed her mind and told her husband to call the police and report her for having a gun. The police took her to a psychiatric hospital, after which she was convicted on a weapons charge and sentenced to four months in jail followed by probation. At the start of her probation, distraught over a business failure and his mother's death, Lana's husband committed suicide, and Lana and the children moved from a city to a rural part of the state to be near her parents' residence. The probation agent in the rural area connected Lana to the local community mental health agency. "She [the agent] paid attention to the fact that my family was hurt by the committed suicide and [my] drinking, that there was a lot of family dynamics that were going on. She just set me up with CMH [Community Mental Health] . . . had them come in and do counseling work with the kids and I just kind of rebuild that with me." In addition to therapy, Lana thought a woman-only alcohol group helped her because it did not include anyone who used recreational drugs or with addictions to cocaine, methamphetamine, or heroin. The group leader did not just respond to her diagnosis, "bipolar," but "looked at everything that went on." She interviewed Lana's children and gathered information from professionals who knew Lana before she moved. Lana saw benefit in the attention to her specific needs and, like Raven, the recognition of the centrality of her children in her life.

Multiple treatment program features and life events created a turning point for Hope at age 44. Over many years, she completed several terms of probation, vacillated between using and not using drugs, and took part in seven substance abuse treatment programs. She lost six children to the state after CPS responded to Hope's mothers' dropping them off at the police department; lost another because he was born with drugs in his system; and then went to another state, where she bore two more children. She left the state so CPS would not automatically remove the newborns from her care. Back in Michigan, after Hope left her nine-year-old son home alone while she was on a "crack binge," the school staff and the CPS worker arranged for her to enter a four-month residential substance abuse treatment program. The probation agent warned her, "I better stay there. I gotta make sure I report still." Hope found the program effective because "half of the [staff] people that was there were recovering people and it was, like, it was real motivational to—wow. I can actually be clean a few years down the road and be this person. . . . I can help someone in church. I can help. I can be a good mother." She gained insight in the program: "I was upset because I lost my kids to the State, and I didn't realize how much pain and hurt I was really carrying around. And it was this, it kept reliving, over and over in my head, and I smoke [crack]. It was just—and I got tired of living that same dream. Can I get out of this nightmare, you know?"

The program challenged Hope to focus on stopping drug use and taking responsibility for the two sons who lived with her. In a group session with 17 other women who were required to complete the program to maintain child custody, another participant impressed upon Hope that she must devote her attention to taking care of her sons,

> [The other participant said,] "You always talking about your mama, your mama, your mama. Your mama didn't lie down and have them babies. You did." [Hope went on] Wow, it's like her coming to me and like, bam, slapping the shit out! . . . So that's when the growing up came with the, with [son M] telling them [he was living alone], you know and me having to go—either you play on those streets and keep on smoking crack, or you grow up and own up to your responsibility. These are your children. They didn't ask to be here. You didn't give them up for adoption. They're yours. You handle them.

After Hope completed the program but while she was still on probation, Hope's 19-year-old son, who grew up in foster homes, raped the 7- and 10-year-old sons who lived with her. She decided against making a violent attack on her older son in front of the younger boys. She realized the older son had been sexually abused himself in foster care, and the two younger sons would be traumatized by witnessing the attack. As an alternative, she engaged herself and the young sons in family counseling to address the trauma from their being raped. Hope had shifted from coping with crises by taking violent action and smoking crack to seeking and using the help of family counseling. Like Kiara, Raven, and Mallory, Hope found it helpful to discuss traumatic events that she had not discussed for many years. Like Lana and Raven, consistent with the high importance women attached to family making, Hope valued family counseling for herself and her children.

In contrast to the accessibility of trauma-oriented family therapy to address Hope's two sons' being raped, Hope had a hard time accessing medication to treat her own psychiatric problems. She outlined the steps involved:

> I already take the boys to therapy, so in order for me to get a psychiatrist I'm going to have to get a therapist in order to see a psychiatrist, and then that is not like, okay I go this week, or I go two visits and then I see the psychiatrist. No, I have to wait, like, four maybe six months for them to sit down and talk to me every week for an hour and hear me bitch and cry and go through my emotions before they can diagnose me. Then we got to find the psychiatrist that's going to see you. Once you with the psychiatrist then he's booked up and then we've got to wait, like, another like three to four weeks before we can get you some medicine.

At the time of the life story interview, Hope was waiting for the appointments to open up. A year later she did not note whether she ever received mental health treatment or not. She had completed probation after 18 months of supervision.

Exit Ramp from Supervision to Mental Health Support

With the help of supervising agents or on their own, some women with long histories of breaking the law and drug use desisted after completing substance abuse treatment, obtaining mental health care, or both. Establishing a network of continuing mental health services to provide long-term treatment and support gave women an exit ramp. Fiona took this exit ramp from criminal justice–agency involvement to mental health services. She attributed mental health problems to her stepfather's repeatedly beating her, her father's visit from another state during which he beat her and engaged her in cooking meth during her childhood, and the time when she ran to escape warrants for her arrest and lived with her father out of state. While she was living with him, Fiona and her father cooked, used, and sold meth, and he repeatedly raped and brutally physically attacked her.

Motivated by desire to bring up her child, Fiona moved back to Michigan and away from her biological father and located and completed a substance abuse treatment program. She said the substance abuse treatment staff helped her link to mental health agencies that provided treatment and necessities such as clothes and diapers. She also became heavily involved in the self-help group, Narcotics Anonymous (NA). By the life story interview, Fiona had married a man who earned a good salary, and they had two children together. Fiona described her current substance use and mental health:

> I've been in recovery four years. I had a relapse two years ago. I thought I could smoke weed and be successful. No, that was bad. But I'm doing really well. . . . It's a lot better than what it was. I still have my craziness, but it's a lot better. . . . My therapist, my psychiatrist, my case manager—they're a huge part of my life.

Fiona talked extensively about her "craziness" when she told her life story. "Each phase in my life, even with recovery, it's front and center." She described herself as having bipolar disorder that started when she was a child and PTSD due to the abuse she experienced throughout her life. Fiona explained her current symptoms:

> The manic, I talk so fast, my mind goes so fast. Fast, like, I over think, I over-analyze everything. From the smallest thing, I am a psycho about, I'm obsessive compulsive. My whole house, even right now, it looks clean—no. There's like fifty things I could clean right now. It takes over my life. The psychosis that I'm going through right now, I got two little babies [in addition to her oldest child]. I got help from my sister. I should be happy and it's this over-consuming mental [thoughts] that's driving me out of my mind.

She told the interviewer about the effects of PTSD: "I get scared. I panic in large crowds. I can't learn in a classroom because . . . I panic. I need a teacher to teach me, so I can't do it on the computer." She said her violent tendencies influenced mental health practitioners to overmedicate her: "They want to dope me up so much that I'm on the couch, but I need the meds, but I don't want to be a . . . zombie." Drawing on what she learned from therapy, Fiona reasoned that given the combination of the "ghetto" environment where she grew up and being fathered by a "monster of a man," her mental illness was expected. "I've had a lot of therapists tell me that I have the perfect melting pot to be a drug addict [and] it was almost inevitable that I turned out the way that I did with who I was related to and my environment." Because her husband made a good living, Fiona lived in an upscale community and did not struggle with poverty or neighborhood crime. Her change in economic status and extensive help from mental health professionals contributed to her desistance from drugs.

Residential substance abuse treatment programs were time limited, usually 30 or 90 days. Outpatient programs varied, but they often imposed a limit on the length of treatment. Jasmine, who chose to stay in both residential and outpatient substance abuse treatment longer than supervision required, described on-demand therapy well after supervision ended:

> I have a therapist. I go to see a doctor once a month. I talk to him. I talk to my therapist. I see him like, either once a week, every two weeks, whenever necessary, whenever we feel I need to come back. So, it just kind of helps, and then it helped me talking to other people and seeing other people that have overcame it, like, at the AA [Alcoholics Anonymous] meetings and stuff.

Given the multiple and life-changing traumas that contributed to many women's substance misuse, continued access to treatment played an important role in women's maintaining desistance. For Jasmine, whose supervising agent had helped her connect to a housing program, having a permanent residence rather than being on the brink of homelessness also supported desistance.

Another exception to time-limited treatment was methadone treatment clinics, which served some people for many years. Linsey transitioned from supervision to reliance on the services of a methadone maintenance clinic that not only dispensed methadone but also gave her access to counseling. Her move out of a deteriorated area of Detroit to a prosperous suburb supported this transition. Linsey eschewed methadone clinics in "bad neighborhoods that you don't want to go to because the drug dealers are there waiting for you to get out." She compared that type of clinic to the one she relied on: "But this one's in a strip mall right behind, like, the Olive Garden [chain restaurant]. So, it's like, you know, it's in a really safe neighborhood."

The counselor and other staff at the methadone clinic gave Linsey considerable ongoing support:

> I've had him for a few years now and he's like the most awesome person ever. He's so kind and so understanding, I never feel scared to talk about anything with him if I ever have a problem. He's been very open about having my fiancé come in. He knows my daughter since she was two. He's seen her grow up and everything. They've just really been, just everybody there has been so awesome and helpful.

When Linsey completed probation, funding ended for her to take part in the methadone program, but the clinic director cut the weekly costs from $80 to $40, which Linsey could afford. The price reduction showed Linsey that staff saw her as a person, not just a number. Clinic staff had given her food; loaned her gas money; and "just every way possible that they could help, they have always helped." The clinic worked out for Linsey because it was not a place with "drug addicts just passing out everywhere and, you know, all kinds of craziness. It's a lot of mothers that come here with their kids." Largely because of its location, visits did not threaten or stigmatize her.[10] As it did for Fiona, who also had the advantage of being White and more easily leaving urban high-crime neighborhoods, moving to a low-crime, high-resource area facilitated Linsey's exit out of the justice system and into ongoing treatment.

For Margo, immersion in NA provided the consistent, motivating support that enabled her to step out of the criminal justice system into a self-help group.[11] Starting in her twenties, she and her husband "got caught up in drugs and life spiraled a down[ward] path." After time on probation, she spent three years in prison because she could not "drop clean," and then for years she went back and forth between periods of abstinence and use. She completed multiple 30- or 90-day substance abuse treatment programs. Three decades later, at age 55 she thought, "I do not want to turn another year older in active addiction." She achieved four years clean by first going to a residential treatment program for 90 days, and then staying away from "the hood" where she had taken drugs and supported herself with a retail fraud operation.

Like other Black women in the study, Margo did not move out of the city, but she extracted herself from the area she called "the hood" by insisting that substance abuse treatment program staff find her transitional housing in another neighborhood. After that, she steered her way from program to program until she lived independently in stable housing, immersed herself in NA, and negotiated a relationship with her children that let her prioritize NA activities and thus her sobriety. Margo referred to the moves toward transitional housing outside of the hood as "my own journey, you know, my own mission to get my own place." After her time was up in transitional housing, she found out that a newly established substance abuse treatment program provided housing for people waiting for Section 8 subsidized housing approval. She moved to a temporary furnished apartment. Even after she had approval for the Section 8 subsidy, landlords' responses to her felony record prevented her from moving to her most desired neighborhood, but a staff member from the temporary housing program knew she would "pay the rent," so she helped Margo secure housing in a neighborhood better than where she lived before. By the life story interview, Margo was receiving disability insurance, medical insurance, and food assistance, and she saw herself as "fully self-supported now."

Margo impressed upon the interviewer that to understand her, the interviewer should read up on a basic principle of NA, "'Step Three—Turning your will and your life over to the care of God as you understand Him. Letting go and letting God [handle things] and getting out the way.'" Margo fully engaged with NA, which she referred to as "the fellowship." She described herself "chairing the meeting, running around collecting money, [and] putting up the secretary table, the literature table." When she could afford a car, she anticipated visiting and talking to "girls who are doing thirty, ninety, maybe one-hundred days" in the county jails to provide literature and lists of resources they could use after release. Maintaining sobriety now and in the future became the central focus of Margo's life. When her daughter complained about the time she spent with the NA group, Margo told her, "Girl, keeping my sobriety is a lifetime thing, because people with twenty-six years has relapsed. So it is something—a top priority—even over the children." Margo summed up her feelings about NA: "I know they saved my life, and it's a lifetime process . . . it's an ever-going process." For Fiona, Jasmine, Linsey, and Margo, in addition to mental health and substance abuse treatment, getting out of high-crime, low-resource neighborhoods facilitated access to people and groups that supported desistance. In part by moving, the women encircled themselves with professionals and self-help groups that enabled them to sustain desistance from drug use and crime.

Medical Insurance as a Barrier to Treatment

Eddie said her childhood was so bad that she did not want to talk about it. During interviews, she digressed from one topic to another, but she did share some parts of her life story. She called herself the "stupidest bitch in the world" for degrading sexual acts she did on the street for $2 a time to get money for drugs. She regretted losing children at birth because she had drugs in her system and leaving children with people she hardly knew so she could go out and get drugs. Finally, she felt bad about being with a man for five years, only to find out that he molested his nieces. She said she had been diagnosed with paranoid schizophrenia, schizophrenia, psychosis, bipolar disorder, PTSD, and drug addiction.

Eddie started using cocaine soon after release from prison and was in and out of residential and outpatient treatment programs because she left them before completion. The agent responded to positive drug tests, dropping out of treatment, and periods of not reporting with placement in different programs, including the only dual-diagnosis program that would accept her, which was on the other side of the state. Eddie cut off her tether equipment multiple times. She remembered the parole agent and the "tether agent" warning her that she was going to "end up in a dumpster." At the life story interview, she said, "Even after treatment, it's all inside and hurting." Eddie's continuing addiction and noncompliance with requirements that she complete programs resulted in her parole being extended for a year. Although she was dismissed from parole after two years, she remained on probation in absconded status for at least three more years. Tampering with the tether device resulted in the extended probation.

Amid the chaos of moving in and out of different residences and programs and just after she left prison, Eddie had no medical insurance. During the first interview, she noted, "I applied for the medical insurance through the State, and they won't . . . they're saying that it's not enough funding or whatever. Basically, it's because all the funding is getting cut on everything." Over a year later, she finally qualified for insurance. Like Marion's story, Eddie's story exemplified how even when agents made referrals to numerous programs and services, some women continued to use drugs. It also shows how a woman with serious mental illness can have an additional burden imposed by sporadic retraction of the safety net, in Eddie's case medical insurance.

Grace's history and her emotional state indicated her need for mental health treatment, but lack of insurance stood as a barrier for her too. Her stepfather beat her from ages five to seven, and her mother did not intervene even though she knew that her "lady friend" repeatedly molested Grace when she was 13. Grace said she was depressed, angry, and violently abusive to other people when she ran away to live on the streets. At 21 she joined a man selling drugs and started selling drugs herself and holding people's guns, wrapping them (covering them with tape to avoid picking up fingerprints), and moving them from person to person to make money. She described her mental state: "This all started when I was 21 and I still have episodes. I have suicidal thoughts. I have burned myself, cut myself, and abused drugs when I'm out of prison. I've tried to kill myself and others."

Grace told her life story in prison. Between the start of the parole that brought Grace into the study and her return to prison for retail fraud, she took part in a dual-diagnosis program that she found helpful: "It was structured. The facilitator deals with domestic violence and anger management and is part of the anger management team. So, it helps deal with multiple things and my dual diagnosis of mental health issues and anger." Grace liked the educational aspect of the program. "This program teaches us more about the medicine we take, how it affects us, the side effects, and it teaches us more about our illness." She also liked the wraparound programming. "They take us on, like, outings and . . . they help us, like, if don't have placement and we need clothes, so pretty much it, it's very beneficial for me." The program had many positive features, but it fell short in helping Grace because she did not have medical insurance:

> I've been struggling really hard trying to stay focused. . . . A lot of the times it's overwhelming to me because I'm not getting proper medicine. . . . The program—they only pay for my Lithium, so I'm not able to even take my medicine to really stay stable, so I'm kinda like off balance. Sometimes I'm up; sometimes I feel like committing suicide; sometimes I'm very depressed.

Grace recognized that even though programming brought benefits, lack of insurance severely tempered those benefits.

Again showing the damaging effects of sporadic availability of medical insurance, a delay in Carley's receipt of Medicaid resulted in her loss of access to mental health counseling. Carley experienced two types of trauma that likely contributed to her depression and anxiety. As a child, she saw her dad severely abuse her mom. At age 21, she saw her fiancé stabbed in the heart and watched him bleed out. "I couldn't sleep 'cause I'd dream about it, so I would drink until I didn't dream." She had a history of retail fraud to take care of herself starting at age 13, and once she started drinking heavily, she turned back to retail fraud to get necessities to support herself and her two children. The conviction that brought her into the study was for a third instance of driving while intoxicated.

Before starting parole, Carley completed treatment for substance abuse in a special unit of the prison. While she was on parole, MDOC initially paid for her appointments to see a counselor one on one at least once a month for depression. The funding stopped, and by the time she got on Medicaid the doctor she had seen previously had no openings. The agent helped her figure out where to go and how to get her medication back. "She gave me the paperwork on the places that took the insurance that I have for the things that I need. She just gave me the steps to do it, to get there, because I didn't really know. I had always gone to the same people since I was 21 [until 40] and they were full." Three months later, Carley still had no place that accepted her as a patient, and the agent had no recourse. "But I mean there's nothing she can do about that. It's not her fault that I don't have medical insurance." Carley thought that even though the agent was powerless to help her get medication,

> it should be a concern because [without medication] then you do stupid things. . . . Like I really need a counselor to talk to so that I don't lose my mind. I can't share half of the things I think with my family or my friends. You know because then they worry about me, and I don't want to worry anybody else.

When she told her life story, Carley expressed her concern about still lacking Medicaid: "And I really only want it for . . . the counseling part of it so that I can share the things that I can't share with other people." The limitations on what the agent could do to give Carley access to Medicaid put both her and the agent in an untenable situation, unable to alter the larger economic and social policies that blocked her access to medication and counseling.

CONCLUSION

Several women's successful exit from supervision depended heavily on a robust set of accessible community-based treatment and social services independent of being on probation, on parole, in prison or jail, or in a reentry program after incarceration. James Kilgore has raised the possibility of diversion of treatment resources from "bare bones social services in communities" to treatment and social services within jails and prisons and systems of community supervision.[12] He provides examples of how, in the name of making incarceration gender responsive, women's high prevalence of substance and mental health disorders opened the door to move resources from community-based services to jails for women. I did not find evidence of this phenomenon in Michigan. However, Michigan women who spoke about treatment needs described instances when they could access needed help and support only while under supervision or incarcerated. Conviction made them eligible for time-limited treatment that, if more abundant in their communities, might have prevented illegal behavior and substance misuse in the first place and that women needed to improve their lives before, during, and after supervision. Women in sparsely populated areas had few choices for treatment, and women in better resourced areas seemed to have greater access. The limits on treatment access and disparities in access show the importance of building community treatment resources apart from correctional institutions. Showing the acute problem of limited resources in marginalized communities, for abolitionist feminists the solution is to build community capacity to address drug use and illegal activity and end funding of criminal courts and correctional agencies.[13]

In the present study, even when women had strong motivation to stop illegal activity, took part in the treatment available in prison, received gender-responsive treatment matched to their specific needs, and believed that by changing their thinking they could improve their lives, the erratic and retracting social safety net could undo progress toward desistance. Jolene described her thoughts in prison: "I was going to end up killing myself with the way I was choosing to live." Based on this realization, she took all the programming, including substance abuse treatment, she could. Jolene feared returning to her hometown where she had used drugs, so MDOC staff arranged for her parole to Detroit to complete the parole board requirement of a 90-day residential substance abuse treatment program. The women-oriented program was intense, with groups meeting from 7:00 a.m. to 7:00 p.m. Jolene felt that this program was especially helpful because it educated her about what was going on inside her mind:

> It helped me to . . . just when I get the feeling or the urge to just let it pass, like, it's a feeling, you know, if you let it pass. And not only that, but just to be able to play your tape all the way through, like, consequences of what, you know, some of the decisions you make. Yeah, and pretty much learning to forgive people. Learning to forgive your past, you know, and not just dwell on it so much. And learning to change . . . like your negative thoughts into something simple and positive.

Jolene felt her substance abuse counselor had "real hope" for her, and she and the counselor were "real close, like if I was crying, like, she'd hug me." Signifying Jolene's success in the program, staff selected her as group leader and chose her to share her "stories at podiums in front of a lot of people." Jolene's comments show that she benefited from social support and from cognitive behavioral treatment, the counseling interventions recommended by feminist theorists and experts in correctional psychology alike.[14]

The parole agent also arranged for Jolene to receive a sequence of interventions that met multiple needs over time, and she developed a relationship marked by caring and trust rather than punishment. When the transitional housing counselor limited Jolene's time away from the residence because she kept coming back late, the agent advocated for her:

> She [the agent] came up there and put that lady [housing counselor] in check. She's like, "I'm going to tell you right now, she's not from around here. She just got out of prison. . . . She don't even know how to ride a bus and if she's not out being able to get on these buses, she's never gonna know how. She needs to look for jobs. She needs to be able to do this stuff. She don't . . . have to be here. She's being here because she's trying to help herself."

Jolene took delight in the agent's reaction when the counselor called Jolene a liar:

> And agent Summer looks at her and she goes, "You know a liar is a really harsh word to call somebody. Do you know that?" I like her a lot. She's so blunt though it's funny. And then, like we were walking out of my counselor's office and she starts giggling and she goes, "If you need anything else, call me. . . . I'm on your side. I'm here to help you, you know."

The agent referred Jolene to a job preparation and placement program, helped her get mental health treatment, and encouraged her to enroll in college courses. Except for staying in transitional housing for a while, Jolene did not follow up with most of these programs and services. Displeased with the continuing restrictions in transitional housing and without any friends or relatives in Detroit, Jolene moved back to her small hometown (about 10,000 population) in a distant part of the state. She let a cousin live with her in the hopes that she could support his effort to stop using drugs, but "kicked him out" when he stole her rent money. She blamed herself for his relapse, overdose, and death right after he moved out, and she started using drugs to quell her bad feelings.

Jolene struggled to get off drugs again. The area had just one outpatient substance abuse treatment provider, and she had been to groups there "at least five times" before. She did not find the groups helpful: "When I am in group there, it's the . . . the same people that I've used with, so it's like you know, half of them are still using." She signed up for a program to receive Buprenorphine, which would keep her from feeling "sick" during withdrawals from heroin, but they stopped the medication after four days. Staff ignored her complaints that she was back in withdrawal, so she left the program. Jolene located and enrolled in a program that used an alternative medication, Suboxone, which helped her withdraw from heroin as long as she continued taking it. She started a full-time job and got a car. Then the MDHHS cut Jolene's Medicaid and food assistance because of her income from work. She made $400 every two weeks and paid $700 a month in rent, and she could not cover the cost of Suboxone. To eat, she and the man she lived with stole food from stores. At other times they placed food orders at restaurants, claimed the orders were incorrectly filled, and ended up with free food. At that point she described herself as "right in the middle of my relapse." Relatives and friends tried to raise money to pay the $197 for the Suboxone monthly prescription being held at the pharmacy, and she was trying to get Medicaid reinstated.

Jolene reasoned:

> If I could get my Medicaid back, then I can get back on my Suboxone. When I get back on my Suboxone, my job told me that I could have my job back anytime. . . . But I can't because I'm using, you know, to keep my body normal because I don't have . . . I don't have my Suboxone, because I don't have Medicaid to get it. . . . So, and I don't use heroin to, you know, get high. I use it to keep me well because otherwise I can't get out of bed unless I'm using it.

Jolene had greater access to heroin than to prescription medication to stop using it. She reflected on the policies that negatively affected her recovery:

> I just feel like there needs to be more resources for the poor . . . the poor people. No, I just think that people that don't have, I guess a whole lot of support. . . . I think that there just should more opportunity. . . . What do people expect? I mean they don't want people to commit crimes, but then they don't want to give people the resources not to. That doesn't make any damn sense to me. Yeah, like, you know, they don't want people to use drugs, but they don't want to give them the resources to not use them. You know, like they want to punish people for being an addict. Like that's stupid.

Despite her continuing addiction, Jolene remained motivated and took action to stop using drugs. After being arrested and charged with possession of methamphetamine between the life story interview and the final interview, which was over a year later, she returned to Detroit and enrolled herself in a nine-month residential treatment program. She described the program: "I gained structure back in my life. It helped me to gain employment. It helped me to be involved in other people. It helped me to open up, and it helped me to identify with other people. It helped me to . . . I don't know, everything." Jolene attributed her motivation to change her life to her pregnancy: " It helps me I guess to give me a reason to want to live and to continue to do what I'm doing, if not for myself, for my child." Back in court in her hometown, the judge sentenced Jolene to probation, which she successfully completed in a year.

Jolene depicted opposing effects of jail, prison, treatment, and access to medical insurance. Starting when she was 17, time in jail educated her to cook meth and enticed her to start shooting up drugs. Prison provided substance abuse treatment and motivation to change herself. After release from prison, residential treatment in a program designed for women helped Jolene change the way she thought by emphasizing cognition and provided a caring relationship with the counselor. The parole agent followed best practices by arranging for a continuum of care after the end of residential substance abuse treatment and advocating for Jolene's empowerment in transitional housing. Jolene still felt restricted in transitional housing and challenged to manage in Detroit, so she moved to her hometown. After she had a relapse, staff in one detoxification program did not listen to her and did not help her, but she found a substitute in long-term treatment with Suboxone. She started working. Even with a very low income, she lost eligibility for food stamps and Medicaid, could not afford Suboxone, and relapsed onto heroin. Local substance abuse treatment did not meet her needs, but she found long-term residential treatment across the state. This mix of helpful and undermining correctional and treatment programs and fluctuating benefit eligibility shows how correctional and safety-net programs put people motivated to desist from substance use in the middle of countervailing forces—with some pulling them away from substance abuse and others pushing them into substance abuse. Jolene's story provides a good transition to consideration of the job market and safety-net programs that had major effects on many women.

CHAPTER 6

Marginalization

Various combinations of limited education, mental health and substance abuse challenges, employer reluctance to hire people with a history of convictions, and the costs associated with community supervision left most of the women in the research that informed this book living in poverty. Especially for Black women who faced racially based housing discrimination and limited options to move outside distressed cities, poverty affected the type of neighborhoods and communities where they lived, which in turn further limited their access to jobs.[1] In the larger sample of Michigan women on probation and parole, Black and other minoritized women disproportionately lived in communities lacking job opportunities, and this spatial mismatch between residential location explained Black women's high unemployment at the end of the first year of supervision. The women's statements revealed additional challenges felt by minoritized women, so throughout this chapter I note women's designation of their race and ethnicity. As described in chapter 1, neoliberal ideologies and economic downturns prompted state and federal legislators to reduce safety-net benefits, and this reduction further marginalized women regardless of race and ethnicity. In this economic context, women frequently spoke of the dismal job market, cuts in welfare and food assistance, years-long waiting lists for housing subsidies, and shutdowns in taking applications for medical insurance. They also noted how employers' responses to their prior convictions magnified their poverty.

The women shared considerable information about the legal and illegal ways they generated income, difficulties covering expenses, and efforts to access social safety-net benefits. In five of the interviews spread across the seven years of data collection, when responding to the question "What have you done to make your life better?," women talked about efforts to secure employment and benefits. During the first three interviews, they recounted discussions with agents about employment and financial problems. Four times before the life story, interviewers asked women if they needed social safety-net benefits in the form of cash income, housing, food, medical insurance, medical care, and funding to support education, and they followed up affirmative responses with questions about efforts to obtain needed benefits and the outcomes of these efforts. Finally, just before women told their life stories, interviewers asked about the material and emotional effects of not receiving needed benefits in the past and engaged women in a discussion of barriers to access.

The accounts and stories of the six women highlighted at the start of this chapter and of the women considered in the broader analysis show how they navigated both legal and illegal ways to bring in income, including job possibilities and potential sources of benefits. They reveal how women managed within the economic context and how outcomes of their efforts affected them and their desistance from crime.

TOUCHSTONE STORIES

Persisting Marginalization

Carmen's long-standing health challenges and difficulty regaining disability payments after release from prison left her feeling incapable of securing an income. She saw herself as unemployable because of frequent seizures resulting from the brain injury sustained in elementary school. Fear of situations that triggered the seizures prevented her from attending school: "Like, I want to go to college for cosmetology, but I have a bad anxiety problem where I can't be around more than twenty people or I'll have a seizure." Worsening her financial situation, while Carmen was in prison her mother collected and spent Carmen's disability insurance, so the state cut off payments and medical assistance after her release. Carmen expressed frustration that the state did not reinstate disability payments after two years of effort on her part: "It kinda makes me feel like . . . it's just not even worth it . . . 'cause I just sit there and call and call and they just give me the same number and it's not the number and it makes me wanna give up." Carmen hoped to live on her own in the future, but due to lack of income, she lived with her boyfriend. She narrowed her vision of the immediate future to exclude supporting herself with both employment and disability insurance.

Criminally Disqualified from Work and Safety-Net Benefits

Bree lived in one of the cities hardest hit by Michigan's economic decline. She summed up her thoughts about the type of job she could get to support herself and her newborn in a depressed economy:

> There's not too much to offer here. The schools are all closing, businesses are closing. . . . With my background, it's kind of easy to get a job as far as trying to provide for my family, but that job is not like a, you know, a great job. It's an okay job, but it's not a great job to where you wouldn't have to worry or still struggle at the end of the day.

Even though her immediate supervisor appreciated her hard work, Bree's criminal history jeopardized her low-paying employment at a gas station. When an upper-level manager discovered Bree's criminal record, Bree almost lost her job:

> And the manager over my manager, she did a background check, and the background check came back, and she ended up calling a little meeting with me and was asking me, am I still selling drugs in her store and, you know, just, kind of, judging me before she knew me. So, it's kind of hard. My manager—the person under her which was over me—she ended up speaking up and saying that I was a very hard worker and good worker and she, you know, if she could that she would prefer to keep me. I was one of the best workers that she had.

The immediate supervisor's intervention saved Bree's job, but the low earnings left Bree in poverty. She could not receive food assistance because past drug convictions left her "criminally disqualified." A criminal history not only jeopardized Bree's employment, but it extended punishment for past offenses beyond criminal justice sanctions to disqualification from food assistance. In effect, the social welfare agency added its own punishment to the judge's sentence.

Stigmatization and Social Marginalization

At the start of the study, Carla felt shut out from employment and housing because of the nature of her crime. She remembered that at a job fair she had attended at the start of parole, potential employers made it clear that her felony conviction ruled out employment: "Selling drugs or manufacturing drugs is a no-no." Living in housing provided by MDOC and looking for a place to rent, Carla faced barriers in the private housing market. "They [landlords] won't even deal with me, because of my felony, operating and maintaining a meth lab." Based on her research into jobs open regardless of criminal history, Carla decided cosmetology training would be feasible, but school was unaffordable, because when she had begun using drugs, she had defaulted on student loans and become ineligible for more loans.

Toward the end of the study, Carla moved from her hometown to another small town in a nearby county. Showing a negative effect of a hometown where people knew each other, Carla experienced not only economic marginalization but also a more general stigmatization by people who knew of her criminal past.[2] She described the social marginalization that continued even after she moved:

> I had to go pay my costs and fines [in my hometown] before they put me in for release from parole. And just bein' down there and runnin' into everybody I know, and it's just like, "Oh God," you know what I mean? It's like . . . oh my gosh 'cause everybody down there knows. I've hit the paper, I've hit the news. . . . Where I'm from, my name's just garbage, you know, because I just got so low and so that's what I'm known for is just grimy, you know. And then like it sometimes it's even embarrassing because there'll be times that people come into my job [in the new town] that knows me from my past. I don't want to go back to . . . bein' that person . . . bein' some loser drug addict with no money, no nothing, you know, like havin' to go hustle up money.

Exemplifying White women's greater residential mobility than Black women had, moving enabled Carla to secure employment and housing and avoid constant stigmatization by people who knew about her past criminal behavior. Looking back, she reasoned that rather than being ashamed of her past, "I should be proud of that 'cause that's who I am, that's made me who I am today, 'cause I'm not that same person." Employed and living in a new town, Carla saw herself as a new person who could dismiss past illegal activity incompatible with who she had become. Narrative identity theorists identify this process of dismissing the past as one mechanism to tie negative past events to a current positive identity.[3] Moving was key to Carla's improving her situation and distancing herself from illegal activity.

Cut Off from the Safety-Net and Geographically Marginalized

Raven, who lived in a high-crime, low-resource Detroit neighborhood, made ends meet despite supervision costs, periods of no or low-paying employment, supporting five children, and being cut off from TANF because of newly instituted statewide time restrictions. Hoping to requalify for TANF, Raven enrolled in Work First, the program intended to transition people from government aid to employment:

> I started Work First and that's the step you have to take before you start getting your cash. It's in the form of a job. You have to be there from eight to five and you have to turn in these job search logs. Before it was you had to go every day, now it's just a couple days out of one week, and then you do four weeks of job search, and then they bring you in and you do four weeks of volunteer work. Then if you don't find a job by then you do another four weeks of job search and then two weeks of volunteer and then so on and so forth, until you find a job.

By the time of the life story interview, Raven was receiving food assistance and a housing voucher, but no cash assistance. Her depiction of Work First shows the underlying assumption of the program, that people without a job need to be trained to work eight hours a day for five days a week through mandated classes and volunteer work. In this system, caring for children and making ends meet on little or no income is not counted as "real work." This devaluation of women's heavy responsibilities for household labor is widespread in U.S. society.[4]

Raven contradicted the stereotype that people receiving government assistance lack a work ethic, so without Work First requirements, they are satisfied to remain unemployed. She made considerable effort to secure employment: "[I] obtained my medical assistant, my resident medical assistant, my phlebotomy, my patient care tech [certifications]." Even with the certifications, Raven could not find a job in the medical field— according to her because of her felony record. During the study, she worked temporarily in a "barbecue joint" for seven months, her longest tenure at a job "in a long time." That was the only employment she secured. Raven sized up the potential for future employment:

> Yeah, I wanna finish, go back and finish my social work [degree] because that's about the only field I can get in with a felony. I researched that, like I researched a couple of different careers that will hire you, you know, you can go into, you can get degrees or certificates with being a felon. That's why I went into the medical assistant field because I was still able to get my

certificate while I had a felony. I don't understand, like, why I can't work as a medical assistant with a felony. If I obtained my degree while I had a felony, I should be able to work with a felony, but it just don't work like that.

With no expectation of permanent employment, Raven cobbled together a living from housing and food assistance, her live-in partner's contributions to the household (in violation of probation prohibitions against associating with a felon), and income from sporadic employment. The family lived on the margins of financial viability. When her partner could not find work as a contractor, "That's when the shut off notice and stuff keeps coming." Neither Work First nor earning several certificates propelled Raven into the workforce, so she managed without a steady income. She did still have hope for the future—she thought she could secure employment by earning a social work degree.

Because she took part in Work First, Raven secured a housing voucher to help pay the rent, but this did not result in a move to a safe neighborhood. Illustrating how a combination of financial marginalization and being Black kept women in high-crime neighborhoods, the family lived not only on the margins of financial viability, but also on the margins of staying alive in their neighborhood, which Raven called "the hood." She described the threat of "gangbangers":

> You would know if something going on because they walk up the block in a group. That's how you know something's gunna go down because a group of them will walk up the block or a group of them would be standing on the corner or something like that. That's how you know when something about to happen or something does happen and they gunna retaliate or something like that. The best bet is just don't be by them, be in your own area, don't go by the windows, none of the above.

Raven had her children sleep upstairs so they were safe from stray bullets. She saw her children's friends smoking weed and breaking into houses at an early age, so she expended considerable time and energy keeping her children away from the streets and in programs. She established a family routine. "On Mondays they go to church from five to nine, Tuesdays they go from four to eight, Wednesdays they go from five to nine, Thursdays they go from six to ten, Fridays they go from five to ten thirty, Saturdays they go from nine to twelve, and Sundays they go from nine to five." For self-protection, Raven only left the house to search for jobs, check the mailbox, or walk the children to and from programs. The combination of benefit cuts, difficulty finding work with a felony record, and the type of housing available to people using a housing voucher made Raven a prime example of an economically and geographically marginalized woman. She coped by heavily supervising her children and making the most of food and housing assistance and sporadic income. Housing vouchers were intended to help individuals move to mixed-race neighborhoods with more advantages than racially segregated, high-crime urban areas. Nationwide, the low funding level for the housing voucher benefit, procedures for obtaining and using vouchers, limited resources for housing searches, and landlord discrimination have prevented this ideal outcome from becoming a reality, especially for minoritized groups.[5]

Disconnected from All Means of Financial Support

For decades, 55-year-old Mallory supported herself and her heroin addiction by boosting high-end products stolen from department stores. She had been in prison 10 times for a total of over 16 years. She attributed her current efforts to stop stealing and stay drug free to her age: "I'm not young anymore. My health is not what it used to be [because of chronic illness due to hepatitis C]. I can't take the concrete and the cells and the cold." Consistent with this view of herself, Mallory said that the message she most recalled and that affected her behavior the most was from the supervising agent who said, "You're getting too old."

Mallory lived in MDOC transitional housing during the study period. Fifteen prior felony convictions disqualified her from housing assistance that would have enabled her to move out. Denial of her application for disability insurance left her discouraged and depressed. "I don't have money. Not having an income is hard, very hard." Mallory had taken college courses in prison but felt she could not continue after release because she found learning difficult. She suspected she had an undiagnosed learning disability. At least in the short run, her struggle with learning made her plan to work as a social worker unrealistic. Mallory was motivated to avoid breaking the law, but she remained disconnected from all means of financial support and thus in a very precarious position for falling back into illegal means of earning money.

Illegal Income

Marion lived completely outside the legitimate economy and lacked motivation and a plan to find another source of income. During the research, she resided in shelters for the homeless until the very last interview when she moved into a small, subsidized apartment. Retail theft brought in a steady income before, during, and after the six interviews. She described her illegal behavior and herself:

> I think shoplifting is an addiction and the more you do it, the more you become seeing if you can get away with it. Closer and closer I got to the door, I felt an adrenaline rush. Yeah, and it was addicting. It became addicting. Then I had to dress a certain way to be a certain way. . . . I was stealing to keep my gambling going, as well as my cocaine use. I would steal name brand items and go down in the hood, like the neighborhoods, like they say the hood, and sell it. . . . I came up in Detroit, but in Detroit the security is more evident than out in the suburbs. So, I would catch the bus, because I didn't have a ride, I didn't have a car. So, I catch the bus and go steal and come back. When I get off the bus people would say, "Whatchya got, whatchya got?" You know and it was . . . that was a rush in itself, just 'cause people—I became noticeable. And I know they knew I had some stuff and I had bags and bags of stuff. I was addicted to shoplifting. Still is, but I have it under control because I do want to get off parole.

Marion had no close living family members, partners, or friends. She presented her boosting operation as bringing more satisfaction and income than any relationships or other accomplishments.

Reactions to Marginalization

Carmen, Bree, Carla, Raven, Mallory, and Marion differed in their efforts to be part of the legitimate economy and their capacity to do so. Except for Marion, who felt exhilarated by her skill at retail theft and boosting the goods and the recognition she received from her customers, they envisioned building human capital through education and securing a satisfying job. Carmen had only a vague sense of engaging in legitimate pursuits, but by the end of the research she had stopped breaking the law and thought that someday she would have an income and her own place to live. Bree scraped by without benefits due to being, as she put it, "criminally disqualified," and subsisted on earnings from a low-wage job. Carla experienced employer and landlord rejection because of the nature of her convictions, but moving out of her small hometown enabled her to eventually find work and housing. Raven took steps to prepare for a career in the medical field, but prohibitions against hiring a person with felony convictions kept her from steady employment that she considered meaningful. As a part of a statewide reduction in welfare rolls, her cash benefits were cut. Her subsequent participation in Work First did not lead to employment but did bring in food and housing assistance. Some women responded to living at the margins of financial viability by accepting a limited future, which is what Carmen did. Alternatively, Bree, Carla and Raven managed the best they could and hoped for improvement in the future. Mallory's age and health gave her reason to avoid breaking the law, but short of success in a future appeal for disability insurance, she expected to manage without income. Marion relied on shoplifting for income and had no alternative plan. To expand on these findings about the six women, the next section presents information about additional women's efforts to secure and maintain income and on what their experiences tell us about themselves, work, and safety-net programs.

THE LARGER GROUP OF WOMEN

The Legitimate Job Market

The combination of feeling stigmatized by potential employers' knowledge of probation or parole status, their reactions to felony convictions, and Michigan's failing economy stood in the way of women's finding what they considered to be meaningful work that brought adequate income. At the start of supervision, Tina, who identified as White, avoided job interviews because of the stigma she felt when she told potential employers about supervision:

> Because then you have to tell people why you need one day a month off. . . . It's just another slap in the face. It makes you feel degraded all over again. It really does. You know, so sometimes you avoid certain things. Sometimes I'm not going to go to certain interviews because I don't want to tell them because eventually I'll be off [supervision] and I don't want to be running into those people.

Anticipated stigma can act as a powerful influence on women's behavior in their search for employment.[6]

Women who overcame the barriers to applying for jobs faced several other obstacles to their employment search. Louisa (Black) attributed her difficulty finding work to a long history of convictions for prostitution; retail fraud; assault with a dangerous weapon; and possession of drug paraphernalia, cocaine, and narcotics. At the start of parole, she saw the convictions for prostitution as especially problematic:

> Yeah, I can't get a job cause of the nature of my felony. But like they say about the prostitution, "Oh we can accept the fact that you did drugs, but

we can't . . ." like it's like a sexual offense to them because of my prostitution cases. They never call me back. Even the worst jobs won't call me.

At the time of the life story interview, Louisa's unrealized goal was to "land a permanent job and to stay there for time so I can say I can re- tire from this job, 'cause I never held a job out of 42 years for a whole year. Even in being clean [for seven years] I never worked a whole year, so that's crazy." She continued to explain the importance of steady paid employment: "Yeah, like not being able to provide for myself, or even for my husband, or for my kids and my grandbaby, that's what it developed from. Not having nothing. Can't pay . . . make the bills, none of that. I'm gunna get a job and keep faith that I can keep it, yeah." Louisa tied her lack of steady employment not just to difficulties paying her bills, but also to supporting her husband, children, and grandchild.

For some women, a criminal history blocked the actualization of ca- reer preparation and plans. Like Bree and Raven, Hope, a 44-year-old Black woman from Detroit, expressed frustration about how her record of convictions limited the types of jobs she could get: "I wish I could go to my name and just shred all my past away, for real. . . . With all this on me, I can't get a decent job in the medical field or anything, you know. And it's real discouraging, 'cause I want to work. I want a career." Even though she had completed a year of college courses to be a radi- ology technician, Kiara (30, Black) similarly saw her plans permanently derailed by convictions for using and selling marijuana and narcotics. "I can't continue my medical career. I only have clinicals left for radiol- ogy. Like I can't get into the field at all for the rest of my life." The desire for meaningful work that requires specialized training, coupled with a sense of the unattainability of such jobs, runs through Hope's, Kiara's, Bree's, and Raven's statements. Despite motivation and efforts to pre- pare for employment, they saw insurmountable barriers to working at the jobs they wanted and trained for.

Even if they secured employment, women might be fired because of prior convictions and assumptions about their continued illegal activity. Bree was nearly fired from work at a gas station after a manager com- pleted a background check, but her immediate supervisor intervened and pointed out how hard she worked, and she kept the job. Abby did not fare as well when a new supervisor took over at her workplace. Abby found considerable fulfillment in assisting people preparing to take the GED, because she could relate well to the many court-involved stu- dents. Ignoring the prior program manager's high evaluation of her job performance, the new manager carried out a background check and terminated her employment based on prior convictions.

Some women found steady employment and even fulfilling jobs despite statewide economic downturns and records of felony convictions. Their opportunity and strategy for securing employment differed depending on employment before conviction, job skills, relatives' capacity to teach skills or link them to work opportunities, and entrepreneurial aspirations and feasibility. Securing employment also depended on opportunities for work near their residences, which in turn were related to race for women featured in this book. White women lived in a more diverse range of communities and more often moved between communities than Black women, who almost always stayed put in high-crime neighborhoods in cities with failing economies.

Several White women found legitimate employment in small towns and rural areas. After leaving prison, Jenny, a 35-year-old White woman from a rural area, started out with the advantages of a high school degree and a history of employment in the landscape business. Past disadvantages included a stepfather who physically abused Jenny, her mother, and her sister, which influenced Jenny to move in at age 16 with a man who introduced her to drugs. While in prison for two years on convictions for producing methamphetamine, Jenny suffered additional hardships. Her mom "lost her mind" because Jenny was unavailable to break up fights with her stepfather, her stepfather left her mom, and Jenny's mom's home burned down with all of Jenny's belongings in it. Yet Jenny described herself as successfully transitioning from prison, which showed her that "I have mind over matter, that I'm strong-willed. I'm outgoing because, you know, I didn't stop. . . . I put in probably 150 applications." She compared herself to other women who left prison: "The way I look at it, is that they didn't have kids out here to go home to. I had something out here that I needed to strive for." Jenny attributed her success after release to personal drive and having a child, but as revealed by comments from women who did not find work, some of them, for example Raven, also demonstrated drive to secure good employment and the motivation to provide for their children. Jenny accepted the neoliberal emphasis on individual responsibility for outcomes regardless of context. Her statements show how the prevailing ideology of individual responsibility can be embedded in the beliefs of women who break the law, or more generally how the standpoint and interests of individuals with power—legislators and other policy makers who ignore contextual and structural influences—can be incorporated into the beliefs of women on probation and parole.

In addition to drive and motivation, Jenny had a prosocial community that welcomed her home and provided employment. Within six months of starting parole, Jenny got her previous landscaping job back, regained custody of her daughter, and lived in a house with a new law-abiding boyfriend. She was about to be released from parole. "I think I got pretty much everything covered but the supervision fees and the tether bill. But she [the agent] says I can get off parole even if I don't pay them. They'll just go to collections, so . . . and that's like 3,000 dollars for three months of tether, and 700 supervision fee." Largely because she returned to the job she held prior to incarceration, Jenny exemplified an idealized form of *reentry* and *reintegration*—that is, a return to a former good situation—that very few women in the study experienced:

> When I went back there [to work], there was this lady that worked there . . . and she took right to me. I mean she's like my everything now. She was my boss, my landlord, my friend, my mom, my sister. Yeah, she is. I mean, like I said, when I told you earlier that people came out of the woodwork, they came out the woodwork. I never thought I had so many people on my side, you know.

Jenny's boss helped her buy a car and get her license back, and he provided training for certification to work with a greater range of chemicals. Unlike most other women, Jenny could actually reenter society after prison, because she had been integrated into a work environment before. She had a high school education, a legitimate job she could go back to, and a prosocial social network at work.

Further exemplifying how personal resources and residential mobility enabled women to do well financially, Social Security benefits resulting from her husband's suicide and reconnecting to her parents provided Lana, a 44-year-old White woman who moved from a distressed city to a rural area, a way to support herself. She had been estranged from her parents since her mother "disowned" her because she was a pregnant teenager. Lana and her recently deceased husband argued frequently and drank heavily, and she had past convictions for driving under the influence and most recently, possession of a gun. After her husband committed suicide, Lana moved out of the city where the family had lived and where she had been arrested and convicted. With income from Social Security payments to widows, she and the children settled in a small town near her parents' home. After an initial focus on addressing her and her children's mental health needs, by the life story interview Lana had reconnected with her parents and was working part time with her father, who taught her carpentry. Two years later, Lana, her dad, and her mom planned or ran multiple businesses. She and her father took classes to learn how to invest in real estate, and Lana helped her mother run a start-up mail order business. Lana envisioned a meaningful present and future: "The investment venture is something that I . . . it's made me a very positive and self-sufficient individual with a whole different lifestyle with different viewpoints. . . . I can say, well if I had never messed up and got myself incarcerated this stuff might not have happened." Lana's perspective provided a classic example of a person making good from the negative aspects of arrest and conviction—a step in the process of desistance.[7] The opportunity to move, income from Social Security, and the chance to earn income with her parents facilitated her making good from past negative events.

Though they did not envision as bright a future in the work world as Lana, a few other women drew on relatives' resources to secure an income. Andy, a 32-year-old White woman who lived in a rural area, worked in her aunt's tax business so she could pay for her drug tests. Pamela, a 39-year-old White woman who lived in an urban neighborhood populated by houses that looked well kept, could not continue studying nursing because of her convictions. She worked with her mother cleaning houses. Although she and her husband divorced after she started dating another man and accumulated convictions for multiple episodes of driving while intoxicated, 53-year-old Sami, a White, Hispanic woman who lived in a suburb, still worked in the company her husband owned. For this research, compared to Black women, White (or for Sami, White and Hispanic) women more often had education, access to jobs, and relatives who facilitated finding a job.

One Black woman (age 36) without these advantages relied on entrepreneurship to earn a good living. When she was 12, Latrelle's family left a city dominated by the declining auto industry and moved to a predominantly White Detroit suburb, where Latrelle and her brother were targets of racially motivated bullying by schoolmates. She gravitated back to the city of her origins, where peers accepted her but then influenced her to sell and use drugs, which she did for 10 years. On probation for drug-related convictions, Latrelle started an office cleaning business. She described the collision of her legitimate cleaning business with a police drug raid on her house:

> Now at this time I'm building on to, I'm starting the cleaning business, so of course I've got nothing but stock of cleaning stuff, mop, buckets, you can just imagine, new brooms, dust pans, Swiffer [household cleaning equipment

brand] this, Swiffer that. And I know in my heart I didn't have anything [drugs], and they [the police] came in there and said they found something.

Latrelle thought that either someone she knew left the drugs in the house or the police planted them because of her history of selling. Undeterred by the resulting new conviction, Latrelle built up the business so much that she ended up in the hospital from overwork, after which she started turning down jobs. Her life projects were to open a chicken wing vending truck business and challenge the court cases resulting from the raid on her house. Latrelle saw herself as a successful entrepreneur with the potential for future expansion. She did not have any additional convictions.

Women's social networks and low monetary capital can make entrepreneurship infeasible. Marie, a Black woman from Detroit, saw owning a hair salon as the way out of poverty, but she recognized network and race-related structural barriers that prevented her from taking this route:

> It's my desire to take a whole bunch of Black people and own a lot of businesses because, I feel like, us Black people don't own a lot of things, and we don't support each other enough. . . . So, yeah, I want to be a Black business owner one day. And that's another reason I feel like I don't want to get a loan, because I feel like I'm a still be workin' for somebody 'cause I'm gonna be payin' you back. . . . So I want to own my own business. When I mean my own, my own!

Marie never had a credit card or any major purchase that would help her build a good credit rating. She needed a network of Black business owners for support, and she needed access to start-up capital to make her entrepreneurial aspirations a reality.

Women who did start businesses built on human and social capital. Lana benefited from a connection with parents who had resources and partnered with her. Latrelle, who grew up moving back and forth between a predominantly Black neighborhood in a distressed city and a well-to-do community on the outskirts of Detroit, could provide cleaning services in part because she had a car, no caregiving responsibilities, and a history of traveling to different areas of the state. For both women, mobility increased the feasibility of entrepreneurship.

The Informal Economy

Some women generated income in the informal economy, often referred to as working "under the table," where the government does not regulate the jobs or the workers. Employers did not deduct taxes or social security, and they did not follow minimum wage and other regulations. Kirsten, a 50-year-old White woman who, by the end of the study, lived in a suburb, worked in the informal economy after she left prison. She highlighted how a record of felony convictions and the potential for stigmatization influenced her to avoid applying for other jobs, and the resulting downside of working under the table. Her account also shows that working in the informal economy coupled with mobility between communities could provide a steppingstone to a better financial situation.

At the start of parole, in exchange for tips Kirsten dried cars at a car wash that her husband's alcoholic sister managed. Similar to Tina, who avoided applying for jobs so she did not have to tell people she was on probation, by working in the car wash Kirsten avoided telling potential employers she needed time off to report to the parole agent. Over time Kirsten grew increasingly troubled by her husband's and his family's heavy drinking (for example, family binges that lasted for five days). Kirsten pressured her husband to move far away from her in-laws. When she and her husband could not pay the rent at their new rental unit, the landlord hired Kirsten's husband to work off the debt and earn money by living in decrepit trailers, often along with other workers, and fixing them up so they were livable.

As a worker in the informal economy, Kirsten experienced gender-related financial exploitation when she lived with the work crew and did odd jobs to support them, the boss, and his girlfriend. She recalled telling her husband, "I do more than my share. I friggen help you work, . . . I do the dishes, I cook dinner for everybody, I pick up after your slobs. I fricken scrub the tubs, the toilets. Oh my God, I can do everything. Anything you can do, I can do better."

Kirsten revealed how the boss exploited her by disregarding the "women's work" that she did:

> I've done a lot of work around there for free. He doesn't pay me like he does the guys and, you know, he does give me money here and there and stuff, but I feel that I'm worth more than that, and I've come to the conclusion that he doesn't want to pay me a paycheck at the end of the week like he does everybody else, instead just give me money here and there.

The reality of her living situation conflicted with Kirsten's family-making aspiration to be a housewife like her mother had been. "I want an old fashion house, you know what I mean? I want a big yard for my grandkids to play in." During the life story interview, Kirsten communicated her ideal future by telling the interviewer to imagine a house with a white picket fence in the field across from the fast-food restaurant where they sat.

Kirsten completed a final interview a little over a year after she told her life story. She took pleasure in having moved with her husband into half of a duplex house equipped for good housekeeping. "I have my own backyard, front yard, you got a basement, washer, dryer, you know, I have everything I need." Kirsten worked at a major combination grocery and department store chain. She had reunited with her daughter, who visited once a week, and she took care of her grandchildren "all the time." The jobs at the car wash and the trailer park served as stepping-stones from social exclusion to inclusion through a job in the legitimate economy and decent housing. The trailer park owner's helping hand to Kirsten's husband in the form of relief from rent debt, income paid to the husband, sporadic payments to Kirsten, and the couple's mobility away from the husband's family and later out of the trailer park made this steppingstone effect possible.

Kirsten and her husband amassed enough money to leave the trailer restoration work arrangement, which especially exploited her, but other women had more negative experiences in the informal economy. Having absconded from supervision for 15 years, Lena, a Black woman from Detroit, found prostituting and hustling to meet basic needs increasingly aversive. Work in the informal economy brought no relief: "So then I would try to find me some under the table jobs . . . that was it. I got tired of that 'cause I was getting cheated out of my money." Unable to seek legitimate jobs, cash checks, use her mother's address, or apply for food stamps without risking arrest for having absconded, and with no hope of making enough money in the informal economy, Lena gave her legal name to police who stopped her for driving a truck without license plates so she could "claim" her name back. Because Lena had absconded, the judge sent her to prison, where she stayed for seven months before being paroled.

Lena told the interviewer she could not read and she had difficulty seeing. Thus, it was not surprising that she made no progress on signing up for let alone completing GED classes required by parole. Lena managed on food assistance and by living with and caring for her ailing mother. She was denied medical insurance after starting supervision, and she worried that she would not be able to stay in the house if her mother passed away. She remained cut off from paid employment and both food and medical assistance and reliant on her mother for housing.

Alice also found that working under the table, in her situation for a friend, gave her little financial help, in part because she needed frequent 15- to 20-minute breaks because of back pain. The MDHHS staff found Alice eligible for medical insurance, but she could not access treatment because the state temporarily "froze" this benefit due to the Michigan economy. She described the temptation to steal from stores at the mall: "Oh, yeah, because that's like fast money and everything. . . . It pops up [in my mind] but it won't pop up like every day or nothing like that." Barriers to legitimate work and the high probability that work in the informal economy would be exploitative or infeasible due to disability influenced some women to consider breaking and act to break the law to earn "fast money."

Illegal Work

Communities with drug markets and demand for stolen goods and that lacked legitimate employment opportunities made illegal work a viable option for residents. Like Alice, Tova, a 39-year-old Black woman in Detroit, felt tempted to fall back on illegal income when she could not get a job. "Prior to getting caught, coming to prison, I used to work my two little jobs, do my little illegal things on the side to keep a little extra dollars in my pocket, but I'm trying to change that because I do not want to go back to prison." She admitted that selling drugs had crossed her mind: "Cause my brother used to sell drugs, and I used to be with him sometimes, well a lot of times, and you know, I just didn't get caught." The supervising agent cautioned Tova to stay away from her family members because they sold drugs, but Tova lacked resources to move. She saw herself as stagnant: "You know, just basically treading water, just trying to stay out of trouble, trying to get off parole, because she extended it, of course, for a year because I absconded." She admitted, "It do get real frustrating a lot." Tova said she had not succumbed to the pull toward illegal earnings, but she felt that pull from her family and in her community.

Mary (32, Black) briefly extracted herself from living on fast money from drug sales in her racially segregated, high-crime Detroit neighborhood. She moved to a job and a home in the suburbs, where she worked at an auto manufacturing plant. "I was making money where I was going to a different lifestyle, you know what I mean? I was living in the suburbs, and I got cars, I got insurance, I got things I need to take care of."

Before she started working at the auto plant, Mary was on probation for making and selling counterfeit copies of movies. She violated probation requirements and spent time in prison for the violation, and the company found out about the current and past convictions and terminated her employment. Paroled from prison, she detailed her failed effort to find a new job and her resumption of illegal work:

> You've only been out two days before that background check comes back [to potential employers]. Hell, I went to Bob Evans [a chain restaurant], I've been to McDonalds [a fast-food restaurant], I've been all over trying to keep a good job, but I've got too many felonies. Since I've been home you ain't got no choice but to come out here and do something illegal and then you're getting more felonies. Yeah, that's what's been going on with me right now. That's about it. It was good while it lasted. I had a great job making twenty-seven dollars an hour. . . . Moved to the suburbs and everything. Beautiful. You learn the difference in life. It can be better. It all depends on where you live.

Before continuing with Mary's story, I want to emphasize her comment, "It all depends on where you live." The message in this comment runs through women's lives and through this book. Where women lived affected the costs of conviction, exposure of themselves and their children to the threat of crime, access to mental health and substance abuse treatment, stigmatization by the local citizenry, and the topic of this chapter, opportunities for legal and illegal work.

After moving back to Detroit, Mary reestablished herself selling counterfeit movies to a combined liquor store and gas station in the neighborhood. Selling movies brought a good profit: "I go buy 100 pack of DVDs for 12.99. . . . You sell them for 5 dollars a piece that's 500 dollars, you go through 3 of them a day that's 1500 dollars. You could make 10,000 a week off movies." Mary was carrying earnings from this work when a group of men tried to rob her and shot her as she ran away. She sized up her situation: "So now I went from making money and living good to now I'm back to hustling and it's looking like I'm on my way back to prison. . . . If I get in any more trouble, the guidelines say I got fourteen or fifteen years." Even though Mary was the victim in the attempted robbery and shooting, she was known to the police and on record as on parole, so the police contacted the agent, who could return her to prison for this police contact.

In an unusual mix, Mary had educational advantages even though she grew up largely on her own. She graduated from a private high school that she paid for with drug-sales earnings, and with tuition paid by a job-preparation program, she earned an associate's degree that gave her a certificate to work as a medical assistant. Disadvantages she faced include seven felony convictions and residence in a high-crime, low-resource neighborhood. The neighborhood, which she described as "drug infested," provided ample opportunity for selling drugs and counterfeit movies. Mary's record of convictions prevented her from keeping a good job in an auto plant in the suburbs as well as from obtaining a low-paying job at a fast-food restaurant near her residence. The push out of legitimate work and the pull into illegal work influenced Mary to resume breaking the law, though to reduce her chances of more prison time, she sold counterfeit movies in lieu of drugs.

Influenced by different circumstances than Mary, relatives, including her adult son, and her years of addictions seemed as much if not more influential over 58-year-old Shannon's illegal income generation than job opportunities in the neighborhood or barriers to moving to a new area. Shannon identified as White. She and family members had always lived in one of the larger Michigan cities that had a relatively diverse economy, and thus the city did not suffer economically as much as other Michigan urban areas, though there were some high-crime areas. Shannon earned money from various illegal activities for nearly four decades and had no realistic alternative plan to secure income. Her sister pressured her into prostitution as a teenager, and Shannon described herself as a lifelong drug dealer.

Shannon supplemented her illegal earnings with money earned in the informal economy. None of Shannon's income sources or plans to generate income—legal or not—seemed lucrative or stable. She cleaned out the rentals of neighbors who went to jail or died and stored the items until she held rummage sales in her yard. According to Shannon, because she was high on drugs at the last rummage sale, she paid people more to help her than she made. The remaining "date" Shannon saw regularly had reduced his payment to her from $800 eight years before to $80 after he retired. Drug sales (pills) were now problematic because her memory problems made it impossible for her to keep track of what people owed her. Shannon also worked as a babysitter and planned to decrease her illegal activity and make up for the lost income by babysitting more children. She continued to break the law for many years, she supplemented her earnings with any safety-net benefits she could access, and she did not see desistance from illegal activity in her future.

Working for a Living

The women's accounts of work in the legitimate, informal, and illegal economies show the importance of Mary's insight, "It all depends on where you live." A quantitative analysis of the larger sample of 402 Michigan women on probation and parole showed that Black women reported more types of criminal activity in their neighborhoods, and they lived in census tracts with greater disadvantages and higher residential turnover than did White women.[8] Another analysis of data from that larger Michigan sample showed that Black women tended to live in communities that lacked job opportunities, which explained their unemployment.[9]

The racial segregation evidenced for the 402 Michigan women on probation and parole and the subsample considered in this book mirrors statewide patterns. An analysis of the American Community Survey and the 2010 U.S. Census data showed that at the start of the research, the Detroit, Warren, and Livonia region and the Grand Rapids/Wyoming area were among the most highly racially segregated metropolitan areas in the United States.[10] Nationally, racial segregation persists at the census tract level, and a growing proportion of minoritized individuals in nonmetropolitan areas live in clusters of people who are poor.[11] In the subsample considered here, Black women usually remained in communities with more opportunity for illegal than legal work. White women experienced financial distress, but more of them moved to a new community, took advantage of social network members' connections to the world of work, or in other ways improved their financial situations. The racial difference is not without exception, but it is apparent in the women's words. It takes considerable motivation and effort to overcome the dual pressures of limited or no legitimate work opportunities and plenty of illegal ones.

SAFETY-NET PROGRAMS

Women whose physical disabilities or mental illness prevented them from working, or who like Raven could not find work, invested considerable emotional and action-oriented energy into securing help from assistance programs. Like Carmen, a few of them resigned themselves to living in poverty and without assistance, at least for the time being, or like Marion they engaged in regular illegal income production. As noted in the first chapter of this book, for individuals living in poverty, who constituted most of the women, increasing reductions and restrictions that applied to all people limited access to a variety of safety-net benefits. A history of convictions further narrowed eligibility for benefits. This section shows how shrinkages in myriad safety-net benefits had a combined effect.

The statewide shortage of affordable housing and financial assistance to pay for it, combined with both racial discrimination and housing commission procedures and policies, created barriers to both finding a place to live in a safe neighborhood and paying the rent. Just the belief that subsidized and public housing was closed to "felons," which was not always the case for local housing commissions that determined eligibility, dissuaded women from even applying. Early in the study Diana, who lived with her father, worried that when he passed away, she would be homeless because a felony conviction made her ineligible for housing assistance. The interviewer's questions about housing restrictions prompted Diana to say, "That's something I have to look into." By the time of the life story interview, Diana described the positive impact of securing public housing: "And thank God, my rent is only 525 a month where I'm at now, or else I don't know what I'd be doing."

Diana met qualifications for housing aid, but the statewide shortage of funds created an insurmountable barrier for other women. At the first interview, 47 of the 118 women said they needed housing assistance, but only 11 were receiving it, and these proportions held over the course of the study. In Michigan and in other parts of the country, it was common for women deemed eligible for housing benefits to wait years for help.[12] Carley said, "I signed up like six years ago and never heard anything." Vivian had the same experience: "I filled out an application for Section 8 [housing voucher]. I never heard anything back, so I really don't know how to go about it." Some women described going to great lengths to establish eligibility for assistance. Lydia identified the steps she took: "I've done everything they've told me to do. I went and stayed at the shelter for three days. I've done all that stuff and I'm not getting any help. I'm very frustrated." Molly lacked the access to technology and time needed to sign up for housing assistance: "I got the Sunday paper, . . . and I saw a listing saying 'public announcement, Section 8 sign-up.' You gotta use a computer to sign up and you had like a week or two and in two weeks we had, like, back-to-back appointments. I could not for the life of me get the bus down there one day where I could finally go and use the computer." Women did not bother to apply for housing assistance because of local freezes on taking new applications; the long wait before and after determination of eligibility; requirements to stay in a shelter to prove need; and the realization that even if they reached the top of the application list, they might be deemed ineligible, and even if they were eligible, they might not be able to find affordable, safe housing that would accept vouchers.

Although a high proportion of the women received food assistance (almost three-quarters of the women, or 84 of 118), some found it difficult to apply. Tina, who at first avoided applying for jobs to avoid the stigma of revealing she needed time off to meet with a probation agent, did eventually start work at a restaurant. She earned very little, so during work hours she subsisted on the daily cup of soup and serving of salad that the restaurant allowed workers. Tina believed she qualified for food assistance, but the MDHHS required in-person or online applications, and Tina did not have a computer with internet access or time to use the library's computers. Persistent hunger also contributed to her not applying. She expressed her frustration: "I would apply if I were allowed to without having to go down there. They say go to the library and apply online. . . . I cannot [go there], so I can't. You know I'm trying to do this on my own, but I'm trying to work without food day after day." Marie, whose agent counseled her to resist the lure of fast money to pay electronic monitoring fees, found that applying for food assistance conflicted with maintaining employment: "It's just they ask you to do so much to get it [food assistance], including missing work, and then they'll want you to go to Work First to find a job that they made you lose." For some women applying for food assistance intensified poverty and stress rather than alleviating it. Even if women receive food assistance, nationwide it falls far short of lifting them out of poverty and meeting nutritional needs.[13]

Criminal history did not restrict women's eligibility for medical insurance or care, but other barriers did. In the first year of supervision, Patricia told the interviewer how Medicaid restrictions made her ineligible for insurance: "I think you got to be pregnant or disabled. They got a lot of different criteria now for you to get Medicaid." Low-income women ineligible for Medicaid had the option to apply for a variety of county insurance plans, but they assessed them as too expensive or inadequate. Simone did not enroll in a county "spend down plan" that paid for medical expenses after the participant covered substantial costs during each month. Unable to afford the premiums and potential costs, she did not get routine care for diabetes:

I have a doctor that I go to, but I don't really see him because I can't afford to get my blood work done. . . . Probably the income that I make. I mean, I probably could get it but it'd be like a spend-down type thing and I don't spend that much a month to even afford it. It'd be good for like hospitals if I was going to the hospital or something.

Lack of medical insurance jeopardized not only Simone's physical health but also her mental health. "As soon as Community Mental Health stops paying for my therapy, how am I gonna get my medications? I'm gonna be right back in prison. But that's where I get frustrated. It's when you do need the help, you want the help, you're doing right, you're doing what you have to do, but you can't get no help."

In 2010, the U.S. Congress passed the Patient Protection and Affordable Care Act (PPACA, often referred to as Obamacare), which established a marketplace to purchase subsidized insurance, and in 2014 the Michigan legislature expanded access to Medicaid. Between the first interview and the life story interview, these changes improved insurance access for nearly 1 out of every 3 of the 118 women featured in this book. Nationally, the PPACA improved coverage and care in essential areas of mental health, preventative, and reproductive health for women living in poverty.[14] Yet given the common pattern for substance-involved individuals to relapse and spend time in jail, prison, or treatment, the gaps in even PPACA coverage created erratic assistance for women who spent time incarcerated or in treatment programs.

Eligibility for food and medical assistance through the WIC (Women, Infants and Children) program changed depending on whether women were pregnant or had just borne a child, had a child under 2, or were supporting a child under 18. Both Marilyn and Bree said they qualified for medical assistance only when pregnant or just after they gave birth, and Tova said the statewide plan, Plan First, only covered obstetrics and gynecological care, not treatment for her high blood pressure.[15] Brenda gave detail about her urgent need for medical care and the better access to care she would have if she were pregnant:

I'm sick. And I need prescriptions and I need to go to the doctor. My kidney is failing, one of them. And I have to have dialysis. Well, it's very expensive. Easter Seals is paying for it right now, but the State won't give me Medicaid because the program is closed to adults. If I had my kids, I would get it. The lady actually told me to get pregnant and then it would cover it. Like, oh that's going to help my kidney.

Medical coverage restricted to the period around childbirth, lapses in insurance after leaving carceral institutions or treatment programs, and county and state cuts and freezes in medical coverage led to churn—repeated transitioning on and off insurance plans. Churn is common for low-income women in the United States and is associated with poor health.[16] The health and medical literature presents churn as problematic, but the Michigan women on probation and parole accepted churn as the status quo and a matter of following the rules for eligibility. Those rules reflected greater investment in protecting the health of a fetus and newborn than the health of the mothers who carried, bore, and cared for the children.

Interconnecting Safety-Net Benefits

Eligibility for one benefit depended on receipt of other benefits, which caused frequent changes in women's resources. Recall that because she obtained a low-paying job, Jolene lost her medical insurance that paid for Suboxone, so she relapsed back to using heroin. Cassie contended with a slight increase in disability payments that resulted in a much larger decrease in food assistance. During the study, her disability insurance payments increased by $24 a month, which led to a drop in food assistance from $171 to $16 a month. When she appealed this decrease, MDHHS staff found her ineligible for any food assistance at all. Cassie reasoned that she could not refuse the disability payments because they made her eligible for "excellent medical care." She continued, "That's why I would never get off disability, because nobody's gonna hire a felon and give me the benefits that I have. With the disorders I have, I need the medical." Cassie listed these disorders: "ADHD [attention deficit hyperactivity disorder], bipolar, manic depressive, borderline personality." Cassie's struggle to manage with decreased food assistance provides a glimpse into life with very low income: "I mean I get 250 a week if you break my Social Security [disability] checks down. I get 250 a week and the only thing I get is excellent medical and they pay my Medicare cost yearly. . . . So if you figure I'm going to eat 40 dollars a week, there is 160, so I'm going to have 90 dollars a week plus I gotta pay bills. You know there's nothing left over, nothing."

Women talked about the necessity of applying for disability insurance repeatedly, enlisting the help of lawyers, and obtaining multiple physical and mental health assessments to qualify. Candece believed that back problems and bipolar disorder qualified her for disability payments, but in another example of the interrelated nature of benefits, lack of medical insurance to pay for an evaluation stood in the way of proving her need. Based on what she described as "ten minutes with me and a few questions," a psychiatrist determined her ineligible. She went on to say, "They didn't get enough data because I have no way to get medical proof of, like, X-rays of my back and stuff. I thought they were gonna send me to their doctors and they didn't." Grace also suffered from mental illness and substantial physical problems:

> I can't stand long [after having two knee replacements], I can't function long. I can't lift nothing because it's like when trying to work this shoulder, right here, it slips out of disk. . . . They have to pop it back. So pretty much it's just so much going on with my body to where, you know, I'm consistently backward and forwards [getting] MRIs, X-rays.

At the start of data collection, disability personnel had denied Grace's application twice, so she did not qualify for medical insurance to treat the physical problems or to pay for medications prescribed for mental illness. With a lawyer's assistance, she protested the decision in the courts. After being denied a third time, she speculated that her next application would be approved, because "I think I got more medical records, more doctors, and MRIs, and I got all the paperwork now."

Maintaining Poverty

Living arrangements could make women ineligible for safety-net benefits. Andrea traded eligibility for cash and food assistance for the chance to get parole from prison. Seeing no other option, she agreed to live with her child's father at the start of parole. Even though she paid him rent and other expenses, his income made her ineligible for cash and food assistance. In another example, Cynthia had worked at a discount department store until her back problems worsened. She applied for and then received disability insurance, and her daughter, who worked at an auto plant, moved in to help her out. Based on the total household income, the reduction of Cynthia's food assistance from $198 to $16 a month offset the relief from her daughter's picking up some household expenses. Women made hard choices about using the common strategy of doubling up to handle limited affordable housing and financial resources.[17] For Andrea and Cynthia, neither reliance on benefits nor reliance on doubling up improved their financial situations.

Just like access to legal and illegal work "all depends on where you live," and the costs of conviction depend on the court jurisdiction, access to benefits varies by the county offices that administer benefit programs and to some extent by the individual making the determination of eligibility. Barry Feld coined the phrase "justice by geography" to highlight the variation in how rural, suburban, and urban juvenile courts responded to youth who broke the law.[18] Illustrating "benefits by geography," the 118 women's descriptions of their lives and experiences in court and on supervision revealed differences by counties rather than the urban-suburban-rural differences Feld documented. Linsey, who moved from a university town in a high-resource county to a poor neighborhood in Detroit, set forth a telling example of benefits by geography. In the university town, she received food stamps because she was a low-income, stay-at-home mother caring for a young child. After moving to Detroit, the newly assigned worker told her she had to participate in Work First even though she only wanted food assistance, not cash benefits. Linsey wanted to stay home with her child, which she could not do if she took part in the Work First program that prioritized devoting eight hours a day to preparing for employment, seeking employment, and eventually working. Linsey resisted pressure to spend her time in Work First and seek employment, but the trade-off was that she was living in abject poverty by the last interview, when she resided in a run-down motel with her daughter and partner. Linsey's experiences with Work First show a well-documented drawback of using a one-size-fits-all approach, insistence on employment, to assist low-income families.[19]

To receive federal support, states had to document that a required proportion of TANF recipients took part in Work First. Linsey felt pressured to take part in TANF, which required she enroll in Work First, to qualify for food stamps even though she wanted to stay home to care for her child. Other study participants described unrealistic pressure to participate in Work First given their capability to work and the availability of jobs. For instance, 45-year-old Maya listed several conditions that made working difficult if not impossible: "Carpal tunnel, anxiety, depression, fibromyalgia, rheumatoid arthritis, and a bulging disk in my back." TANF staff terminated cash, housing, and food assistance because Maya exceeded the lifetime limit. The human services worker told her to get a letter from her doctor verifying her disability, which she did, but then pressured her to enroll in Work First. Maya wondered, "So why am I going to Work First if I can't work?" A probable explanation of the insistence that Linsey and Maya take part in Work First is that to avoid reductions in federal funding, state agencies had to show that a certain proportion of TANF recipients were taking part in Work First.[20]

For women motivated to stop breaking the law, receiving benefits can be fundamental to desistance from substance use and illegal activities. They reduce the pull into getting fast money by illegal means to pay for such basics as food and housing.[21] Medical insurance provides treatments and medication that reduce women's reasons to misuse substances and support substance misuse through illegal activities. Benefits clearly reduced some women's illegal activity, but barriers to receipt were high.

CONCLUSION

Probation and parole agents can help women address individual-level challenges such as addiction, depression, and anxiety, but they cannot alter the contexts and structures that disadvantage people who have a criminal history, live in poverty, or are in minoritized groups. No matter the individual supports provided, many women remained confined in low-resource, high-crime neighborhoods; could not overcome barriers to employment; and lacked financial resources to meet their own and dependents' basic needs for food, housing, and medical care. Supervising agents, physical and mental health professionals, and women with multiple convictions found themselves "in a box" that limited their power to improve the women's lives.

Rules and regulations for each safety-net benefit rather than a holistic understanding of women's needs determined the resources women could access. The prior chapter on mental health and substance abuse treatment services showed how unexpected, sporadic cuts in food, medical, and other assistance wreaked havoc in the lives of women in financially precarious positions. Successful application for disability payments depended on the quality of mental health and medical assessments, which in turn depended on medical insurance. When one benefit increased, another might decrease, and some medical benefits were tied to pregnancy and childbirth, so women found themselves constantly juggling different streams of income, mental health care, and medical care. Some women ended up disconnected from all means of financial support. Racial group marginalization in distressed communities and disability, which often came with aging, intensified these negative effects.

CHAPTER 7

Endpoints

This chapter describes where women ended up at the point of the final research contact, and for records of convictions, the last check of official data. It highlights the women who generated the touchstone stories and those whose circumstances are best known to the reader based on the content in prior chapters. It addresses these questions: How did women make sense and meaning of their lives? Did some women feel their lives made no sense and had no meaning? Did women continue or stop substance misuse and illegal activities?

As part of their life stories, women told of making good from trauma as children and adults; challenges of motherhood; and difficult times when they were addicted to drugs, misusing alcohol, or breaking the law. Narrative identity theory helped to understand how women portrayed such difficulties and connected them to their current identities. In the general U.S. population, people favor life stories that include what are called redemption sequences that show how a challenging, traumatic, or negative experience ends in growth, making one's life meaningful or showing the resolution of a difficulty.[1] Criminologist Shadd Maruna's application of narrative identity theory to people who broke the law—mostly men who committed property crimes in Liverpool, England—showed how they made good from past periods of illegal behavior, for example by learning or recovering from their experiences or using knowledge gained to help other people.[2] Life stories also include contamination sequences in which one or more events spoil future events and result in stagnation rather than growth and change.[3] In this chapter, women reveal various ways they handled and adapted to negative events in their pasts and their current circumstances with either good results or, alternatively, stagnation marked by little or no positive change, but instead feelings of despair or continued substance misuse and illegal behavior.

The life story interview generated most of the information about how women made sense and meaning of their lives. Questions elicited information about key episodes in each woman's life (for example, high points, low points, and turning points), and especially important for understanding how women create meaning, information about what each episode tells a woman about herself. In theory and empirical research, these constructions of identity influence behavior.[4] Questions also asked about religious and spiritual experiences, life themes and projects, challenges, and future plans and expectations. Apart from the life story, in five of the interviews, women responded to a question intended to reveal their exercise of agency: "How have you made your life better?" The responses to the full compilation of questions gave insight into what mattered most to women and how they saw themselves and their futures. A final piece of information, official records for an average of just over 10 years after they began participation in the research, documented women's official convictions.

TOUCHSTONE STORIES

A Limited Future

At 23 Carmen calculated that since she was age 17, court and probation agents' responses to violations had led to jail time totaling three years "on and off," and because she opted for prison instead of more time on probation, she spent two and a half more years in prison followed by eight months on parole. Counting time incarcerated plus time supervised in the community, she was "on papers" for nearly seven years. Carmen identified increased self-control to avoid criminal justice involvement and the GED she earned in prison as the good that came out of time under correctional control. A year and a half after the life story interview, Carmen said she had not done anything to make her life better. To use a concept from narrative identity theory, Carmen described herself as in a state of stagnation.[5] Her story showed a few gains (the GED and self-control) counterbalanced by powerful constraints created by prior traumatic events.

Carmen pruned her vision of the near future to exclude living on her own with income from disability payments or work, relationships with romantic partners, and having children. Narrative identity theory researchers document how trauma can be so threatening that it forces a person to narrow her view of herself and her future.[6] Carmen described the trauma: "I've had my heart broke with two kids already [a miscarriage caused by abuse by the father and a baby stillborn in prison] and abusive relationships. I really don't want shit to do with that now. You know like, later on in life where I'm doing good and I have my own place, but not now." Ineligible for disability insurance because her mother collected it while Carmen was in prison, she saw no way to have an income that would support her living on her own. Carmen had recently forged connections to her sister and newborn niece, but the relationships seemed distant and tenuous. She had never seen the baby, yet she felt "inspired" by her birth because although the child was diagnosed as autistic and having Down syndrome, she was happy and "pushing for the positive." Broken relationships with her parents and barriers to safety-net benefits and employment left Carmen lacking meaningful ties to other people and dependent on a boyfriend, with whom she did not see much of a future, for a place to live.

Carmen created meaning in her life by producing 20 notebooks of poems and stories, which she stored in a safe and kept private. She said she started writing at age 10 because, "It was easier for me to focus on that than to focus on the bad things that was goin' on." She took pride that before she started to fail in school, she won a writing award. She continued to add to her collection of written materials and noted that she had always imagined being a rich book writer, though she also wanted to be a hair stylist. The anxiety she felt attending school and her lack of income made attaining these goals unlikely, but her writing served as a private accomplishment.

Family Making, Living in Poverty

Bree came into the study on parole after spending two years in prison for convictions for carrying a concealed weapon and possession of narcotics with intent to deliver while she was absconded from probation. She described herself as "settling down" because of the aversive nature of life in prison, "Well, dealing with correctional officers for two years, that was a major toll. When you go from having freedom to having limited freedom, that alone can just make a person go crazy, and so coming home from that, I guess, that would have to be a major turn because I didn't want to go through that again." Bree successfully completed supervision by completing required programming and using money she had put aside before prison to pay conviction-related costs and restitution.

Bree had a newborn, and she and the baby's father were "trying to build a family." Having her first child motivated her to "turn things around." At the time of the life story interview, Bree and the baby's father had just bought a house, an act that showed Bree she was "responsible" and "thinking ahead in life." Describing her values, she said, "Both mother and father are supposed to be in the house with the kids." This vision of a nuclear family contrasted sharply with Bree's parents' splitting up when she was 11; her time living with her father out of state, then living with her mother who suffered from drug addiction and had minimal contact with Bree; and finally her moving into her own trailer at 16. As part of her story, Bree talked about her father's current refusal to talk to her because she did not want to meet the woman he now lived with. She reasoned, "Since I was 11, I've met more [of her father's partners] than I can count on both of my hands. . . . If they're not gonna be around, then I feel that it's no need to keep bringing your associates around." Bree regretted coming to Michigan as a teenager and starting to sell drugs, but she saw a silver lining, "If I didn't come up here, I wouldn't have my kid or, you know, my child's father or the life that I do have now."

Bree found purpose and satisfaction in the family she had formed, but financial precarity persisted. The house she bought was in an economically distressed Michigan city; the neighborhood houses looked run down and the yards were strewn with trash. Bree received income and food assistance to support her newborn son, but because of her convictions she remained "criminally disqualified" from receiving assistance to cover expenses. Bree wanted to start a business, but she had no idea what sort of business. She hoped to move out of the distressed city where she had spent her adolescence and now lived. Until she could move, she thought she could focus on buying "a couple more houses," fix them up, and rent them. Pressed by the interviewer for more information about this plan, she noted that she was still in the process of fixing up her own house and joked that to finance buying and fixing up houses she would "have to hit the lottery." Bree saw herself as successfully establishing a family with mother, father, and child, but the family lived in poverty, and Bree lacked feasible plans to bring in more income.

Ten years older than Bree and raising five children, Raven also prioritized family making. After being cut off from cash assistance, she identified her children as a reason to avoid illegal behavior. "If I wanted to, I can retreat back to the old me, but why? . . . That's not going to get me nothing but more trouble. So why not keep it moving ahead, trying to do something better, trying to find something better, because like I feel like I have to show my kids something different." A series of strokes left Raven's mother partly paralyzed, so Raven anticipated taking on increased responsibility for her physically and mentally challenged adult brothers. Raven explained how family caretaking conflicted with her hopes for finding a good job outside of the city where she had been convicted and continued to live: "I want to move from here. I really do, but I don't want to leave my mom." Raven's motivation to show her "kids something different" and her sense of obligation to help her mother care for her brothers locked her into taking care of children, siblings, and a parent. "That's my fire; that's why I live, for my kids, my mom, and my brothers. That's why I live, to help them, to be there for them." Showing the force of gendered expectations that women nurture other people, the three occupations she imagined, but could not realize right now because of family demands and a record of felony convictions—nursing, social work, and medical aid or nurse—involved taking care of people. A combination of heavy family responsibilities and prohibitions against hiring a person with a felony record kept her in poverty. Raven had stopped using heroin and crack several years before she told her life story, and she had stopped smoking marijuana more recently when she decided it impaired her thinking.

Showing how she built on prior negative experiences to create positive experiences, Raven used her mother's shortfalls as a parent to fashion a better way to raise her own children:

> Like my mom wasn't there for me to talk to her. She wasn't that ear that I needed as a teenage girl with certain stuff that you need to know. . . . That's not how I want to raise my kids. So, everything that my mom didn't do, I'm doing, you know? Everything she didn't teach me I taught my daughters so there will never be a repeat of what happened to me.

A high-crime neighborhood compounded Raven's child-rearing burden. While Raven was in jail for stealing and cashing fraudulent checks, her 15-year-old son was charged with a felony for possession of promethazine, an antihistamine used with opioids to intensify the high. Since her release, Raven had spent her energies keeping him and his younger brother "out of the streets." Raising five children with no help from their fathers (one died from a gunshot shortly after the birth of the first child;

the other had been in prison for nearly a decade) convinced Raven she was stronger than anyone she knew.

Family Making and Supportive Supervision

Like Bree and Raven, Carla aimed to be a good parent. While pregnant in the first year of supervision, she reasoned that she was not in a position to parent, so arranging the adoption of the baby showed she cared about the child. She developed a relationship with the mother who adopted her two older children so that she could be in their lives, and by the time of the life story interview, Carla was raising a newborn. She also improved her relationship with her uncles and mother: "We have a relationship so different now. We have an actual relationship and we, you know, that's helped out a lot too." Seeing a new connection to her natal family, Carla anticipated living with and caring for her aging mother. All of these family-making actions gave Carla commonly valued gender-typical roles to fill.

Carla also planned to help other women by sharing the actions she took to overcome adversities. She would volunteer at a shelter for battered women, schools, or prisons:

> I want people to see where I've been through. Like I've been through everything in my life that you can imagine, from being a low income family, to not having nothing growing up, to, you know, like death, just everything you can imagine, I've had it happen in my life. And I just want to help other people see that, hey, you don't have to go and be miserable on drugs and to cover your feelings like, you know, there is hope out there.

Carla wanted women who knew her just for "drugs and alcohol" to see that she had completely turned her life around. Sharing her story would help other women and reaffirm her changed identity.

A connection with God helped Carla make sense of seemingly inexplicable points in her life. In jail she complained to the Bible study group leader: "I'm so tired of coming to jail, reading my bible and being Christian like, [then] I just take one step out and I'm getting high in the parking lot." Carla remembered the group leader's response: "Have you ever thought maybe God's bringing you here because it's the only time you'll even listen, and you slow down enough?" Just before hearing this, Carla felt something spiritual tugging at her heart that, combined with the Bible study leader's comment, showed her that God was pulling her back to jail to slow her down and form a relationship. To make sense of repeated times in jail and the drug use that got her there, Carla drew on her connection to God to interpret her past and present circumstances, stop using drugs, and change her way of thinking. "I don't want to go back to bein' that person, bein' some loser drug addict with no money, no nothing, like havin' to go hustle up money." Carla experienced a form of religious redemption, in which God steered her in the right direction and helped her stop using drugs.

Decades of Drug Use and Crime

Mallory and Marion, both in their mid-fifties and with a string of convictions going back decades, shared similar life events. Both had witnessed abuse between their parents, were addicted to drugs by early adulthood, stole and resold goods to support their addictions, and took part in numerous substance abuse treatment programs. Safety-net programs affected Mallory's and Marion's lives. The newly passed PPACA opened Mallory's access to previously unavailable physical and mental health treatment, but she could not qualify for disability payments and, except for time in jail, lived in a shelter from the start of supervision to the life story interview. Different from Mallory, Marion established eligibility to receive disability insurance and moved out of a shelter, only to find that she could just afford a small, poorly equipped apartment. Her experience exemplifies the finding that for the lager Michigan sample, the receipt of safety-net benefits kept women in poverty.[7] Mallory's and Marion's endpoints are consistent with theory and research showing how the disadvantages of childhood followed by persisting drug use and lawbreaking in adulthood accumulate to a state of ongoing exclusion from the labor market and reliance on the state for a place to live and, for Marion, reliance on disability insurance for an income.[8]

Marion stood out by virtue of a complete lack of close relationships:

> I'm the loneliest person in the world. I'm by myself. I've never had children, never could, and my mother and my grandparents on both sides, my sister, is gone. Everybody is gone, and it's like, you know, everybody go through unhappiness. It's a given for life, I mean, pain and misery, but I don't . . . it's nobody like me.

Showing very limited connections to other people, when Marion lived in a shelter, she became attached to a young woman and the woman's children but feared she would soon grieve the loss of them when they moved out. She also became attached to the driver on the bus she took regularly, but she lost track of him when she left jail and discovered he had retired, and she had no way to contact him. Finally, Marion said the high point in her life was seeing the birth of a baby after she and two other women volunteered to be the mother's support people. This made her feel "sadness and happiness" as she thought about "what I missed."

Neither Mallory nor Marion talked about drawing on past negative experiences to improve their lives or to help other people. Mallory used her time and energy trying to qualify for disability payments and making up for lost time getting the medical and mental health treatments she needed. Marion hoped to work for pay in a domestic violence program, not to give back or use her own experiences with abuse to help others, but to support herself "in a certain lifestyle," that is, earning more than she could working in "some greasy spoon." At a follow-up interview Marion expressed dissatisfaction with the apartment she could afford: "I got an itty bitty apartment. I can't even afford a bathtub. It's just a walk-in shower, it's so little, no tubs nothing." In contrast to women who found meaning and reason to stop using drugs and breaking the law in making family, Marion expressed the most excitement about life when she described customers who anxiously gathered around to see what she had stolen from stores and brought into the neighborhood. She could not identify any theme that characterized her life, and she presented a dismal picture of her past, current, and future circumstances:

> Twisted in the system, twisted in bad decisions. You know, life becomes a ball of twisted yarn just unraveling all at the end and you gotta mess. That's the only thing that I can come up with is that life is a mess, truly. It was just obvious when I turned 56. I don't own anything. I don't have anything, and now I lived most of my life that I'm gonna live. I'm just, like, "Don't be like me." For the next one, "Don't be like me, miserable, all broke down, old." I'm close to a senior citizen. It's just craziness, it really is.

Between first contact with research staff and the life story interview, Mallory had two convictions, the first for first degree retail fraud and the second for second degree retail fraud two and a half years later. She was sentenced to jail for a year for the first offense and for 90 days for the second, and both times she incurred conviction-related costs. Between the first interview and the life story interview, Marion had seven convictions for first-, second-, or third-degree retail fraud. She received probation sentences or jail time ranging from 10 days to a year for four of these offenses plus numerous orders to pay restitution, sometimes over $1,000, and various other costs, or in a few instances sentences to probation. After the life story interview the one other conviction was for "obstructing by disguise," when she dressed to hide her identity during the commission of retail fraud.

Conclusion from the Touchstone Stories

Carmen, Bree, Carla, and Raven had no further convictions after the life story interview, and their statements and actions signaled desistance from drug use and illegal activity. Mallory had one conviction during the first year of supervision but none after that, and Marion kept up the pace of repeated convictions for retail theft before, during, and after supervision. The following content shows that a large proportion of women found purpose and meaning in their lives by creating family and nurturing family members and others. A smaller proportion found meaning and purpose by giving back or finding uses, benefits, or silver linings in their past adversities. Women's ages and racial/ethnic identification did not affect these patterns. The value of motherhood manifested in bearing and raising children for younger women and in being a grandmother for older women. The chapter ends with an account of women like Marion, who never gave up drugs and illegal activity, at least not fully or before the last check of official convictions, and who struggled to find meaning and purpose in life.

THE LARGER GROUP OF WOMEN

Family Making

In the United States, being a mother and more generally caring for and nurturing family members are culturally emphasized scripts for women.[9] Although it is possible to break with societal scripts, the largest proportion of the 118 women, just over one-third, experienced redemption from negative life events by nurturing others.[10] Women talked more about struggling with concerns about being a "bad mother" than about reconciling past criminal behavior with a new self that no longer used drugs or broke the law. Stage of life affected whether women viewed their lives as meaningful in anticipation of a child's birth, while raising children, reconnecting with adult children, caring for grandchildren, or caring for a sick or aging parent. With one exception, the women whose statements comprise this section on family making had no convictions after supervision started. The exception, Jolene, had recently relapsed, but she completed a lengthy residential treatment program and expressed a commitment to avoid drugs now that she was pregnant. Although becoming a "good" or "better" mother (or grandmother or daughter) created meaning and purpose in many women's lives, it did not always influence women to stop breaking the law.

Expecting a Baby

At the follow-up interview after she told her life story, Jolene described a relapse, a new sentence to probation (that she successfully completed), and long-term residential substance abuse treatment. She talked about the essential nature of building connections with her newborn baby and other family members: "That's what people do. That's what humans want. That's what we're supposed to be doing. We're not supposed to be killing ourselves and being miserable and lonely and empty." Consistent with what we know about gender, for the women in this book a meaningful life required relationships with others.[11] Becoming a mother presented a readily available prosocial role they could fill, and having a child offered them a chance at a caring relationship that their childhood and adolescence had often failed to provide.

Raising Children

Like Carla and Raven, Fiona immersed herself in the day-to-day care of children. She named the current chapter of her life "Diapers" because all day, every day she worked to meet the needs of her children and maintain the large suburban home where she lived with her infant, a toddler, a daughter by a previous relationship, and her husband. Fiona made sure her first-born daughter lived with them because she believed that even though her daughter was too young to be diagnosed, the child had bipolar disorder like she did. Fiona envisioned breaking a cycle of "just constant mess ups" that ran through generations in her family by addressing her daughter's mental health needs, including a recent diagnosis of attention deficit disorder:

> That's why it was so important to get her here with me. I've got it. I know what she needs, how to fix it. I know. I've talked to these damn psych doctors, not like my mother with no idea. I know how to help her, so she doesn't turn out like me. Plus, then [growing up] I was so isolated. Both of us take damn medication in the morning so she doesn't feel so isolated. She's taking her medication, but so am I.

In addition to immersion in the daily care of the three children, Fiona helped other people in need. She remembered that as a child growing up "dirt poor," the Lion's Club and the Salvation Army had fed her, and after a fire, charities had replaced the family's furniture and given her mother money. These experiences prompted Fiona to donate to charities. In the future, Fiona wanted to attend college and work as a drug counselor, "to go work at a rehab and to help somebody like me. To help somebody get better 'cause there were people there for me and I'd want to be able to give back, to be able to do what they did for me."

Fiona identified the theme that ran through her life:

> Drugs and poverty. Hoping the next 20 years will be a lot different—so far, so much better. But the two years of good and better is nothing compared to the 25 years of gutter, you know. It's just now . . . I'm 27 years old. It's just now starting to get better and getting out of the ghetto, getting out of the bad neighborhoods, and getting away from the drugs and the bad things. So, it's in the bigger scheme of my life, it's so much smaller.

Marriage to a man with a good income lifted Fiona out of poverty, but unsure that the marriage would last ("He's a great guy, but I learned a long time ago that men will fail you."), she pursued eligibility for disability insurance for herself and her daughter. Fiona's statement about the duration of the "bad" as opposed to the "good" in her life is telling. Many of the women had survived powerful and persistent adversities that dwarfed the immediate impact of even marriage to a person with financial means and the extensive mental health support Fiona was receiving.

Being a Grandmother

Lena created meaning in her life by caring for her granddaughter, whose custody she had recently gained because of sexual abuse that Lena's daughter-in-law and son ignored. Caring for her granddaughter redeemed Lena for not being what she considered a good mother to her son:

> Failure was I wasn't a good mom, because of drugs, but I trying to help be the best grandmother. So, I missed that time with my son like when, I didn't do it then so now I can do it in her like "See this girl? She need it bad." And even if she wasn't abused and molested, she need a be here.

By replacing past inability to parent with current investment in grandparenting, Lena quelled her depression about people she knew who were dying and aging. "And then I got my grandbaby so that helped a lot. So, you know, that took a lot of that negative out and put a positive on, you know? Your grandchild looks up to you, so you know you want to have a good impact on your grandchild." Caring for her grandchild gave Lena meaningful work, though she lived in a precarious financial situation without income.

Reconnecting to Children and Their Children

Tova also strove to make up for not raising her children, which was her greatest regret. She said:

> Anytime they [adult children] need, almost anytime, I feel like they need me, I try to do what I can, anything I can for them or whatever. It had put like a gap in some of me and my kids' relationships or whatever. We working on it—a little anger problem with some of the kids, whatever.

Tova stated that she needed to act her age and be a mother and grandmother to her offspring. She acted on this sense of what women should do at her stage in life with her youngest child, whom she was raising. Because her aunt exposed him to "drugs, guns, all that stuff" while she was in prison, Tova contended with raising a child she called a "thug" in a high-crime neighborhood: "Right now I been dealing with it by working, working, working, working, working. So, I be too tired to do anything, you know. Working, shoot my son, you know try to keep him busy so, me keeping him busy keeps me busy." Tova worked at a job, and she worked to keep her son out of trouble.

Faced with the conundrum of helping her family while avoiding breaking the law, Tova altered her typical response to calls about fights involving family members who expected her to retaliate on their behalf. In a recent episode, when her niece had called to say her baby's father was hitting her, Tova talked to them and calmed them down instead of grabbing a gun on her way over to stop him. After that, she arranged through the court for the baby's parents to use her as their go-between, "They drop the baby off over my house and I take the baby over there or he come and get it." Tova explained that "changing over" by not grabbing the gun was a struggle. Her efforts to change over and act her age seemed to have good effect. By the follow-up to the life story interview, she remained employed and had opened a bank account, purchased a house, bought a new truck, and regained her driver's license.

Tina also reconstituted family to recreate meaning in her life by the end of the research. She described her life project: "I don't know, my kids just need me, and they are my project." After leaving prison, Tina immediately took steps to get custody of her 11-year-old daughter. When her daughter was born, Tina's husband was not the biological father. Regardless, her husband's parents cared for the child while Tina was in prison, and they went to court with a legal team to fight for their son, whom Tina had divorced, to have custody so they would remain involved in raising the child. Tina remembered convincing her ex-husband to waive all rights to the child by telling him the judge was not going to give him, who had never been part of the child's life, custody, and even if he did, he would face 11 years of unpaid child support. After obtaining custody, Tina formed a relationship with a new partner and joined him; her ex-husband, whom she called her "best friend;" and her offspring at family get-togethers: "I thought that was going to be weird, but last Christmas and this Christmas, you know, he came with me over there [ex-husband's place] early in the morning and we all celebrated it together with the kids and the grandkids."

Tina expected to stop working and move north to a rural area in Michigan with her new partner. She felt that since leaving prison, she had taken a long time to stop feeling worthless and thinking that whatever she tried to do, felony convictions slapped her in the face: "It's always following you. It's not something you wanna tell people about. . . . It's still a judgment that you carry inside yourself." She named her life theme "resilience." Her ability to reconstitute family seemed to be a bright spot in her life, as did her anticipated move with her new partner.

Making Good from the Past

Examples presented earlier show how mothers and grandmothers learned from their own adverse childhood experiences—being on their own at a young age, abuse, adults' disbelief or inaction after sexual abuse—to avoid recreating those experiences for their children and grandchildren. Women also stopped the erratic care they provided their children during periods of addiction and lawbreaking. Drawing on negative past childhood events in their lives or their children's or grandchildren's lives to change and "make good" fit previously documented gender-related, structurally available opportunities and cultural expectations that emphasize women's role in raising children and caring for others.[12]

Narrative identity theory also identifies redemption by giving back for help received and using lessons learned from experiences with crime and punishment to help other people. This process of making good allows a person to connect past drug use or lawbreaking with a present prosocial self, a person who helps others.[13] In addition to forming a blended family, to help other women Tina drew from her experience of abuse by a man she had dated several years before the start of the research by volunteering at a shelter that had helped her. "I have a passion for a few things, and one of them is women in domestic violence situations, and you know it's very hard. And you can only stay at the shelter for ninety days. That's not a lot of time to put your life together." Tina realized that women leaving shelters needed very basic things, like a can opener, so she collected donations and organized and stored them in her garage. When women left shelters, they could pick out what they needed.

Linsey also helped other people in order to make up for her past crimes. She wanted to right the wrongs she had done by committing more than 30 burglaries, larcenies, and fraudulent transactions while "in addiction." She viewed the damage to victims as an indication that she had lost herself, her purpose in life, and her strong spiritual beliefs that people should help, not harm, others. She redeemed herself by giving back to other people as much as she could. At Christmas, she helped a friend collect donations for presents for a family with no money for the holiday. She volunteered at the methadone clinic that provided her treatment, and she drove a friend there every day for no charge. She watched people's dogs and cats, and if needed she tried to find homes for the animals. Linsey's generosity was large in relation to her means. By the follow-up interview a year and a half after the life story interview, because of the family's limited income, Linsey was living in a motel room with her daughter and the daughter's father. Like Carmen, private artistic expression gave her purposeful activity. When her daughter was at school and her partner was at work, Linsey did "a lot of art," painting and coloring to keep herself busy.

To help peers and assist staff in a residential program, Molly shared her knowledge of substance abuse, jail, and treatment:

> Okay well when we were in our groups, and stuff like that, they used to pick on me mostly to speak to the group, because I had more knowledge. And then people don't see certain things that people say. Like they'll try to say something, and they'll take it a different way, in the meaning of a bigger picture, and not meaning exactly what the words are. It means something bigger. And then as I moved up, I was able to sit in and be like a counselor's helper. Like I was allowed, I was trusted with their paperwork.

Molly explained her reason for sharing her life with other people: "I want people to know my experiences because if it teaches anybody . . . one person, and they get it, and they learn from it. 'Cause if only people knew what I've been through, man." These experiences showed Molly she was "a giving person." She elaborated by pointing out that she planned to "continue to pay society back, because I'm that type of person. I know how to volunteer." Tina, Linsey, and Molly avoided new convictions. This finding is replicated for the 118 women, who were somewhat more likely to stop illegal activity if they made good from past illegal behavior by using their experiences to help others.[14]

A Higher Power

Spiritual forces helped some women reduce the dissonance between past drug use and crime and their current law-abiding and sober identities. Kirsten had established herself as an integral part of her daughters' and grandchildren's lives and realized her dream of living in a home fully equipped with household appliances. She drew on her belief in God to make sense of her past illegal behavior. Police had pulled Kirsten over when she had absconded from supervision, was under the influence of drugs, and did not have a valid driver's license. According to her, God pressed her foot on the gas pedal: "It wasn't me. It was like somebody just jumped inside me, and vroom I was gone." She led the police on a high speed chase "like a race car driver" that ended with her crashing into a telephone pole. She interpreted this event and the fact that she had just one bruise as "a wake-up call" orchestrated by God to end her drug use. After stopping drug use, she and her husband eventually bought the home she had dreamed of as a place to care for grandchildren, and she had no additional convictions.

In another example of spiritual redemption, God forgave Hope for loosing seven children to CPS. At age 28, Hope had worked as a prostitute to support six of the children and an addiction to "51s" (crack and weed mixed in a cigarette). While Hope was "out on a binge," a man she stayed with dropped the children off at Hope's mom's house. When Hope's mom had to go to work, she dropped the children off at the police station, which triggered CPS involvement. Hope indicated that initially she did not realize the papers she signed gave up her custody rights. She despaired at the loss of the children, but years later, with the help of residential substance abuse treatment program staff, she felt redeemed by God's forgiveness for losing custody of them and a younger sibling born drug affected. In treatment, Hope rejected the label "the crack-head dope fiend person" and replaced it with "a strong, willing, capable human being." Speaking about three younger offspring she was raising, she said, "God says that I'm a nurturing mother and I deserve these children." She remembered the message she had heard in the program as reinforcing her focus on fulfilling her role as mother: "Wait five years. Get yourself off of them drugs. Don't do nothing. Focus on the children." Hope had one conviction for larceny in a building a year after her first interview and no further convictions after she completed the residential treatment program.

Combining the account of spiritual redemption in the treatment program with acquiring knowledge about parenting, Hope prided herself on having learned to raise her children better than her mother had raised her. In contrast to her mother blaming her as a teenager for being raped by the mother's boyfriend, Hope believed her two sons' claims that an older son raped them. Further differentiating her parenting from her mother's, Hope learned what she could do to help the boys deal with the trauma, and she recognized the connection between the older son's sexual abuse in foster care and his abuse of the younger brothers. She characterized herself as working hard at self-acceptance and change:

> And I know that I can change. Oh yes, you know that's part of working on it and because something tragic happened and. . . . [M]ore counseling is needed, required with me and my sons, so I have to, I have to try my best to attend trauma groups and everything to learn about how to deal with the, you know, trauma that they experienced.

Redemption through God's forgiveness released Hope from bad feelings about losing seven children to the state. It put her in a position to self-affirm a capacity to parent by engaging in counseling, where she learned how to help her traumatized sons.

Making Sense through Therapy

Hope changed her response to her sons' trauma in family therapy and by educating herself about trauma. Fiona changed herself through ongoing support from a team of mental health professionals who convinced her that a combination of biology and environment had led to her mental illness and heavy drug use. Lydia also took the mental health treatment exit ramp out of drug use and illegal activity to put her past behind her. With the support of the supervising agent, instead of following the judge's order to attend AA, Lydia expended considerable effort to get the mental health care she needed:

> I'm taking DBT [dialectical behavioral therapy] classes through the borderline personality disorder [program]. . . . I kept telling them, I'm not being treated for that, and I need to be. Everybody wants to treat me for bipolar. I need to

be treated for borderline personality disorder and finally I have the perfect therapist. She's DBT trained. . . . I feel like people are listening to me, finally.

A year before she told her life story, Lydia said that in the last two months, after "fighting for it" for 10 years, she was seeing a renowned psychiatrist who gave her the help she needed: "And he couldn't believe it. He read my records, he said, 'I see you been tryin' to see me since 2007.'" She was working hard with a therapist when she told her life story. "Yeah, I've been really proactive with my treatment at CMH [Community Mental Health], like with my therapist and trying to . . . define what my goals are and then trying to figure out a way to get closer."

Lydia's church had disfellowshipped her for smoking cigarettes, which meant she could not talk to her adoptive parents, biological sister, or any congregation member. With these family and church ties broken, Lydia made sense of her life with the insights she gained on her own and during treatment. She described efforts to figure out the meaning of her life and the discovery of her agency in therapy:

> I want to leave some sort of a legacy and I feel like a lot of it is poor choice that I've made, some of it I feel I was given a bad break with the court system, but a lot of it was bad choices. But I'd like to spend the rest of my life figuring out how my life matters, you know. So that's what I'm focusing on now, and I seem to have the right group. I've got the right psychologist, the right psychiatrist, the right doctor. I've got a really good group around me now. And sticking up for myself, I've never done that. . . . When you're in the court system, you can't stick up for yourself. You have to do what they tell you to do unless you want to battle with them and, you know, but, yeah, I just want to matter.

The therapist helped Lydia deal with family and fellowship rejection by pointing out, "Jesus died for our sins. We're forgiven, you know? We don't need another human being to tell us." Lydia increased family social support by acting to reunite with two adult daughters. As a first step in "mattering," Lydia talked to her CMH payee, who managed her disability payments because the diagnosed mental illnesses caused her to "overspend," about occasionally buying a $5 gift certificate for a world mission or another charity.

IN A BOX

Chapter 1 opened with Tina's depiction of herself and the supervising agent boxed in by limited resources and influence to fully help Tina improve her life. Except for Marion and, depending on future events, possibly Carmen and Mallory, most women described so far made sense and meaning in their lives within the constraints of their resources and circumstances. The next women included in this chapter had endpoints severely constrained by context, structure, addiction, and their choices that kept them using drugs and breaking the law for decades. Dependence on a partner who enabled drug use, an abusive intimate partner, family members who used drugs and lived on illegal income, and distressed communities could keep women vacillating between desistance and persistence, or like Marion, seeing no end to illegal behavior.

Francesca said she had been arrested 50 times between ages 18 and 35. Her convictions were drug- and prostitution-related before and during the supervision that brought her into the study, and she continued to prostitute and use drugs up to the time of the life story interview. When she was stressed, she still went to a crack house. Even though Francesca had a new conviction for prostitution during supervision, the agent continued to use a combination of control and caring marked by warnings, limit setting, and expressions of concern. Francesca said that as a result, she saw her counselor more often and used some of the coping skills she learned. The counselor encouraged her to leave the man she had lived with for 17 years, the man who had supported and enabled her drug use and encouraged her to prostitute almost two decades before. At the final interview a year and a half after she told her life story, Francesca had taken the counselor's advice and left the man. She gave her increased sense of empowerment as the reason: "Because I can work, and I'd rather enjoy my life and be able to do what I want to do. I'm depending on myself and not another individual." Between the life story interview and that final interview, Francesca lost her driver's license after a conviction for driving under the influence. After that, she began paying to regain the license and paying off her court and supervision-related debts. Just under three years later, Francesca had another conviction for driving while impaired and without a valid license, but no further convictions for prostitution.

An abusive partner kept Lynette from realizing her goal of avoiding new convictions and keeping custody of her youngest child. At the time of the life story interview, Lynette's husband of six years was physically abusing her, and when she left the home, he called her every 10 to 15 minutes demanding she return. He put all household expenses (gas, water, electricity) in her name and then worked in another state earning substantial income, but sent her a pittance to cover the household costs. He threatened to set her up for arrest so her youngest child would go to foster care. Lynette planned to divorce him, but she never got to that point. After the life story interview, she was convicted of possession of a controlled substance and maintaining a drug house, soliciting another person to obtain ephedrine or pseudoephedrine, and operating and maintaining a methamphetamine lab, and she spent time in jail and in prison. She was discharged from correctional oversight three and a half years later. I am not privy to the details of how Lynette ended up in prison, but there is an earie similarity to this endpoint and her description of her husband's threats: "I'm in a war of wits right now in my life right now actually. It's getting away safely, and not without anything. You know, 'cause he could destroy my career, he could destroy my . . . me having my son. He told my family he was . . . straight up said he was gonna set me up, and I was going to prison."

Shannon's parole ended just a few months short of two years, at which point her statements and official reports indicated she was drug and crime free. She did not have further convictions, but at the time of the life story and the follow-up interviews, Shannon was using a mix of highly addictive drugs, generating illegal income, and viewing her life as meaningless:

> My life has been nothing but tragic ups and downs, just living the lifestyle of just drugs and illegal activities . . ..It hurts me to know that I put myself through that. . . . I always felt like I wasn't that good. Men tell me and boyfriends tell me that, "You ain't shit." A lifestyle of drugs and running the streets was what I did and [it] wasn't really a life. Just a life of messing up and getting high and living the best I could.

Shannon's family pushed for, assisted, and accepted Shannon's drug use and crimes from her early teen years to her late fifties. Five years after the start of supervision, Shannon was living with an aunt who had supplied her with pills to sell for years and the sister who had told her as a teenager that if she wanted to eat, she needed to start prostituting. This sister smoked crack daily in the house where Shannon lived. The adult son who lived with Shannon had recently traded $300 worth of marijuana for a truck he gave her. Shannon said her son had just stopped using other drugs by taking her prescribed methadone. Until recently, Shannon had been making $1,000 a month selling her prescribed methadone, but the program discontinued her participation because she "dropped dirty," which showed she was using illegal drugs. The force of a family immersed in drug use and crime dwarfed the effects of Shannon's perceptions of the downside of continued use.

Mary provided the final example of how context and structural location promoted continuing illegal activity. Mary's difficulty finding work, with her long history of violent and other felony convictions; her motivation to raise her younger siblings; and her view that a house and car were essential hindered her from stopping criminal income-producing activity, though she did cut back after release from prison. Since she was a teenager, she had supported herself, her mother, and siblings with income from drug sales. Her mother's death while Mary was in prison left Mary pressing to get out, get custody of her brother and sister, and avoid arrests for new offenses. For young Black men in a distressed California community, Nikki Jones depicted "half and half," the transition out of making money illegally but taking it up when other sources of income dried up; Jamie Fader described "falling back" when young Black men in Philadelphia left a juvenile institution that instilled values and a way of thinking that were largely abandoned after the return to communities with high crime and low work opportunities.[15] Mary followed a similar pattern when she felt constrained by court-ordered restitution, her record, and the need for a house and car:

> Like I said, sometimes they put you in a box and sometimes you stuck in that box, and you got to take everything that in the box and you've got to go with it. I ain't no robber and I ain't no thief, so I had to go [stop stealing], so it is what it is. Once you get right [get in the right mindset], you don't take two in [think twice]. You take a few that will put you able [steal a few times for financial stability].[16]

Mary further explained that once a person gains financial stability and can meet basic needs, she should stop breaking the law or she will be "stuck" in a life of crime. She applied this principle to herself: "I just needed a few [dollars] to get the basic essentials and everything else. . . . If you can make your life more secure, everything else gunna fall in place. So that's how I do it." After outlining a half-in, half-out reliance on illegal income when she told her life story, at a follow-up interview Mary said that in the last year and a half she had made her life better. When the interviewer asked Mary how she managed to do this, Mary said, "FAFSA. You want the truth? Because that's the truth." FAFSA stands for the Free Application for Federal Student Aid. Mary did not state that she used a substantial amount of the financial aid for living expenses as opposed to tuition and educational materials, but she made it clear that this financial aid contributed to paying for "essentials."

Like mothers who learned to raise their children by avoiding what their parents had done, Mary raised her siblings so they would not break the law as she had done. Mary's mother had accepted the drug sales earnings that Mary contributed to the family from her early teens. Mary responded to her brother very differently. She recalled saying in an emotional scene when she found her cousin and brother "cutting up some dope," "Man, you don't wanna be like me. I was straight until I started doin' this bro." She told the interviewer, "I don't know the emotions that came on me. I was crying. It made my brother cry. He never cries. He never shows emotion. He barely talk. So, for this mother fucker to cry, it was like I did something good that day." Mary identified the source of her wisdom to respond this way as "experiences, bad experiences." She transformed her bad experiences into wisdom to steer her brother away from selling drugs.

Two years after Mary's final interview, she went to prison for first-degree home invasion, aggravated stalking, and larceny in a building. Her discharge from correctional control was approximately two years later.

MAKING SENSE OF ENDPOINTS

Most women depicted themselves as purposely and actively making positive changes in themselves and their lives. They changed how they raised and related to children, sought out and received mental health treatment, and found and worked at jobs. Some women reproduced their own chaotic childhoods for their offspring during periods of drug use, but later altered the family dynamics or took steps to repair strained and broken relationships. For several women, mental health treatment for themselves and their children enabled change. Women's heavy investment in making family and securing income often took precedence over giving back or making good in other ways, though some women drew on past experiences with drug use and conviction to help others or planned to do so in the future. The gender-related emphasis on creating family and assuming responsibilities for others in the family persisted across women differing in race, stage in life, and community type.

Developmental life course theories stress social learning that leads to reproduction of the values and behaviors exemplified by parents and other caretakers.[17] Shannon and her relatives' ongoing illegal income–

producing activities and their use of drugs provide an extreme example of the power of this socialization mechanism. However, social learning from parents and peers is not the full explanation of where women ended up. Most women in this book and in the full Michigan study sample indicated they had motivation to avoid crime-related behaviors (like misusing drugs and spending time with crime-involved people), change how they made decisions, and engage in school or work.[18] Though many women valued these goals, several social forces and policies made it difficult to escape poverty, access needed treatment, fully achieve their aims, and avoid additional convictions.

CHAPTER 8

Reform

This chapter shifts away from the prior chapter's attention to individual-level change, redemption, and outcomes and toward reform of programs, agencies, contexts, and social structures that affect the lives of women who have broken the law. Throughout this book, women describe circumstances that show the need for development and reform of programs, practices, and policies. They highlight living on their own as girls while no one looked out for them, drift and pushout from school, and disbelief and disregard in response to childhood sexual abuse allegations by institutions that should have protected them. The women clarify myriad ways that legal financial obligations inhibited successful completion of supervision, created stress, and maintained poverty. Jail time rarely gave women access to needed medical, mental health, and other services and often left jailed women's children poorly supervised and at risk of being drawn into illegal activity. Women describe benefits from supervision coming from new MDOC procedures and policies. To a lesser extent, some experienced deviations from the ideals of the reformed supervision approach. In the book, several women talk about the ways that mental health and substance abuse treatment empowered them, but others had trouble accessing treatment, especially after probation and parole supervision ended. Women reveal how they overcame barriers to finding work despite restrictions resulting from histories of felony convictions. Often the jobs they found did not match their education and the type of work they wanted to do. With low pay and sporadic employment, even women with jobs relied on food and housing assistance to meet day-to-day expenses. Both unemployed and working women talk at length about struggles to access safety-net benefits and the low levels of financial help they received. This chapter revisits women's revelations about needed systemic change, describes the issues more broadly in Michigan and other states, and identifies a selection of promising reforms. In keeping with the voice given to women's insights, women's accounts drove the selection of needed changes discussed here.

RESPOND TO GIRLS

Chapter 2, "Starting Points," called attention to the large proportion of women who started life on their own during or before adolescence and schools' use of suspension, expulsion, and reports to the police when girls acted aggressively or seemed defiant. It showed not just family members who failed to believe or stop sexual abuse of girls, but in a pattern of institutional betrayal, police, court, and school staff who failed to believe and protect them. Taking notice of and helping the many girls who live on their own; reducing drift and pushout from school; and ensuring that police, prosecutors, and juvenile court judges believe and act to stop abuse of girls would reduce the transition from girlhood to convictions as adults.

Girls On Their Own

Women described being incentivized to leave their homes to escape heavy sibling care and housekeeping responsibilities, neglect, family violence, parental rejection, parental desertion, or some combination of these circumstances. Researchers and practitioners use the term *unaccompanied minors* to describe youth living on their own. Any count of unaccompanied minors is an undercount because of problems accessing this group, but even those undercounts are high. A 22-community study of youth on the streets, in shelters, runaway, kicked out, and couch surfing generated an estimate of at least one in 30 adolescents (age 13 to 17) being an unaccompanied minor during a year.[1] The number over multiple years would be higher. In a nationally representative survey of households, 4.3 percent of people surveyed from over 25,000 households indicated that an adolescent from the household currently lived apart from the family due to running away, being told to leave, or couch surfing (sleeping anyplace available).[2] Complicating girls' circumstances, an estimated 10 percent of 13- to 17-year-old girls living on their own are pregnant or have a child.[3] A disproportionate number of unaccompanied minors, a designation held by several women in this book, are Black, Hispanic, and LGBTQ+.[4] They experienced abuse in their families and, after they separated, in whatever places they found to spend their days and nights. Feminist criminological studies going back decades and continuing to the present have found that girls who leave home due to abuse in the family turn to illegal survival strategies like prostitution, theft, and drug sales to meet basic needs.[5] In this book, for example, Bree lived on her own and supported herself by selling drugs after her mother stopped providing food or supervision, and Mallory and Vivian left home to escape their parents' violent abuse of each other.

For youth living on their own, cash assistance with no strings attached and access to safety-net benefits reduce illegal behavior and drug and alcohol use.[6] However, youth rarely access safety-net benefits because of the knowledge and stamina needed to deal with the multiple agencies that administer them, staff suspicions of fraudulent eligibility claims, and the complexity of required documentation and paperwork.[7] Also, in a familiar pattern in the women's lives, policies and programs work at cross-purposes, with benefits provided by one source offset by reductions in benefits provided by another. For example, no-strings-attached payments can make youth ineligible for food and housing assistance.

Urban Institute researchers recommend concrete steps to open safety-net benefits to youth living on their own: designate welfare agency staff to work with youth, reach out to unaccompanied minors, simplify applications, require fewer documents to establish eligibility, recognize needs for mental health and trauma-informed supports, avoid punitive responses, and coordinate benefits so increases in one type of assistance do not result in decreases in other types.[8] Because of high rates of trauma among youth on their own, cash transfers and safety-net benefits help youth the most when paired with psychological support and assistance accessing multisectoral services.[9] Adoption of these reforms and procedures requires overcoming the punitive and rejecting turn that safety-net programs have taken. Without massive reorientation of benefits, case managers with small caseloads, mentors, or navigators are best positioned to guide and advocate for youth (and adults) needing assistance.[10] These approaches help some youth, but they leave the current arrangement of safety-net benefits difficult to access and sparse.

Pushed Out of School

Abuse at home precipitates fights and verbal aggression in school that lead to girls' suspension, expulsion, and arrest. Carmen attributed her fighting in school to frustration and anger stemming from rejecting parents who moved her between their homes and school districts every month to receive disability payments intended to help the family meet Carmen's needs. Administrators barred her from the entire school district for fighting in school. After her mother did not believe that her brother had sexually assaulted her, Sally's persistent anger led to fights at school and expulsion. School personnel's biased perception that Black and Latina girls are older than their chronological age and therefore more culpable for breaking school rules (a process called adultification) results in the girls' especially high rates of in-school suspensions that remove them from classrooms (11.2%) and out-of-school suspensions that remove them from the campus (13.3%).[11] Schools also remove nontrivial proportions of White girls from classrooms (10.2%) and campuses (7.9%). The dynamics leading to school pushout differ by race, with different stereotypes and biases operating, but the outcomes are similarly negative. Zero tolerance policies first instituted to reduce drugs and guns in school, but then spread to sanction a multitude of behaviors, have magnified the problem of removal of girls from school.[12] Reformers address the bias against girls of color by providing them with support, raising public awareness through campaigns about adultification and training defense attorneys on adultification bias, and for all girls (and boys), spearheading community action to establish alternative approaches to punitive school discipline.[13]

Heavily publicized and lauded programs to prevent school-based aggression and violence focus on reforming youth by building their problem-solving skills, clearly communicating rules, and establishing reasonable consequences for misbehavior.[14] They do not address trauma, anger, and felt needs for self-defense. Reducing the number of girls who are disciplined, suspended, and expelled from school and helping them cope with trauma and threats to safety that promote rule breaking can reduce the number who become women in trouble with the law. School personnel need training to take trauma into account and to address racial and gender bias when they make sense of and respond to students' aggression.[15]

Victims Betrayed

Describing the aftermath of childhood sexual abuse, women identified police officers who discounted their reports and school personnel who failed to respond. Even though her older sister corroborated the abuse, the police did not pursue Carmen's report that her brother had sexually abused her. When her mother threatened Anna with permanent separation from the family, the police accepted Anna's explanation that she had made up the entire detailed report of six years of sexual abuse by her stepfather. Raven's high school counselor did not keep her sexual abuse confidential, and the resulting taunts by other students caused Raven to drop out of school. These actions disregard trauma-informed practices promoted by the U.S. Substance Abuse and Mental Health Services Administration.[16] Trauma-informed professionals know that culture and gender can prevent reports of abuse, recognize signs and symptoms of abuse and trauma, provide person-centered support, and avoid retraumatization so that survivors feel safe and have voice and choice.

CUT THE COST

The MDOC's efforts to handle violations of probation and parole conditions without resort to jail or prison and to address client needs, including women's unique needs, are routinely undermined by costs associated with court appearances and judges' use of jail time and extended supervision in response to nonpayment. Judges' decisions left Carmen cycling back and forth between inability to pay supervision fees and jail as punishment, to the point that she chose to go to prison to end community supervision. When she could not pay costs associated with probation, Bree absconded to avoid an extension of supervision. Carla could not afford further education because she paid court and supervision costs instead of paying back student loans, which meant she could not get additional loans. The many financial obligations and requirements for supervision in two different court jurisdictions left Mallory stressed and emotionally drained. Fiona no longer used drugs, and she immersed herself in multifaceted mental health care, but the judge prolonged supervision until she could pay off her debts. Compared to women on probation, the situation for women on parole and therefore supervised by MDOC agents was somewhat better due to department policies stipulating that once individuals met time and other requirements, MDOC ended parole and referred any debt to the state collection agency, which established a payment plan. This solution released women from supervision but left them with a debt burden.

Nationwide there are documented uneven and uncoordinated costs levied within and between court districts and variable efforts to tailor costs to the financial resources of convicted individuals.[17] Also, in locations besides Michigan individuals accumulate court and conviction costs simultaneously in multiple jurisdictions.[18] Widespread concern about injustice and unintended consequences of legal financial obligations motivated several U.S. foundations, research institutes, and advocacy groups to document the effects nationwide and to strategize and act to reduce or eliminate these costs.[19] Analysis of Harvard Law School's national database on legal financial obligations shows that states authorize assessment of between 9 and 118 different fees and surcharges after a person is convicted of a felony, misdemeanor, or traffic offense.[20] Fees for supervision, court appearances, and assigned counsel for people without means to pay a lawyer are the most common.[21] By Michigan law, until the passage of reform legislation in 2021, nonpayment of one or more of the 38 different monetary charges related to conviction could result in increased fines, wage garnishment, incarceration, requirements to establish an installment plan for payment, collection of interest, and property liens. The costs place extra burden on women, who are more disadvantaged than men in securing employment, who have responsibilities for children that judges sometimes disregard when they determine what women can reasonably pay, who more often contend with trauma and substance disorders, and who often manage on their own without an intimate partner or other supportive adults.[22]

In addition to the personal toll of conviction-related costs, there is a perverse connection between safety-net benefits and charges for being processed through the court, supervised in the community, and locked up in jail. In a nationally representative sample, about half of people with legal financial obligations received safety-net benefits.[23] Even meager safety-net benefits can justify a judge's finding of willful nonpayment and an order for additional punishment.[24] In a dynamic that increases a person's financial need, money received to alleviate poverty goes toward supporting supervision, incarceration, and other government functions, leaving people who depend on state support unable to cover basic needs, such as rent to secure a stable place to live.[25] To pay off conviction-related debts, women described diverting meager income from safety-net benefits or low-paying jobs from meeting their own and often their children's basic needs. When they fell short, they were punished with jail or extended supervision, which brought additional costs. Because Black Americans have less capital and credit than White Americans, Black and other minoritized groups suffer the greatest burden of legal financial obligations, and these obligations reinforce racial economic inequality.[26] Further showing the disutility of legal financial obligations, the costs of extracting payments from people living in poverty and the low payment compliance rates raise doubts about the worth of the return on investment in collecting this money for state and local governments.[27]

Public, media, and scholarly attention to the injustice of high conviction-related costs relative to low or no income and successful legal challenges showing these costs to be unconstitutional and discriminatory have fueled state-level reforms. In 2016, the Michigan Supreme Court required judges to assess ability to pay and reduce payments before jailing individuals. The ruling fell short of fully ensuring justice because it left judges to use different approaches and criteria to figure out how to assess ability to pay, and this resulted in considerable disparity.[28] In 2020, for people who set up a payment plan and made the payments, the Michigan legislature eliminated driver's license suspensions as a penalty for unpaid court costs and fines. This helped people who could make payments but left those who could not pay without a license. Also starting in 2020, the Michigan State Legislature responded to the futility and potential harm of charging people with little or no income for their own supervision by limiting the MDOC monthly supervision fee to $30 a month (down from $135 a month) or, if the person wore an electronic tether, a total of $60 a month. Even these fees are high in relation to the financial situation of most of the women who contributed to this book. They struggled to make payments while living on, for example, disability insurance amounting to just over $700 a month.

The Fines and Fees Justice Center, a multistate advocacy group, identified numerous examples of states' successful elimination of fines and fees and practices to discharge several types of debt.[29] In a parallel effort to promote change, the Harvard Law School prepared extensive recommendations for state legislative, judicial, and executive branch reforms and case examples of states that instituted each reform.[30] For example, state legislatures should cap and then lower the percent of revenue that jurisdictions raise from court fines and fees, and legislators should require courts to conduct standardized ability-to-pay assessments before levying penalties for nonpayment. For the judiciary, there should be monitoring and elimination of racial disparities in court financial charges. And for the executive branch of government, as occurred in Michigan, policy should dictate that failure to pay court, jail, and other conviction-related costs should not result in suspension of driver's licenses.

Recommended reforms differ in whether they make the current system fairer and more reasonable versus abolishing the practice of charging people for court processing, supervision, and incarceration, then using the money to support police, courts, correctional agencies, and other governmental functions. Although Beth Colgan recognizes that tailoring monetary sanctions to the ability to pay lessens many individuals' debts, she criticizes graduation of costs because the more feasible payments could engage more people in financially supporting criminal justice agencies, often from the money they receive to alleviate their poverty.[31] Alternatives are to fund justice agencies through the usual budgetary process, as is common in several European countries, and use graduated financial sanctions and restitution as an alternative to supervision and incarceration rather than a supplement, thereby downsizing the number of people under correctional control.[32] More generally, ending the cycle of high monetary costs of conviction followed by jail or extended supervision and additional costs for failure to pay would reduce the number of people with lengthy periods of community supervision or time in jail.

REDUCE INCARCERATION

In 2020, Michigan's prison for women held 1,704 women, most of whom were serving a sentence for drug or property offenses.[33] Compared to other states, Michigan has the eighteenth lowest rate of women in prison. For every 100,000 women age 18 and over, 34 (compared to the average of 44 for all other states) were in prison.[34] The combined state emphasis on reducing the prison population and numerous MDOC reforms that started in the early 2000s have supported the goal of reducing prison populations.[35] Further reducing the number of women in Michigan's prisons is a laudable goal, but relevant to community supervision, the women who provided data for this book moved in and out of jail much more often than they returned to prison.

Reduce the Number in Jail

In the women's accounts, jail stood out as crime producing rather than crime reducing. When 17-year-old Jolene stole to support herself after her mother left her on her own, a judge sent her to a jail where older women taught her to cook meth, and during a second time in jail, convinced her of the terrific high achieved by shooting up drugs. Jolene described a better approach: "Yeah, now if they would have placed me in a placement home or something and gave me resources as to how to change my life with the problem that I had with drinking instead of putting me in jails full of 31-year-olds and 40-year-olds that are fucking there for meth labs, then maybe I wouldn't have got out and cooked meth." A judge sent 17-year-old Carmen to jail for resisting arrest for being a minor in possession of alcohol. In the holding cell, Carmen violently attacked a cellmate who was kicking her. The judge dismissed the charge for resisting arrest but sentenced Carmen to a year in jail for the attack. Unlike jail, diversion to mental health treatment in the community or a residential setting would have directly addressed the "anger problem" that Carmen knew she had and wanted help with. In an example of being jailed in response to a mental health crisis, the police arrived just after Lana aborted a suicide attempt and, in what seemed like a cry for help, told her husband to call the police because she was a felon with a gun. Recognizing that mental illness drove Lana's behavior, the police took her to a psychiatric hospital. However, instead of being channeled into mental health treatment, her conviction on a weapons charge resulted in four months in jail followed by probation. Probation supervision turned out to be helpful because the agent connected Lana to local community mental health services, but there is no indication that time in jail provided any help. The women's statements show how police and court handling of a mental health crisis, sentences to jail, and incarceration for debts maintain high numbers of women locked up in jail without adequate mental health care.

Considerable information confirms that throughout the nation, women are especially likely to spend time in jail. Between 2008 and 2019, the number of women in U.S. jails increased by 11 percent, while the number of men in U.S. jails decreased by 9 percent.[36] Also showing the disproportionate jailing of women, consistent with the pattern in Michigan, in the United States more men are in prison than jail, but more women are in jail than prison.[37] One of every four women in jail is being held for low-level drug crimes (like possession), and just under a third for property offenses, often committed because of substance dependence.[38] Demonstrating the widespread use of jail time, between 2010 and 2019, rural, suburban, and urban women experienced nearly equivalent increases in arrest followed by jail.

Affirming the experiences of many women in this book, most jails lack programming and deprive people of privacy, autonomy, social support, and medical and mental health care. Even though Lily no longer used drugs, she did not turn herself in after her time absconded because of the possibility she would be sent to jail, where staff would deny her life-saving medications. She remembered being in jail with a woman who did not want to be on the top bunk because she was epileptic. The woman had a seizure and fell onto the floor, knocking out all her teeth. The guard told her to go back to sleep, they'd deal with it in the morning. The failure of most jails to provide safety and need-driven care and programming is a national problem. In a sample of U.S. jails, most of the budget went to pay employees, a smaller but substantial amount went to maintaining the physical facility, and less than 5 percent went to programming.[39] Given the limited educational, mental health, and medical assistance, it is no surprise that one in four people in jail return more than once in the same year.[40] Along with the limited benefit, jails constitute a disproportionately large expense to local communities, making it more cost effective to invest in community programs and services than to keep people locked up.[41]

The high co-occurrence of both women's mental illness and substance misuse with being jailed after an arrest, and then of being sentenced to jail, begs for a way to break the connections. Evaluations of alternative police responses to people with mental illness show minimal effects, so without further refinement and development, police training and monitoring are unlikely to substantially reduce the number of people in jail.[42] Evaluations of intensive case management programs suggest that a focus on jail diversion, coordination between mental health and criminal justice agencies, and comprehensive services (for example, addiction treatment, housing assistance, and vocational services) show promise for reducing arrests and incarceration.[43] Mental health and drug courts benefit some participants, but for others the combined court control and monitoring of treatment compliance clash with empowering mental health treatment driven by clients' desires and understanding of their needs for change.[44] Agents' split-role relationship that separates mental health and substance abuse treatment from community supervision and diversion away from jail and prison toward mental health treatment offers alternatives when mental health and drug courts are unavailable or the expectations of monitoring and control by supervising agents cannot be reconciled with client-centered, empowering mental health approaches.

Legislative reform is likely to have the greatest effect on the use of jail time. Following principles developed by the Pew Charitable Trusts, a nongovernmental organization that advocates and provides technical assistance to reduce the number of people under correctional control, Michigan legislators passed 20 jail reform bills in 2021.[45] The Michigan legislation responded to a task force report finding that from 1960 to 2016, the state's jail incarceration rate tripled while the crime rate dropped to its lowest in 50 years, and the finding that many jailed people were awaiting trial or serving sentences for offenses that do not threaten public safety. The Michigan reforms include allowing police use of citations for a greater range of low-level misdemeanor charges and handling failure to appear in court with a summons that allows rescheduling the appearance instead of arrest. The new laws also prohibit jail sentencing for all but the most serious misdemeanors and low-level felonies, use of alternatives to jail for young people, and elimination of several mandatory minimums for the length of jail sentences. To address the overuse of jail for probation and parole violations, the legislation reduces the maximum probation term to three years, provides incentives for early probation discharge, and limits jail time and arrest warrants for technical probation violations. The legislation requires that all probation and parole conditions be justified by valid assessment of a person's risk for recidivism. To address the connection between mental illness and jail, additional pending legislation in Michigan would invest in community-based mental health (including substance abuse) treatment to divert people from jail.

Alternatives to Prison for Absconders

Women's statements about life while absconded and responses to this violation reveal a way to reduce prison populations. For women on parole, MDOC personnel based the decision to return people to prison on assessed risk, so absent new convictions, policy resulted in efforts to reduce the cause of not reporting. However, even though probation agents made recommendations, judges ultimately decided how to respond when women absconded from probation.

Some women absconded so they could continue illegal activities and drug use. Mallory's official record shows multiple times in prison starting in 1983, repeated releases on parole, absconded status that sometimes led to a return to prison and sometimes to continued parole, and new convictions while she was absconded. A variety of other reasons led to absconding. After Elsie lost access to mental health medication during a transition out of substance abuse treatment, she relapsed on crack cocaine to "self-medicate." Fearing punishment if she told the agent about the relapse, she absconded for more than two years. Rhiannon absconded to avoid complying with the agent's directive to move into transitional housing, where Rhiannon thought another resident would influence her to use drugs, relapse, and jeopardize her life. Lily absconded not only because she feared being denied necessary medication in jail, but because she believed she would be paying conviction-related costs for the rest of her life. Even after she stopped using drugs and reunited with her adult children and grandchildren, publicly available official records listed Lily as absconded for years.

With some exceptions, women who were no longer breaking the law accurately perceived the unpredictability and potential harm of recontacting probation and parole agents after being absconded. A judge sent 45-year-old Lena to prison for not reporting for 15 years, even though Lena had no arrests or convictions during the period. Her two most recent convictions, committed in her twenties, were for breaking into a bakery 15 years earlier and receiving and concealing stolen property, which she described as joy riding in a car. She emphasized the length of time since those incidents—"It's been a long time. Everything's been a long time"—and she characterized her years on probation as "forever." After she gave her name to police who stopped her for driving without license plates, the judge sentenced her to prison; she served seven months and then began a term of parole. She said group meetings in prison improved her self-esteem, but not being able to read and impaired vision prevented her from earning a GED. The cost to hold her in prison made less financial sense than addressing her limited vision and engaging her in self-esteem and literacy classes in the community.

Nationally, a nontrivial proportion of individuals abscond from community supervision. In 2020, 9 percent of the women and men on probation and 7 percent of those on parole were absconded.[46] A few studies identify women's reasons for absconding that the Michigan women did not identify. Research on Missouri women produced examples of one woman who did not want the supervising agent to see injuries inflicted by an intimate partner, because she believed she could not handle being told to leave him at the time.[47] Another woman feared that because the corrections department had approved her living at an ex-boyfriend's residence, she would be sent to prison if she left to avoid his sexual advances. The Michigan women in this book said they absconded because of conviction-related costs, the expectation of interminable supervision, and a sense of injustice when supervision was extended because costs were unpaid. They remained absconded out of fear of being jailed or imprisoned, and for one woman, the thought that she would be in medical crisis after jail staff denied her medication.

The Pew Charitable Trusts presents examples of states where responses to absconding depend on intent, not just missing appointments and becoming unfindable.[48] This sort of judicial discretion has the potential to reduce the number of individuals who end up in both prisons and jails. The same report recommends amnesty for people absconded but desisting from illegal activity for a long time. Amnesty makes sense for women like Lena and Lily, who had long periods without police or court contact. They had already paid dearly by living without identification, a stable address, and legitimate work.

IMPROVE SUPERVISION

Tina, who conceptualized herself and her agent as constrained in a box, attributed the limitations on the help the agent could provide to his large caseload. Shannon felt that the agent's caseload was "to big to care about what a person was going through." When Mallory tried to talk to an agent about her past, she felt rushed and dropped the topic. These experiences contradict the ideals of the MDOC community supervision reforms. They also show that improved supervision hinges not just on skills to hear about and address the difficulties women identified, but also on agents' having adequate time to interact with clients. Fifty-four agents supervised the 118 women. For the 47 agents with caseload information, the range was 43 to 107 clients, and the average was 64.8. A reduced number of people on probation would free agents' time to concentrate their efforts on those most in need of assistance and supervision.

Reduce the Numbers Supervised in the Community

To reduce the number of women (and men) supervised in the community, the majority of whom are on probation, the Pew Charitable Trusts developed a comprehensive list of policy reforms supported by case examples and research evidence.[49] The core recommendation is to downsize the numbers of people at multiple points between arrest and through the point of sentencing. The MDOC does not control many of the recommended actions, notably increased alternatives to arrest, incarceration, and supervision. Diversion into mental health treatment rather than jail and amnesty for crime-desisting absconders would reduce MDOC caseloads. Reflecting many of the adopted Michigan jail reforms, the Pew Charitable Trusts recommend that judges consider the ability to pay when they levy costs, give shorter sentences, focus on goals and incentives, and base decisions on recidivism risks and individuals' needs. The MDOC has implemented Pew-recommended reforms that it controls, including existing procedures to reduce barriers to reporting (for example, instituting virtual reporting technologies), setting limitations on returns to prison, and monitoring and training of supervising agents.

Improve Supervision

The MDOC's gender-responsive (and thus trauma-informed), needs-driven supervision delivered through motivational interviewing techniques benefited many women. Consistent with the intention of reformed MDOC supervision, women especially appreciated and felt helped when agents understood the constraints imposed by neighborhood crime, responsibilities for children and other family members, mental illness, and drug addiction. Agents shared their knowledge of the courts and child protection services and referred and advocated for women to receive multiple types of help as needs changed or became apparent over time. Recognition of needs and successful channeling of women into matching programs provided a way out of drug use and related illegal activities, and advocacy with judges and other agencies showed women that agents cared about them.

MDOC agents became temporary members of women's networks by coaching them to handle supervision by multiple agents and to approach and interact with court staff, child protection workers, and welfare workers. They made referrals that expanded women's social networks to include people who gave access to critical resources.[50] When Pamela could not find a place to live, the agent linked her to a police officer who rented her a safe place to stay. The entire experience of parole supervision, which started with residential substance abuse treatment far from her hometown, exposed Jolene to recovery capital in different types of treatment programs around the state, so when she relapsed, she connected herself to a nine-month residential treatment program that, again, was distant from where she lived, but that met her need for a long-term, comprehensive residential program away from former drug-using associates in her hometown. Agents' many referrals of women to a variety of resources and programs gave them new access to networks that could help them avoid crime and substance misuse and achieve their goals.

A stand-alone follow-up study of 160 women randomly selected from the full Michigan study sample shows the importance of expanding women's social networks.[51] It reveals that a limited number of women's network members could provide access to employment opportunities. Of those who could, many were weak ties or acquaintances such as coworkers and neighbors. In this book, Jenny found work doing landscaping by reconnecting to her former employer, Andy worked in her aunt's tax preparation business so she could cover drug test costs, and Sami returned to work in her ex-husband's business. Most of the women in the network study, however, lacked former employers, relatives, and friends who could link them to jobs. Marva Goodson-Miller, who carried out that research, recommends strategic efforts to grow women's networks to include people unconnected to close family and friends. She also recommends giving women skills to seek support from individuals who can provide novel advice, employment opportunities, and other resources. Agents' actions to build women's resource access and facilitate their participation in programs that provide wraparound services and a continuing support group are particularly important in light of the small social networks of many women entangled with the courts and corrections.[52]

Since the start of the research, the MDOC has continuously developed and expanded training of probation and parole agents in gender-responsive approaches, motivational interviewing, and collaborative case management that focuses on meeting women's needs with evidence-based interventions. The use of the Women's Needs/Risks Assessment tool expanded from matching risks and needs to programming in prison to use at release, to use in preparing presentence investigation reports, and finally to use by probation and parole agents. After the final interview conducted for this book, the MDOC training further evolved so that all new agents receive training with an integrated five-day curriculum in both collaborative case management and gender-responsive approaches during New Agent School. In 2018, during two days initially and a month later a two-day follow-up, MDOC staff trained the 12,000 community corrections, prison, and administrative staff in motivational interviewing.[53] Additional MDOC innovations include educating in-house trainers so the department can sustain this knowledge base among staff and regular computer-based booster training in motivational interviewing. To ensure all personnel work from the same intervention platform, the training is incorporated into the academy for new employees.

There is no national survey of the prevalence of probation and parole agencies' implementation of a combination of evidence-based supervision, gender-responsive approaches, and motivational interviewing. Providing some information, a survey of over 500 supervising agents in seven departments across five states revealed that supervising agents felt comfortable combining approaches that might conflict: evidence-based practices and monitoring, surveillance, and punishment.[54] Research in two districts of one state's probation department found incomplete implementation of motivational interviewing techniques, in part because agents used a mixture of motivational interviewing and authoritarian strategies, or they used only authoritarian strategies.[55] In Great Britain, agents struggled to use gender-responsive strategies with women due to institutional constraints and the inavailability of resources.[56] Together these studies point to problems implementing components of the Michigan model. The multifaceted Michigan approach, which includes continuing follow-up agent training and training of administrators, stands as unique in promoting department-wide implementation and a shift away from punitive approaches.[57] Implementation may be possible because the agency has characteristics known to promote evidence-based supervision, namely department-wide rehabilitation goals, management with advanced training in psychology and other fields relevant to meeting the needs of women under supervision, and extensive and expanding MDOC training requirements that give agents confidence in using motivational interviewing.[58]

CREATE EMPLOYMENT OPPORTUNITIES

Pointing out needed reforms outside of criminal justice agencies, Louisa analyzed programs and practices that prevent people with a record of convictions from finding work. She criticized a national recycling and secondhand store company for hiring people with felony convictions to work for just 90 days, "So they don't ever have to hire anyone 'cause they always use the criminals to do it, but then when they done with the 90 days what you do, just kick them out? So, they right back to do the same thing [breaking the law and accumulating new convictions]."

Research in several settings confirms Louisa's insight that short-term, low-paying employment often fails to lift people with criminal convictions into decent-paying, stable employment.[59]

Louisa also criticized licensing restrictions on the types of jobs that people with felony convictions could hold, "Like the government, why do they still hold us accountable for felonies that we did, when if you really look at it the people who have felonies, they are the ones who will work." She believed that prohibiting employment in specified employment sectors led people to "find a way to get money and to beat the system because we feel like you're not letting us go anywhere or move forward with our life."

To increase women's work opportunities beyond low-paying, short-term jobs, solutions include expungement of criminal history records and elimination of a criminal record as a reason to deny occupational licenses. Researchers joined with justice advocates in Michigan to provide the empirical evidence that sparked a change in expungement laws.[60] They found that only 6.5 percent of eligible people had their records expunged, but those who did had extremely low recidivism and substantially higher wages from steady employment. A 2021 Michigan law made expungement or sealing of files (restricting information access to law enforcement personnel) automatic after a set numbers of years and reduced the expense and complexity of applying for nonautomatic expungement. Michigan and 12 other states have the broadest felony and misdemeanor relief through expungement and sealed files, 23 states provide more limited relief, 5 states give relief for misdemeanors and pardoned felonies, 3 states and the District of Columbia allow expungement only for misdemeanors, and 5 states do not allow expungement or sealed files.[61]

An estimated one-quarter of the U.S. workforce needs a license to work in their occupations.[62] Licensing restrictions often apply to jobs with relative ease of entry and that offer opportunity for entrepreneurship, for example providing care for children, working in the health-care sector, and cosmetology trades.[63] Michigan ranked relatively low among the states for the number of entry-level occupations that require a license and the cost and the amount of training required to obtain a license. Licensing requirements were further reduced in 2020 when Michigan legislation stipulated that restrictions based on criminal history and related judgments of "good moral character" must be for serious crimes directly related to an occupation. Previously, a history of any type of illegal activity restricted people from jobs that included cosmetology, nursing, and several other high-demand, accessible occupations. Michigan's law still falls short because it allows a degree of subjective judgment about what constitutes good moral character, but it is more progressive than laws in many other states. Unfortunately, this law came into effect too late for the women in the Michigan research.

REPAIR THE SAFETY NET

National and state-level reforms have reduced the restrictions on some banned benefits for people with criminal histories. In 2020, under pressure from coalitions of advocacy groups, the U.S. Congress eliminated its 1994 denial of grants to support higher education in prisons.[64] States also softened or eliminated some bans on assistance to people living in poverty and having a history of criminal convictions. For people with felony convictions, the District of Columbia and 29 states (including Michigan as of 2020) no longer or never did ban receipt of food assistance, 21 have a modified ban, and 1 has a full lifetime ban.[65] In a similar pattern, for TANF, 27 states and the District of Columbia have no ban, 17 (including Michigan) have a modified ban, and 7 states have a full lifetime ban. Restoring access to postsecondary education, food assistance, and welfare support makes financial sense given the effects on recidivism. Increased education reduces recidivism.[66] Eligibility for welfare and food assistance at the time of release from prison and living in a state that does not restrict access to TANF for people with a criminal conviction also reduces recidivism.[67] In addition to the economic sense of eligibility for government assistance, it is unjust to extend punishments and prohibitions handed down by criminal courts to denial of safety-net benefits intended to assist people in financial need.

Molly, a White woman with multiracial children from a marriage to a Black man, expressed a keen awareness of the prejudicial injustice of safety-net benefit bans on minoritized women, poor women, and women with substance abuse disorders. She gave an example of a negative comment about people who receive safety-net benefits, "Oh minorities, Black people, they don't need this because they need to get off their lazy ass." She also criticized the use of drug tests for people to qualify for food assistance: "[If] you give them a food card, then leave them alone and let them feed their family." She saw injustice in the lack of public safety, transportation, and grocery stores in Detroit neighborhoods:

> Nobody should have to worry about safety. You should be like how you are in the suburbs. . . . If you can't drive, let there be systems that let you get

places and be on time, or at least somewhat on time. And let there be enough
grocery stores, or certain stores around that—where there isn't—you know
there's not transportation.

Molly believed that stereotyping of minoritized women limited access to safety-net benefits, and the lack of investment in neighborhoods ignored the needs of people living in low-resource, high-crime
neighborhoods.

The historical record confirms Molly's assessment of racist stereotypes and resulting negative attitudes toward parents living in poverty,
especially mothers. The Center on Budget and Policy Priorities' analysis
of TANF history shows the power of politicians' and media's unsup-
ported narratives that have falsely linked mothers' being Black or Brown
to their fraudulent receipt of welfare income through the now defunct
AFDC, use of drugs, inadequate parenting, and disdain for work.[68] The
narratives fueled new federal policies and state actions that continue to
reduce essential income for minoritized individuals the most, but also
for poor families of all races and ethnicities. In 2020, only 11 percent of
poor families in Michigan received TANF.[69] Limiting women's capacity
to acquire better-paying jobs, in Michigan (and other states) not more
than 10 hours of training and education can count toward the required
work preparation and time working at a job to qualify for TANF.[70] As
the women who told their stories for this book recognized, and as research shows for the nation, the TANF requirement to participate in
Work First job preparation and employment requirements often fails to
lift people out of poverty.[71] It ignores the many structural influences that
keep women from finding steady employment with a livable wage, and
for many women in this book, histories that have left them traumatized,
unable to work, and with limited human and social capital that would
lead to good-paying, steady employment.

Like the divide between making legal financial obligations more affordable versus eliminating them altogether, access to benefits can increase through advocacy for individuals, changing TANF, or replacing
TANF as the means to move families out of poverty. Examples of interventions that do not challenge current safety-net program arrangements
but that improve access for individuals include training correctional staff
to guide women through the application process and ensuring that social
service staff help noncompliant clients become compliant with rules before or soon after sanctions cut them off.[72]

Advocating for state and federal transformation of TANF, analysts at the Center on Budget and Policy Priorities show that states spend only a bit over one-fifth of the combined state and federal TANF contribution on the transfer of money to recipients. Michigan spent one of the lowest proportions of funds on actual payments to recipients, just 10 percent.[73] Evidence points to racist stereotypes of Black women who receive TANF as an influence on these patterns. States with a larger percentage of Black residents paid the lowest proportion of TANF money directly to recipients and spent the highest proportion to discouraging single motherhood, as evidenced by Michigan's emphasis on pregnancy prevention and marriage; also, a low proportion of funds allocated to cash assistance occurs in states with a high prevalence of White individuals' stereotyping of Black people.[74] Federal legislation is needed to prohibit the deeply rooted racial inequities that states introduce into TANF allocations.

Two 2020 federal initiatives that responded to the COVID-19 epidemic—the Economic Impact Payments instituted in 2020 and 2021 and the child tax credit available in 2021—exemplify major policy overhauls that could improve the lives of women in this book and more broadly all women living in poverty. These provisions of cash briefly lifted 11.7 million people out of poverty, including more than 61 million children.[75] The effects appear to be short lived because the U.S. Congress acted to end both sources of income in 2022. These policies demonstrated alternatives to government nonintervention to alleviate poverty, and some politicians and advocacy groups continue to work toward reinstating the child tax credit, which reduces the tax burden for all families with children. It helps families that lack income by providing them with a "refund" to support their children.

Elliot Currie proposes major systemic change to reduce violent crime: create good-paying jobs in the public sector—jobs for childcare workers, teachers, social workers, and mental health treatment providers—and provide training and education to prepare people for these jobs.[76] Currie builds the case for moving people from poverty and related crime into the workforce, so they are not drawn to earn "fast money" through illegal means. With fewer people needing safety-net benefits, there would be more resources, and thus a higher quality of life, for people who cannot work. For the women in this book, Currie's proposal could have given child-serving institutions the human resources to prevent the progression from girlhood to adults in trouble with the law. In essence, Currie proposes a massive shift from spending on responding to crime to investment in human development and opportunity as a means to prevent crime. It remains to be seen whether a major overhaul of safety-net systems and investment in people without financial means will take place locally or nationally.

REFORM IN A BOX

A central message of this book is that MDOC community supervision had a demonstrable pattern of desired effects on many women on probation and parole. The MDOC model implemented evidence-based interventions matched to needs, recognized women's unique needs and valuation of relationships, and promoted motivational interviewing to guide agents' interactions with women they supervised. An equally important message is that this reform played out in a larger community, policy, and economic context exogenous to the MDOC. These exogenous forces varied in whether they supported the intentions of the MDOC reform or undermined them. Women's decisions and actions made a difference, but their context and social location had as much if not more effect on their behavior, quality of life, and continuation of drug use and illegal behavior in the short and the long term.

Depending on the point in time and geographic location, public policy affected women in trouble with the law in opposing ways. Medical insurance through the PPACA brought women lifesaving medical and mental health care, and MDOC made it practice to assist people leaving prison to apply before release and to encourage women in the community to apply. Working against MDOC reforms, different from peer countries, the U.S. federal government continues to disallow disability insurance when the primary medical problem is substance abuse.[77] It also bans receipt of TANF for people with a felony drug conviction unless the state modifies this stipulation. The national affordable housing shortage persists, and qualifying for safety-net benefits, which could prevent girls becoming convicted adults and could give women reason to avoid making fast money, requires knowledge, resources, and stamina. At the local level, judges vary in their emphasis on treatment or punishment, and court-imposed costs combined with supervision fees create a severe financial strain for all but the best-off women.

Contradictory policies defy economic logic. Cutting housing and income assistance saves on social welfare costs but increases the cost of criminal justice processing, control, punishment, and rehabilitation.[78] Devika Hazra used available data from 1992 to 2014 for the 50 states to model the effects of government funding on welfare and education versus law enforcement and corrections on different types of crime.[79] She found that public welfare and education funding can lower violent and property crime rates, but law enforcement spending can only lower property crime rates. Correctional spending increased both types of crime. Encouraging women to reduce their needs and risks for recidivism conflicts with policies that maintain these needs and risks, and this bidirectional dynamic is yet another way that counteracting policies waste resources by undoing each other. Legislators and other policy makers either lack knowledge of or disregard the complex ways that multiple policies affect highly marginalized women. Conflicting policies and lack of investment to build human capital and livable communities leave probation and parole agents and the women they supervise working hard to fashion woman-by-woman solutions to society's shortfalls.

Method and Sample Characteristics

Data were collected from two sequential studies of a subsample of 118 of 402 Michigan women on probation and parole for felony offenses. To obtain the sample of 402 women, a random selection of 77 agents across 16 Michigan counties that could be reached in day trips were asked to participate in the research, and 73 agreed. To allow study of agent relationships with women they supervised, for the women agents supervised, eligibility required the start of supervision about two months prior to study recruitment. I or a co-principal investigator met in person to review each agent's caseload records and draw a random sample of 726 eligible clients. Potential participants were contacted via one of the following methods: agent introduction at the reporting center; with permission, agent-provided contact information given to an interviewer; or agent-provided potential participant contact information so the participant could contact an interviewer. The most common reason for nonparticipation was that the interviewer never made contact (typically, because of phones not in service or residence or contact information being unknown to the agent) or the woman did not show up for one or more scheduled appointments.[1]

AGENT CHARACTERISTICS

Fifty-four agents supervised the 118 women featured in this book. Just under half (24, 44.4%) worked in Wayne County, where Detroit is located. Four worked in Macomb County and three in Oakland County, which are adjacent to Wayne County. Four also worked in Genesee County, where Flint is located, and four worked in Ingham County, which includes the state capital, Lansing. Three worked in each of the counties that were a mix of rural areas, small towns, and cities—Jackson, Oakland, and Saginaw; two worked in Kent County, the location of Grand Rapids; and either one or two worked in each of these counties: Calhoun, Clinton, Eaton, Ionia, Shiawassee, and Washtenaw. The 54 agents included 36 (66.7%) with probation caseloads, 12 (22.2%) with parole caseloads, and 6 (11.1%) with combined probation and parole caseloads.

Fifty-two agents identified as women and two as men. One had a high school education, thirty-eight had completed a bachelor's degree, fourteen had a master's degree, and one had a PhD.

Most of the 54 agents supervised just 1 of the 118 women (24, or 44.4%), 14 (25.9%) supervised 2, 8 (14.8%) supervised 3, and the rest (8, 14.8%) supervised between 4 and 7 women. For the 47 agents with caseload information, the range was 43 to 107 clients, the average was 64.8, and the standard deviation was 15.8.

CHARACTERISTICS OF THE 118 WOMEN

The 118 women had a mean age of 40.0 (standard deviation = 9.2) at the time of the life story interview.[2] Most of the women identified as White (53, 44.9%) or Black (43, 36.4%), 20 (16.9%) as multiracial or Hispanic, one as Native American, and one had missing data. A majority (75, 63.6%) began the study on probation and the rest (43, 36.4%) on parole, with a few on parole and probation at the same time. For the 116 with information, most of the women did not hold full-time jobs at the time of the life story interview: 22 (19.0%) worked full-time, 20 (17.2%) worked part-time, 29 (25.0%) were unable to work due to family care responsibilities or disability, and 45 (38.3%) were unemployed but able to work. For education and training, 85 (73.3%) had graduated from high school or had a GED, and 47 (40.5%) had a job-related license. Over half (64, 55.2%) had attended college, but just 14 (12.1%) had a college degree.

Based on official data, before the initial interview, 49 (41.5%) of the 118 women had been in prison prior to the start of the research. Women with prison time spent an average of 46.5 months in prison. On average, the 118 women had 9.5 prior convictions (standard deviation = 5.1, range = 5-36). Most women (91, 78.4%) were no longer on probation or parole when they told their life stories, and seven were in prison.

PROCEDURE AND INTERVIEW QUESTIONS

The first three interviews were conducted in person in private offices at the reporting centers or other private places convenient to participants, and the fourth and sixth interviews were conducted by phone. The life story interviews were carried out in person. Unless women were in prison, where rules prohibited payment for a follow-up interview, gift cards or U.S. Postal Service money orders were provided for all interviews. Payments were T1 (time 1 interview) $30, T2 $40, T3 $75, T4 $40, T5 (the life story) $75, and T6 $40.

The life story interviews asked women to identity chapters in their lives and how they transitioned between them. Once they had the chapters in mind, follow-up questions asked for high and low points in childhood and again as adults, turning points, religious experiences, wisdom events, and to generate information about identity; for each of these, details of the event and what the event says about them as a person were requested.

All qualitative data were audio-recorded and transcribed except for women interviewed in prison, in which case notes were taken. Agents' case notes for 18 months after the start of supervision were kept in qualitative form to serve as a second source of information on agent actions in the analysis phase. Quantitative data collected during interviews were entered immediately by the interviewer into computer software. The state police provided information on convictions before and after the start of the research, and the Michigan Department of Corrections supplied data on time in prison.

ANALYTIC STRATEGY

I compiled the 118 women's qualitative data into three NVIVO software data sets: (1) all qualitative content from the first four interviews and the final interview, (2) all qualitative data from the life story interview, and (3) a data set that summarized the following from the other two NVIVO files plus demographic and justice system contact information. The summary file included (1) key life events in time order; (2) statements about identity (What does this say about you?) in the order of the events, for example with childhood events first; (3) race; (4) future plans; (5) past challenges; (6) experiences with illness of self and others; (7) religious or spiritual experiences; (8) pattern of convictions and prison incarcerations before, during, and after the interviews; and (9) thoughts about telling the life story. This summary file also included extracts from (10) women's descriptions of crime in the community or neighborhood, (11) efforts to make life better, (12) efforts to secure jobs or safety-net benefits, and (13) interactions and communication with the agent. To be constantly aware of women's stage of life, in the summary file I arranged the women's files in order of their ages at the time they told the life story and included that age at the start of each woman's filename.

Multiple readings of the summary data set, revisits of the other two NVIVO files for more detail and to check on the accuracy of the summaries, and my awareness of issues relevant to women in correctional settings informed the choice of book chapter topics: starting points, conviction-related costs, agent actions, mental health and substance abuse treatment, economic marginalization, endpoints, and reform. For these issues I compiled relevant accounts and their variants so I could identify which were common and which were unique, and to understand intersectionality as it affected women differing in race, life stage, community type and conditions, and access to financial resources. I repeatedly went back to the two full data sets, the official conviction and incarceration data, and the agents' case notes to ensure I was getting the fullest and most accurate picture that the data could provide. After identifying policy and theory-relevant findings, I selected key stories and accounts that illustrated common discoveries but preserved complexities unique to a particular woman.

Notes

1. THE RESEARCH, THE CONTEXT, AND THE REFORM

1. Stephanie Covington, *Helping Women Recover* (San Francisco: Jossey-Bass, 2019); Stephanie S. Covington and Barbara E. Bloom, "Gender Responsive Treatment and Services in Correctional Settings," *Women and Therapy* 29, nos. 3–4 (2007); Nena Messina et al., "Examination of a Violence Prevention Program for Female Offenders," *Violence and Gender* 3, no. 3 (2016); Nena Messina, Stacy Calhoun, and Umme Warda, "Gender-Responsive Drug Court Treatment: A Randomized Controlled Trial," *Criminal Justice and Behavior* 39, no. 12 (2012); Nena Messina et al., "A Randomized Experimental Study of Gender-Responsive Substance Abuse Treatment for Women in Prison," *Journal of Substance Abuse Treatment* 38, no. 2 (2010); and Merry Morash, *Women on Probation and Parole: A Feminist Critique of Community Programs and Services* (Boston: Northeastern University Press, 2010).

2. E. Ann Carson and Rich Kluckow, *Correctional Populations in the United States, 2021—Statistical Tables, 2021* (Washington, DC: U.S. Department of Justice, Bureau of Justice Statistics, 2023); Matthew DeMichele, "Studying the Community Corrections Field: Applying Neo-institutional Theories to a Hidden Element of Mass Social Control," *Theoretical Criminology* 18, no. 4 (2014); Michelle S. Phelps, "The Paradox of Probation: Community Supervision in the Age of Mass Incarceration," *Law and Policy* 35, nos. 1–2 (2013); and Faye S. Taxman, "Community Supervision in the Post Mass Incarceration Era," *Federal Probation* 79, no. 2 (2015).

3. Stephanie Bush-Baskette, "Is Meth the New Crack for Women in the War on Drugs? Factors Affecting Sentencing Outcomes for Women and Parallels between Meth and Crack," *Feminist Criminology* 7, no. 1 (2012); Stephanie Bush-Baskette, "The War on Drugs and the Incarceration of Mothers," *Journal of Drug Issues* 30, no. 4 (2000); Seena Fazel, Isabel A. Yoon, and Adrian J. Hayes, "Substance Use Disorders in Prisoners: An Updated Systematic Review and Meta-Regression Analysis in Recently Incarcerated Men and Women," *Addiction* 112, no. 10 (2017); Noelle E. Fearn et al., "Trends and Correlates of Substance Use Disorders among Probationers and Parolees in the United States 2002–2014," *Drug and Alcohol Dependence* 167 (October 1, 2016); and Shannon M. Lynch et al., *Women's Pathways to Jail: Examining Mental Health, Trauma, and Substance Use* (Washington, DC: U.S. Department of Justice, 2013).

4. Mary Bosworth, "Resistance and Compliance in Women's Prisons: Towards a Critique of Legitimacy," *Critical Criminology* 7, no. 2 (Autumn 1996); Peggy C. Giordano, Stephen A. Cernkovich, and Jennifer L. Rudolph, "Gender, Crime, and Desistance: Toward a Theory of Cognitive Transformation," *American Journal of Sociology* 107, no. 4 (January 2002); and Morash, *Women on Probation and Parole.*

5. Pat Carlen, *Women, Crime and Poverty* (Milton Keynes, England: Open University Press, 1988); Kathleen Daly, "Women's Pathways to Felony Court: Feminist Theories of Lawbreaking and Problems of Representation," *Southern California Review of Law and Women's Studies* 2, no. 1 (1992); and Lisa Maher and Kathleen Daly, "Women in the Street-Level Drug Economy: Continuity or Change?," *Criminology* 3, no. 4 (1996).

6. Patricia Hill Collins, *Black Feminist Thought: Knowledge, Consciousness, and the Politics of Empowerment* (Boston: Unwin Hyman, 1990); Kimberlé Crenshaw, "Demarginalizing the Intersection of Race and Sex: A Black Feminist Critique of Antidiscrimination Doctrine, Feminist Theory and Antiracist Politics," *University of Chicago Legal Forum* 14 (1989); Kimberlé Crenshaw, "Mapping the Margins: Intersectionality, Identity Politics, and Violence against Women of Color," *Stanford Law Review* 43, no. 6 (1991); and bell hooks, *Ain't I a Woman: Black Women and Feminism* (Boston: South End Press, 1981).

7. Nicholas W. Bakken and Christy A. Visher, "Successful Reintegration and Mental Health," *Criminal Justice and Behavior* 45 (2018); Beth M. Huebner, Christina DeJong, and Jennifer E. Cobbina, "Women Coming Home: Long-Term Patterns of Recidivism," *Justice Quarterly* 27, no. 2 (2010); Margot Kushel et al., "Revolving Doors: Imprisonment amongst the Homeless and Marginally Housed Population," *American Journal of Public Health* 95 (2005); and Christy K. Scott et al., "Predictors of Recidivism over 3 Years among Substance-Using Women Released from Jail," *Criminal Justice and Behavior* 41, no. 11 (2014).

8. D. A. Andrews and James Bonta, *Psychology of Criminal Conduct*, 5th ed. (Newark, New Jersey: LexisNexis, 2010). For critiques of the emphasis on the individual, see Pat Carlen and Jacqueline Tombs, "Reconfigurations of Penalty: The Ongoing Case of the Women's Imprisonment and Reintegration Industries," *Theoretical Criminology* 10, no. 3 (2006); Marie Gottschalk, *Caught: The Prison State and the Lockdown of American Politics* (Princeton, New

Jersey: Princeton University Press, 2015), 18; and Jill A. McCorkel, "Criminally Dependent? Gender, Punishment, and the Rhetoric of Welfare Reform," *Social Politics* 11, no. 3 (2004).

9. Merry Morash et al., "Narrative Identity Development and Desistance from Illegal Behavior among Substance-Using Female Offenders: Implications for Narrative Therapy and Creating Opportunity," *Sex Roles* 83, nos. 1–2 (2020).

10. Robyn Fivush et al., "Gender Differences in Parent-Child Emotion Narratives," *Sex Roles* 42, nos. 3–4 (2000); and Jefferson A. Singer, "Narrative Identity and Meaning Making across the Adult Lifespan: An Introduction," *Journal of Personality* 72, no. 3 (2004).

11. Robyn Fivush and Kelly Marin, "Development of a Gendered Narrative Identity," in *APA Handbook of the Psychology of Women: History, Theory and Battlegrounds*, ed. Cheryl B. Travis et al. (Washington, DC: American Psychological Association, 2018); and Singer, "Narrative Identity and Meaning Making."

12. Kayla M. Hoskins and Merry Morash, "How Women on Probation and Parole Incorporate Trauma into Their Identities," *Journal of Interpersonal Violence* 36, nos. 23–24 (2021); Shadd Maruna, *Making Good: How Ex-Convicts Reform and Rebuild their Lives* (Washington, DC: American Psychological Association Books, 2001); and Dan P. McAdams, *The Redemptive Self: Stories Americans Live By* (New York: Oxford University Press, 2013).

13. Morash et al., "Narrative Identity Development and Desistance from Illegal Behavior"; and Rebecca Stone et al., "Women on Parole, Identity Processes, and Primary Desistance," *Feminist Criminology* 13, no. 4 (2018).

14. Joanne Belknap, *The Invisible Woman*, 5th ed. (Los Angeles: Sage, 2021); Barbara Bloom et al., *Gender-Responsive Strategies: Research, Practice, and Guiding Principles for Women Offenders* (Washington, DC: National Institute of Corrections, 2003); Covington and Bloom, "Gender Responsive Treatment and Services in Correctional Settings"; Daly, "Women's Pathways to Felony Court"; and Beth E. Richie, *Compelled to Crime: The Gender Entrapment of Battered Black Women* (New York: Routledge, 1996).

15. Dan P. McAdams, "Coding Systems for Themes of Agency and Communion," 2002, https://sites.northwestern.edu/thestudyoflivesresearchgroup/instruments/; Dan P. McAdams, *Coding Autobiographical Episodes for Themes of Agency and Communion* (Evanston, Illinois: Foley Center for the Study of Lives, Northwestern University, 1992); and "The Life Story Interview," The Foley Center, 2008, https://sites.northwestern.edu/thestudyoflivesresearchgroup/instruments/. The life story interview schedule was based on questions and the coding schemes that were central to the development of narrative identity theory.

16. Joey Sprague, *Feminist Methods for Critical Researchers: Bridging Differences* (Walnut Creek, California: Altamira Press, 2005), 169–73.

17. Sprague, *Feminist Methods for Critical Researchers*, 195.

18. For a description of the interviewers' backgrounds, see Merry Morash and Deborah A. Kashy, "The Relevance of Women's Economic Marginalization to Recidivism," *Criminal Justice and Behavior* 49, no. 3 (2022).

19. Emily J. Salisbury, Breanna Boppre, and Bridget Kelly, "Gender-Responsive Risk and Need Assessment: Implications for the Treatment of Justice-Involved

Women," in *Handbook on Risk and Need Asessment: Theory and Practice*, ed. Faye S. Taxman (New York: Routledge, 2017). For a detailed description of the WRNA as modified for the research, see Morash and Kashy, "Relevance of Women's Economic Marginalization to Recidivism."

20. Sandra Morgen, Joan Acker, and Jill Weight, *Stretched Thin: Poor Families Welfare Work, and Welfare Reform* (Ithaca, New York: Cornell University Press, 2010); and Tony Platt, "The State of Welfare: United States 2003," *Monthly Review* 55, no. 5 (2003); Anna Marie Smith, "Neoliberalism, Welfare Policy, and Feminist Theories of Social Justice," in "Feminist Theory and Welfare," special issue, *Feminist Theory* 9, no. 2 (2008).

21. Charis E. Kubrin and Eric A. Stewart, "Predicting Who Reoffends: The Neglected Role of Neighborhood Context in Recidivism Studies," *Criminology* 44, no. 1 (2006); Robert J. Sampson, *Great American City: Chicago and the Enduring Neighborhood Effect* (Chicago: University of Chicago Press, 2012); and Robert J. Sampson, Jeffrey D. Morenoff, and Thomas Gannon-Rowley, "Assessing 'Neighborhood Effects': Social Processes and New Directions in Research," *Annual Review of Sociology* 28 (2002).

22. Alan Mallach, *The Divided City: Poverty and Prosperity in Urban America* (Washington, DC: Island Press, 2018), 34.

23. Douglas S. Massey and Mary J. Fisher, "How Segregation Concentrated Poverty," *Ethnic and Racial Studies* 23 (2010); and Ruth D. Peterson and Lauren J. Krivo, *Divergent Social Worlds: Neighborhood Crime and the Racial-Spatial Divide* (New York: Russell Sage Foundation, 2010).

24. Sampson, *Great American City*, 272.

25. Phil Gramm and Mike Solon, "If You Like Michigan's Economy, You'll Love Obama's," *Wall Street Journal Eastern Edition*, September 13, 2008.

26. Elizabeth McNichol et al., *Pulling Apart: A State-by-State Analysis of Income Trends*, Center on Budget and Policy Priorities, Washington, DC, 2012, www.cbpp.org/research/poverty-and-inequality/pulling-apart-a-state-by-state-analysis-of-income-trends.

27. Economic Innovation Group, *The 2016 Distressed Communities Index*, Washington, DC, https://eig.org/wp-content/uploads/2016/02/2016-Distressed-Communities-Index-Report.pdf.

28. Judith Berman, *Women Offender Transition and Reentry: Gender Responsive Approaches to Transitioning Women Offenders from Prison to the Community* (Washington, DC: U.S. Department of Justice, National Institute of Corrections, 2005); Scott H. Decker et al., "Criminal Stigma, Race, and Ethnicity: The Consequences of Imprisonment for Employment," *Journal of Criminal Justice* 43, no. 2 (2015); Natalie Ortiz, "The Gendering of Criminal Stigma: An Experiment Testing the Effects of Race/Ethnicity and Incarceration on Women's Entry-Level Job Prospects" (PhD diss., Arizona State University, 2014); and Devah Pager, Bruce Western, and Naomi Sugie, "Sequencing Disadvantage: Barriers to Employment Facing Young Black and White Men with Criminal Records," *Annals of the American Academy of Political and Social Science* 623 (2009).

29. Harry Holzer, "The Spatial Mismatch Hypothesis: What Has the Evidence Shown?" *Urban Studies* 28, no. 1 (1991); and Solveig Spjeldnes and Sara

Goodkind, "Gender Differences and Offender Reentry: A Review of the Literature," *Journal of Offender Rehabilitation* 48, no. 4 (May 1, 2009).

30. Lucius Couloute and Daniel Kopf, *Out of Prison and Out of Work: Unemployment among Formerly Incarcerated People* (Northhampton, MA: Prison Policy Initiative, 2018).

31. Karen Heimer, "Changes in the Gender Gap in Crime and Women's Economic Marginalization," in *From the Nature of Crime: Continuity and Change; Criminal Justice 2000*, ed. Gary LaFree (Washington DC: National Institute of Justice, 2000); and Kristy Holtfreter, Michael D. Reisig, and Merry Morash, "Poverty, State Capital, and Recidivism among Women Offenders," *Criminology and Public Policy* 3, no. 2 (2004).

32. At the first interview, 17 of the 118 women reported income over $10,000 a year, and 3 did not answer the question about income. At the end of the first year of supervision, 22 reported income over $10,000 a year, and 2 did not answer the question about income.

33. Kathryn Edin and Maria Kefala, *Promises I Can Keep: Why Poor Women Put Motherhood before Marriage* (Berkeley: University of California Press, 2005); Kathryn Edin and Laura Lein, *Making Ends Meet: How Single Mothers Survive Welfare and Low-Wage Work* (New York: Russell Sage Foundation, 1997); and Kaaryn S. Gustafson, *Cheating Welfare: Public Assistance and the Criminalization of Poverty* (New York: New York University Press, 2012).

34. Scott W. Allard, *Out of Reach: Place, Poverty, and the New American Welfare State* (New Haven, Connecticut: Yale University Press, 2009); and Liz Schott, Ladonna Pavetti, and Ife Finch, *How States Have Spent Federal and State Funds under the TANF Block Grant*, Center on Budget and Policy Priorities, Washington, DC, 2012, https://www.cbpp.org/research/how-states-have -spent-federal-and-state-funds-under-the-tanf-block-grant.

35. Francis Fox Piven, "Welfare Reform and the Cultural Reconstruction of Low-Wage Labor Markets," in *New Poverty Studies: The Ethnography of Power, Politics, and Impoverished People in the United States*, ed. Judith G. Goode and Jeff Maskovsky (New York: New York University Press, 2001).

36. Rebecca M. Blank, *It Takes a Nation: A New Agenda for Fighting Poverty* (Princeton, New Jersey: Princeton University Press, 1997); Janice Peterson, Xue Song, and Avis Jones-DeWeever, *Life after Welfare Reform: Low-Income Single Parent Families, Pre- and Post-TANF*, Women's Policy Research, Washington, DC, 2002, https://iwpr.org/wp-content/uploads/2020/12/d446.pdf; and Nancy E. Rose, "Scapegoating Poor Women: An Analysis of Welfare Reform," *Journal of Economic Issues* 35, no. 1 (2000).

37. Sheldon Danziger et al., "Health Insurance and Access to Care among Welfare Leavers," *Inquiry* 45, no. 2 (2008); Pamela Loprest, *How Are Families that Left Welfare Doing? A Comparison of Early and Recent Welfare Leavers*, 2001, www.urban.org/sites/default/files/publication/61306/310282-How-Are -Families-That-Left-Welfare-Doing-.PDF; and LaDonna Pavetti, *Work Requirements Don't Cut Poverty, Evidence Shows*, Center on Budget and Policy Priorities, Washington, DC, 2016, https://www.cbpp.org/sites/default/files/atoms/files /6-6-16pov3.pdf.

38. Harold A. Pollack and Peter Reuter, "Welfare Receipt and Substance-Abuse Treatment among Low-Income Mothers: The Impact of Welfare Reform," *American Journal of Public Health* 96, no. 11 (2006).

39. Sean R. Hogan et al., "Social Welfare Policy and Public Assistance for Low-Income Substance Abusers: The Impact of 1996 Welfare Reform Legislation on the Economic Security of Former Supplemental Security Income Drug Addiction and Alcoholism Beneficiaries," *Journal of Sociology and Social Welfare* 35, no. 1 (2008); Taryn Lindhorst and Ronald J. Mancoske, "The Social and Economic Impact of Sanctions and Time Limits on Recipients of Temporary Assistance to Needy Families," *Journal of Sociology and Social Welfare* 33, no. 1 (2006); Marcia K. Meyers et al., *Review of Research on TANF Sanctions: Report to Washington State Workfirst Subcabinet* (Seattle, WA: West Coast Poverty Center, 2006); Quinn Moore, Robert G. Wood, and Anu Rangarajan, "The Dynamics of Women Disconnected from Employment and Welfare," *Social Service Review* 86, no. 1 (2012); Jean C. Norris et al., "Homelessness, Hunger, and Material Hardship among Those Who Lost SSI," *Contemporary Drug Problems* 30, nos. 1–2 (2003); Robert G. Orwin et al., "Welfare Reform and Addiction: A Priori Hypothesis, Post Hoc Explorations, and Assisted Sensemaking in Evaluating the Effects of Terminating Benefits for Chronic Substance Abusers," *American Journal of Evaluation* 25, no. 4 (2004); and Nancy E. Reichman, Julien O. Teitler, and Marah A. Curtis, "TANF Sanctioning and Hardship," *Social Service Review* 79, no. 2 (2005).

40. Danilo Trisi and LaDonna Pavetti, *TANF Weakening as a Safety Net for Poor Families*, Center on Budget and Policy Priorities, Washington, DC, 2012, www.cbpp.org/research/tanf-weakening-as-a-safety-net-for-poor-families.

41. Patricia Allard, *Life Sentences: Denying Welfare Benefits to Women Convicted of Drug Offenses*, The Sentencing Project, Washington, DC, 2002, www.opensocietyfoundations.org/publications/life-sentences-denying-welfare-benefits-women-convicted-drug-offenses.

42. Liz Schott and LaDonna Pavetti, *Many States Cutting TANF Benefits Harshly Despite High Unemployment and Unprecedented Need*, Center on Budget and Policy Priorities, Washington, DC, 2011, www.cbpp.org/research/many-states-cutting-tanf-benefits-harshly-despite-high-unemployment-and-unprecedented-need.

43. Sarah Halpern-Meekin et al., *It's Not Like I'm Poor: How Working Families Make Ends Meet in a Post-Welfare World* (Oakland: University of California Press, 2015).

44. National Low Income Housing Coalition, "America's Affordable Housing Shortage, and How to End It," *Housing Spotlight* 3, no. 2 (2013).

45. Schott and Pavetti, *Many States Cutting TANF Benefits Harshly*.

46. Doris L. MacKenzie, "First Do No Harm: A Look at Correctional Policies and Programs Today," *Journal of Experimental Criminology* 9, no. 1 (2013); Benjamin Steiner et al., "The Correctional Orientation of Community Corrections: Legislative Changes in the Legally Prescribed Functions of Community Corrections 1992–2002," *American Journal of Criminal Justice* 29, no. 2 (2005).

47. Michigan Comprehensive Laws, Community Corrections Act., Ch. 791. 401–14 (1988); and Dennis Schrantz, Stephen DeBor, and Marc Mauer,

Decarceration Strategies: How 5 States Achieved Substantial Prison Population Reductions (Washington, DC: The Sentencing Project, 2018).

48. Michigan Department of Corrections, *Michigan Department of Corrections: Field Operations Administration, Community Alternatives (Annual Report)* (Lansing: Michigan Department of Corrections, 2012).

49. Schrantz, DeBor, and Mauer, *Decarceration Strategies*.

50. Krissi Jimroglou, *U.S. Prison Count Continues to Drop*, Pew Charitable Trusts, Washington, DC, 2013, www.pewtrusts.org/en/about/news-room/press -releases-and-statements/2013/03/08/us-prison-count-continues-to-drop.

51. Lori Brusman Lovins et al., "Probation Officer as a Coach: Building a New Professional Identity," *Federal Probation* 82, no. 1 (2018).

52. Merry Morash et al., "Technical Violations, Treatment and Punishment Responses, and Subsequent Recidivism of Women on Probation and Parole," *Criminal Justice Policy Review* 30, no. 5 (2019).

53. Bloom et al., *Gender-Responsive Strategies*.

54. *American Psychological Association Dictionary*, https://dictionary.apa .org/motivational-interviewing.

55. Kristy Holtfreter and Katelyn A. Wattanaporn, "The Transition from Prison to Community Initiative," *Criminal Justice and Behavior* 41, no. 1 (2014).

56. After completion of research for this book, MDOC no longer contracted directly with services but instead relied on the Michigan Department of Health and Human Services, which provides access through Prepaid Inpatient Health Plans and Community Mental Health Services programs. Prioritized groups include pregnant injecting drug users and other substance users, nonpregnant injecting drug users, parents at risk of losing children, and individuals supervised by and referred by MDOC or released from prison and referred by MDOC.

57. The measure used was developed by Jennifer L. Skeem et al., "Assessing Relationship Quality in Mandated Community Treatment: Blending Care with Control," *Psychological Assessment* 19, no. 4 (2007).

2. STARTING POINTS

1. Tim Brennan et al., "Women's Pathways to Serious and Habitual Crime: A Person-Centered Analysis Incorporating Gender Responsive Factors," *Criminal Justice and Behavior* 39, no. 2 (2012); Meda Chesney-Lind and Randall G. Sheldon, *Girls, Delinquency and Juvenile Justice*, 3d ed. (Belmont, California: Wadsworth/Thompson Learning, 2004); Jennifer E. Cobbina, "From Prison to Home: Women's Pathways in and out of Crime" (PhD diss., University of Missouri–St. Louis, 2009); Dana DeHart et al., "Life History Models of Female Offending: The Roles of Serious Mental Illness and Trauma in Women's Pathways to Jail," *Psychology of Women Quarterly* 38, no. 1 (2014); Emily Gaardner and Joanne Belknap, "Tenuous Borders: Girls Transferred to Adult Court," *Criminology* 40 (2002); and Peggy C. Giordano, *Legacies of Crime: A Follow-Up of the Children of Highly Delinquent Girls and Boys* (New York: Cambridge University Press, 2010).

2. Vera Lopez, *Complicated Lives: Girls, Parents, Drugs, and Juvenile Justice* (New Brunswick, New Jersey: Rutgers University Press, 2017); and Amy M.

Young and Hannah d'Arcy, "Older Boyfriends of Adolescent Girls: The Cause or a Sign of the Problem?," *Journal of Adolescent Health* 36, no. 5 (2005).

3. Analysis of the full sample of women uncovered a small number of women whose start in illegal activity was during adulthood. Most were influenced by male partners to use drugs or to drink excessively and to commit a variety of crimes.

4. Monique W. Morris, *Pushout: The Criminalization of Black Girls in Schools* (New York: The New Press, 2016); and Sandra B. Simkins et al., "The School to Prison Pipeline for Girls: The Role of Physical and Sexual Abuse," *Harvard Civil Rights Journal* 24, no. 4 (2004).

5. Regina A. Arnold, "Processes of Victimization and Criminalization of Black Women," *Social Justice* 17, no. 3 (1990); Meda Chesney-Lind and Lisa J. Pasko, *The Female Offender: Girls, Women, and Crime*, 3d ed. (Los Angeles: Sage, 2013); and Meda Chesney-Lind and Noelie Rodriguez, *Women under Lock and Key: A View from the Inside* (Manoa: Youth Development and Research Center, School of Social Work, University of Hawaii, 1983).

6. Malika Saada Saar et al., *The Sexual Abuse to Prison Pipeline: The Girls' Story*, Human Rights Project for Girls, Center on Poverty and inequality at Georgetown Law, and Ms. Foundation for Women, Washington, DC, 2015, https://rights4girls.org/wp-content/uploads/r4g/2015/02/2015_COP_sexual -abuse_layout_web-1.pdf.

7. Kayla M. Hoskins and Merry Morash, "How Women on Probation and Parole Incorporate Trauma into Their Identities," *Journal of Interpersonal Violence* 36, nos. 23–24 (2021).

8. Laurie Schaffner, *Girls in Trouble with the Law* (New Brunswick, New Jersey: Rutgers University Press, 2006), 206.

9. Lopez, *Complicated Lives*.

10. UNICEF, *Ending Child Marriage: Progress and Prospects* (New York: United Nations Children's Fund, 2014); and UNICEF, *Committing to Child Survival: A Promise Renewed*, (New York: UNICEF's Division of Policy and Strategy, 2012).

11. Patricia K. Kerig, "Polyvictimization and Girls' Involvement in the Juvenile Justice System: Investigating Gender-Differentiated Patterns of Risk, Recidivism, and Resilience," *Journal of Interpersonal Violence* 33, no. 5 (2018); and Simon Pemberton, Susie Balderston, and Jo Long, *Trauma, Harm and Offending Behaviour: What Works to Address Social Injury and Criminogenic Need with Criminal Justice Involved Women? Initial Findings*, (Birmingham, England: University of Birmingham, 2019).

12. Matthias Domhardt et al., "Resilience in Survivors of Child Sexual Abuse: A Systematic Review of the Literature," *Trauma, Violence, and Abuse* 18, no. 4 (2015).

13. Kate Theimer and David J. Hansen, "Attributions of Blame in a Hypothetical Child Sexual Abuse Case: Roles of Behavior Problems and Frequency of Abuse," *Journal of Interpersonal Violence* 35, nos. 11–12 (2020).

14. Kathryn C. Monahan et al., "From the School Yard to the Squad Car: School Discipline, Truancy, and Arrest," *Journal of Youth and Adolescence* 43, no. 7 (2014); and Morris, *Pushout*.

15. Alan Carr, Hollie Duff, and Fiona Craddock, "A Systematic Review of Reviews of the Outcome of Noninstitutional Child Maltreatment," *Trauma, Violence, and Abuse* 21, no. 4 (2020); Jordan P. Davis et al., "Longitudinal Effects of Adverse Childhood Experiences on Substance Use Transition Patterns During Young Adulthood," *Child Abuse and Neglect* 120 (October 2021); and Nancy R. Downing, Marvellous Akinlotan, and Carly W. Thornhill, "The Impact of Childhood Sexual Abuse and Adverse Childhood Experiences on Adult Health Related Quality of Life," *Child Abuse and Neglect* 120 (October 2021).

16. Katherine Irwin, Lisa Pasko, and Janet T. Davidson, "Girls and Women in Conflict with the Law," in *Routledge Handbook of Critical Criminology*, ed. Walter S. DeKeseredy and Molly Dragiewicz (New York: Routledge, 2018); Darrell Steffensmeier et al., "An Assessment of Recent Trends in Girls' Violence Using Diverse Sources: Is the Gender Gap Closing?," *Criminology* 43, no. 2 (2005); and Tia Stevens, Merry Morash, and Meda Chesney-Lind, "Are Girls Getting Tougher, or Are We Tougher on Girls? Probability of Arrest and Juvenile Court Oversight in 1980 and 2000," *Justice Quarterly* 28, no. 5 (2011).

17. Elliot Currie, *A Peculiar Indifference: The Neglected Toll of Violence on Black America* (New York: Metropolitan Books, 2020); and Treva B. Lindsey, *America, Goddam: Violence, Black Women, and the Struggle for Justice* (Oakland: University of California Press, 2021).

18. Theimer and Hansen, "Attributions of Blame in a Hypothetical Child Sexual Abuse Case."

19. Domhardt et al., "Resilience in Survivors of Child Sexual Abuse."

20. Robert F. Anda et al., "The Enduring Effects of Abuse and Related Adverse Experiences in Childhood: A Convergence of Evidence from Neurobiology and Epidemiology," *European Archives of Psychiatry and Clinical Neuroscience* 256, no. 3 (2006); Christopher R. DeCou et al., "Evaluating the Association between Childhood Sexual Abuse and Attempted Suicide across the Lifespan: Findings from a Nationwide Study of Women in Jail," *Psychological Services* 13, no. 2 (2016); Shanta R. Dube et al., "Adverse Childhood Experiences and the Association with Ever Using Alcohol and Initiating Alcohol Use during Adolescence," *Journal of Adolescent Health* 38, no. 4 (2006); Kevin Lalor and Rosaleen McElvaney, "Child Sexual Abuse, Links to Later Sexual Exploitation/High-Risk Sexual Behavior, and Prevention/Treatment Programs," *Trauma, Violence, and Abuse* 11, no. 4 (2010); Elaine Loudermilk et al., "Impact of Adverse Childhood Experiences (Aces) on Adult Alcohol Consumption Behavior," *Child Abuse and Neglect* 86 (2018); and Matthew D. Moore and Anthony W. Tatman, "Adverse Childhood Experiences and Offender Risk to Re-Offend in the United States: A Quantitative Examination," *International Journal of Criminal Justice Sciences* 11, no. 2 (2016).

21. Gregor J. Jurkovic, *Lost Childhoods: The Plight of the Parentrified Child* (New York: Routledge, 2014); and Lopez, *Complicated Lives*.

22. Susan Dewey et al., *Outlaw Women: Prison, Rural Violence, and Poverty in the American West* (New York: New York University Press, 2019); and April N. Terry and L. Susan Williams, "On the Outside Looking In: Rural Girls, Trauma, and Involvement in the Criminal Justice System," *Journal of Aggression, Maltreatment and Trauma* 30, no. 3 (2021).

23. Eveline A. Crone, *The Adolescent Brain: Changes in Learning, Decision-Making and Social Relations* (New York: Routledge, 2017); and Meredith A. Gruhn and Bruce E. Compas, "Effects of Maltreatment on Coping and Emotional Regulation in Childhood and Adolescence: A Meta-Analytic Review," *Child Abuse and Neglect* 103 (2020).

3. COSTS OF CONVICTION

1. Alexes Harris, Mary Pattillo, and Bryan L. Sykes, "Studying the System of Monetary Sanctions," *RSF: The Russell Sage Foundation Journal of the Social Sciences* 8, no. 1 (2022); and Ebony L. Ruhland et al., "Monetary Sanctions in Community Corrections: Law, Policy, and their Alignment with Correctional Goals," *Journal of Contemporary Criminal Justice* 37, no. 1 (2021).

2. Mario Salas and Angela Ciolfi, *Driven by Dollars: A State-by-State Analysis of Driver's License Suspension Laws for Failure to Pay Court Debt* (Charlottsville, Virginia: Legal Aid Justice Center, 2017).

3. Ruhland et al., "Monetary Sanctions in Community Corrections."

4. Michigan Supreme Court, State Court Administrative Office, 2016.

5. Mich. Comp. Laws § 771.3(6)(a).

6. Amerian Civil Liberties Union, *In for a Penny: The Rise of America's New Debtors' Prison*, (New York: American Civil Liberties Union, 2010).

7. Amerian Civil Liberties Union, *In for a Penny*; April D. Fernandes et al., "Monetary Sanctions: A Review of Revenue Generation, Legal Challenges, and Reform," *Annual Review of Law and Social Science* 15, no. 1 (2019); and Chris Mai and Maria Katarina E. Rafael, "User Funded? Using Budgets to Examine the Scope and Revenue Impact of Fines and Fees in the Criminal Justice System," *Sociological Perspectives* 63, no. 6 (2020).

8. Amerian Civil Liberties Union, *In for a Penny*.

9. Lindsay Bing, Becky Pettit, and Ilya Slavinski, "Incomparable Punishments: How Economic Inequality Contributes to the Disparate Impact of Legal Fines and Fees," *Russell Sage Foundation Journal of the Social Sciences* 8, no. 2 (2022); Michele Cadigan and Gabriela Kirk, "On Thin Ice: Bureaucratic Processes of Monetary Sanctions and Job Insecurity," *RSF: The Russell Sage Foundation Journal of the Social Sciences* 6, no. 1 (2020); Alexes Harris, *A Pound of Flesh: Monetary Sanctions as Punishment for the Poor* (New York: Russell Sage Foundation, 2016); Alexes Harris and Tyler Smith, "Monetary Sanctions as Chronic and Acute Health Stressors: The Emotional Strain of People Who Owe Court Fines and Fees," *RSF: The Russell Sage Foundation Journal of the Social Sciences* 8, no. 2 (2022); Mary Pattillo and Gabriela Kirk, "Layaway Freedom: Coercive Financialization in the Criminal Legal System," *American Journal of Sociology* 126, no. 4 (2021); and Christopher Uggen and Robert Stewart, "Piling On: Collateral Consequences and Community Supervision," *Minnesota Law Review* 99 (2015).

10. Bing, Pettit, and Ilya, "Incomparable Punishments." This study similarly found that people forwent or delayed education to pay off their debts.

11. Also see Cadigan and Kirk, "On Thin Ice"; and Mary Pattillo et al., "Monetary Sanctions and Housing Instability," *RSF: The Russell Sage Foundation Journal of the Social Sciences* 8, no. 2 (2022).

12. Bing, Pettit, and Slavinski, "Incomparable Punishments"; Harris and Smith, "Monetary Sanctions as Chronic and Acute Health Stressors"; and Breanne Pleggenkuhle, "The Financial Cost of a Criminal Conviction: Context and Consequences," *Criminal Justice and Behavior* 45, no. 1 (2018).

13. For further documentation of this pattern in Michigan and other states, see Amerian Civil Liberties Union, *In for a Penny*; and Marie Gottschalk, *Caught: The Prison State and the Lockdown of American Politics* (Princeton, New Jersey: Princeton University Press, 2015).

14. Harris and Smith, "Monetary Sanctions as Chronic and Acute Health Stressors."

15. Lily Gleicher and Caitlin DeLong, *The Cost of Justice: The Impact of Criminal Justice Financial Obligations on Individuals and Families*, Illinois Criminal Justice Authority, 2018, https://icjia.illinois.gov/researchhub/articles/the-cost-of-justice-the-impact-of-criminal-justice-financial-obligations-on-individuals-and-families. This study of 318 people with court costs in Illinois found that almost three-quarters of them had to choose between buying groceries and paying legal financial obligations, and nearly as high a proportion had to choose between paying utility and rent or mortgages and legal financial obligations

16. Pattillo and Kirk, "Layaway Freedom.

17. The women named the counties, but to maintain their anonymity, these names are not included here.

18. Margaret Costello, "Fulfilling the Unfulfilled Promise of Gideon: Litigation as a Viable Strategic Tool," *Iowa Law Review* 99 (2014).

19. Pattillo and Kirk, "Layaway Freedom."

20. Bing, Pettit, and Slavinski, "Incomparable Punishments"; and Raj Chetty et al., "Race and Economic Opportunity in the United States: An Intergenerational Perspective," *Quarterly Journal of Economics* 135, no. 2 (2020).

4. AGENT ACTIONS

1. Emily J. Salisbury, Breanna Boppre, and Bridget Kelly, "Gender-Responsive Risk and Need Assessment: Implications for the Treatment of Justice-Involved Women," in *Handbook on Risk and Need Assessment: Theory and Practice*, ed. Faye S. Taxman (New York: Routledge, 2017); and Patricia Van Voorhis, "On Behalf of Women Offenders: Women's Place in the Science of Evidence-Based Practice," *Criminology and Public Policy* 11, no. 2 (2012).

2. Patrick. J. Kennealy et al., "Firm, Fair, and Caring Officer-Offender Relationships Protect against Supervision Failure," *Law and Human Behavior* 36, no. 6 (2012); Merry Morash et al., "The Connection of Probation/Parole Officer Actions to Women Offenders' Recidivism," *Criminal Justice and Behavior* 43, no. 4 (2016); Merry Morash et al., "The Effects of Probation or Parole Agent Relationship Style and Women Offenders' Criminogenic Needs on Offenders' Responses to Supervision Interactions," *Criminal Justice and Behavior* 42, no. 4 (2015); and Jennifer L. Skeem et al., "Assessing Relationship Quality in Mandated Community Treatment: Blending Care with Control," *Psychological Assessment* 19, no. 4 (2007).

3. Sheryl Pimlott Kubiak et al., "Differences among Incarcerated Women with Assaultive Offenses: Isolated versus Patterned Use of Violence," *Journal of Interpersonal Violence* 28, no. 12 (2013); and Merry Morash et al., "Characteristics and Context of Women Probationers and Parolees Who Engage in Violence," *Criminal Justice and Behavior* 45, no. 3 (2018).

4. Jennifer Cornacchione and Sandi W. Smith, "Female Offenders' Multiple Goals for Engaging in Desired Communication with Their Probation/Parole Officers," *Communication Quarterly* 65, no. 1 (2017).

5. This type of placement is no longer used by MDOC.

6. Kerwin K. Charles and Ming Ching Luoh, "Male Incarceration, the Marriage Market, and Female Outcomes," *Review of Economics and Statistics* 92, no. 3 (2010); Todd R. Clear, *Imprisoning Communities: How Mass Incarceration Makes Disadvantaged Neighborhoods Worse* (New York: Oxford University Press, 2007); and Bruce Western and Christopher Wildeman, "The Black Family and Mass Incarceration," *Annals of the American Academy of Political and Social Science* 621, no. 1 (2009).

7. Robert Hampton, William Oliver, and Lucia Magarian, "Domestic Violence in the African American Community: An Analysis of Social and Structural Factors," *Violence Against Women* 9, no. 5 (2003); Esther J. Jenkins, "Community Insights on Domestic Violence among African Americans," *Journal of Aggression, Maltreatment and Trauma* 30, no. 6 (2021); Emiko Petrosky et al., "Racial and Ethnic Differences in Homicides of Adult Women and the Role of Intimate Partner Violence—United States, 2003–2014," *Morbidity and Mortality Weekly Report* 66, no. 28 (2017); Sharon G. Smith et al., *The National Intimate Partner and Sexual Violence Survey (NISVS): 2010–2012* (Atlanta, Georgia, Centers for Disease Control and Prevention, 2017).

8. Sandi W. Smith et al., "Communication Style as an Antecedent to Reactance, Self-Efficacy, and Restoration of Freedom for Drug- and Alcohol-Involved Women on Probation and Parole," *Journal of Health Communication* 21, no. 5 (2016).

9. Jennifer L. Skeem, John Encandela, and Jennifer Eno Louden, "Perspectives on Probation and Mandated Mental Health Treatment in Specialized and Traditional Probation Departments," *Behavioral Sciences and the Law* 21 (2003); and Skeem et al., "Assessing Relationship Quality in Mandated Community Treatment."

10. Jennifer Cornacchione et al., "An Exploration of Female Offenders' Memorable Messages from Probation and Parole Officers on the Self-Assessment of Behavior from a Control Theory Perspective," *Journal of Applied Communication Research* 44, no. 1 (2016).

5. TREATMENT

1. "State of Mental Health in America—Ranking the States," Mental Health America, 2017.

2. Department of Health and Human Services, *National Survey of Substance Abuse Treatment Services (N-SSATS): 2011 Data on Substance Abuse Treatment Facilities*, Substance Abuse and Mental Health Services Administration,

Rockville, Maryland, 2012, https://mhanational.org/issues/2017-state-mental-health-america-ranking-states.

3. Community Mental Health Association of Michigan, *Addressing the Systemic Underfunding of Michigan's Public Mental Health System*, 2019, https://cmham.org/wp-content/uploads/2019/03/Systemic-underfunding-of-Michigans-public-mental-health-system-rev.pdf.

4. Hannah S. Bell et al., "Medicaid Reform, Responsiblization Policies, and the Synergism of Barriers to Low-Income Health Seeking," *Human Organization* 76, no. 3 (2017).

5. Michigan Department of Health and Human Services, *Person-Centered Planning Pratice Guideline*, Lansing, 2021, www.michigan.gov/documents/mdhhs/Person-Centered_Planning_Practice_Guideline_702780_7.pdf, 1.

6. Lynne Haney, *Offending Women: Power, Punishment, and the Regulation of Desire* (Berkeley: University of California Press, 2010); Jill A. McCorkel, *Breaking Women: Gender, Race, and the New Politics of Imprisonment* (New York: New York University Press, 2013); Emma J. Palmer et al., "Cognitive Skills Programs for Female Offenders in the Community," *Criminal Justice and Behavior* 42, no. 4 (2015); and Susan Starr Sered and Maureen Norton-Hawk, *Can't Catch a Break: Gender, Jail, Drugs and the Limits of Personal Responsibility* (Oakland: University of California Press, 2014).

7. Rosemary L. Gido and Lanette Dalley, *Women's Mental Health Issues across the Criminal Justice System* (Upper Saddle River, New Jersey: Prentice Hall, 2009); Shannon M. Lynch et al., "A Multisite Study of the Prevalence of Serious Mental Illness, PTSD, and Substance Use Disorders of Women in Jail," *Psychiatric Services* 65, no. 5 (2014); and Coral Sirdifield, "The Prevalence of Mental Health Disorders amongst Offenders on Probation: A Literature Review," *Journal of Mental Health* 21, no. 5 (2012).

8. Patricia O'Brien and Diane S. Young, "Challenges for Formerly Incarcerated Women: A Holistic Approach to Assessment," *Families in Society: The Journal of Contemporary Social Services* 87, no. 3 (2006).

9. Sarah Kate Cameron, Jacquia Rodgers, and Dave Dagnan, "The Relationship between the Therapeutic Alliance and Clinical Outcomes in Cognitive Behaviour Therapy for Adults with Depression: A Meta-Analytic Review," *Clinical Psychology and Psychotherapy* 25, no. 3 (2018); Louis-Georges Cournoyer et al., "Therapeutic Alliance, Patient Behaviour and Dropout in a Drug Rehabilitation Programme: The Moderating Effect of Clinical Subpopulations," *Addiction* 102, no. 12 (2007); and Ruth Howard, Katherine Berry, and Gillian Haddock, "Therapeutic Alliance in Psychological Therapy for Posttraumatic Stress Disorder: A Systematic Review and Meta-Analysis," *Clinical Psychology and Psychotherapy* 29, no. 2 (2021).

10. For a similar finding of the stigma associated with substance abuse treatment that clusters participants together in high-crime neighborhoods, see Polly Radcliffe and Alex Stevens, "Are Drug Treatment Services Only for 'Thieving Junkie Scumbags'? Drug Users and the Management of Stigmatised Identities," *Social Sciences and Medicine* 67, no. 7 (2008).

11. Alcoholics Anonymous has been criticized as inconsistent with empowerment. For a review of criticisms as well as evidence showing effectiveness for

women and their adaptation of the model of recovery to fit their situations, see Sarah E. Ullman, Cynthia J. Najdowski, and Erika B. Adams, "Women, Alcoholics Anonymous, and Related Mutual Aid Groups: Review and Recommendations for Research," *Alcoholism Treatment Quarterly* 30 (2012). For a critique of the limitations of Alcoholics and Narcotics Anonymous groups, see Sered and Norton-Hawk, *Can't Catch a Break*.

12. James Kilgore, "Repackaging Mass Incarceration," *Counterpunch*, June 6, 2014, www.counterpunch.org/2014/06/06/repackaging-mass-incarceration/.

13. Brady T. Heiner and Sarah K. Tyson, "Feminism and the Carceral State: Gender Responsive Justice, Community Accountability, and the Epistemology of Antiviolence," *Feminist Philosophy Quarterly* 3, no. 1 (2017); and Beth E. Richie and Kayla M. Martensen, "Resisting Carcerality, Embracing Abolition: Implications for Feminist Social Work Practice," *Affilia: Journal of Women and Social Work* 35, no. 1 (2020).

14. D. A. (Don) Andrews, "Reintroducing Rehabilitation to Corrections," in *Applying Social Science to Reduce Violent Offending*, ed. Joel A. Dvoskin et al. (New York: Oxford University Press, 2011); Stephanie S. Covington and Barbara E. Bloom, "Gender Responsive Treatment and Services in Correctional Settings," *Women and Therapy* 29, nos. 3–4 (2007); and Stephanie Covington and Barbara Bloom, "Gendered Justice: Addressing Female Offenders," in *Gendered Justice: Women in the Criminal Justice System* (Durham, North Carolina: Center for Gender and Justice, 2003).

6. MARGINALIZATION

1. Ariel L. Roddy, Merry Morash, and Miriam Northcutt Bohmert, "Spatial Mismatch, Race and Ethnicity, and Unemployment: Implications for Interventions with Women on Probation and Parole," *Crime and Delinquency* 68, no. 12 (2022). In the larger sample of Michigan women on probation and parole, Black and other minority women tended to live in communities that lacked job opportunities, and this spatial mismatch between place of residence and jobs helped to explain Black women's unemployment at the end of the first year of supervision.

2. For similar findings about justice-involved women in rural areas, see Dawn Beichner and Cara Rabe-Hemp, "'I Don't Want to Go Back to That Town': Incarcerated Mothers and Their Return Home to Rural Communities," *Critical Criminology* 22, no. 4 (2014).

3. Monisha Pasupathi, Emma Mansour, and Jed R. Brubaker, "Developing a Life Story: Constructing Relations between Self and Experience in Autobiographical Narratives," *Human Development* 50, nos. 2–3 (2007).

4. Scott Coltrane, "Research on Household Labor: Modeling and Measuring the Social Embeddedness of Routine Family Work," *Journal of Marriage and the Family* 62: no. 4 (2000); Erin Hatton, "Mechanisms of Invisibility: Rethinking the Concept of Invisible Work," *Work, Employment and Society* 31, no. 2 (2017); and Jennifer L. Hook, "Gender Inequality in the Welfare State: Sex Segregation in Housework: 1965–2003," *American Journal of Sociology* 115, no. 5 (2010).

5. Stephanie DeLuca, Phillp M. E. Garboden, and Peter Rosenblatt, "Segregating Shelter: How Housing Policies Shape the Residential Locations of Low-Income Minority Families," *Annals of the American Academy of Political and Social Sciences* 647, no. 1 (2013); Rachel Garshick Kleit, Seugbeom Kang, and Corianne Payton Scally, "Why Do Housing Mobility Programs Fail in Moving Households to Better Neighborhoods?," *Housing Policy Debate* 26, no. 1 (2016); Kirk McClure, "Deconcentrating Poverty with Housing Programs," *Journal of the American Planning Association* 74, no. 1 (2008); Eva Rosen, Philip M. E. Garboden, and Jennifer E. Cossyleon, "Racial Discrimination in Housing: How Landlords Use Algorithms and Home Visits to Screen Tenants," *American Sociological Review* 86, no. 5 (2021); and Lauren. M. Ross, Anne B. Shlay, and Mario G. Picon, "You Can't Always Get What You Want: The Role of Public Housing and Vouchers in Achieving Residential Satisfaction," *Cityscape: A Journal of Policy Development and Research* 14, no. 1 (2009).

6. Erin Buchanan and Margaret Ann Keaton, "Anticipated Stereotypes of Female Convicted Felons," *American Journal of Forensic Psychology* 32, no. 4 (2014); Andrea Cantora, "Navigating the Job Search after Incarceration: The Experiences of Work-Release Participants," *Criminal Justice Studies* 28, no. 2 (2015); Adrian Cherney and Robin Fitzgerald, "Efforts by Offenders to Manage and Overcome Stigma: The Case of Employment," *Current Issues in Criminal Justice* 28, no. 1 (2016); and Rebekah Lee and Chris Brown, "The Relations among Career-Related Self-Efficacy, Perceived Career Barriers, and Stigma Consciousness in Men with Felony Convictions," *Psychological Services* (forthcoming).

7. Shadd Maruna, *Making Good: How Ex-Convicts Reform and Rebuild Their Lives* (Washington, DC: American Psychological Association Books, 2001).

8. Jennifer E. Cobbina et al., "Race, Neighborhood Danger, and Coping Strategies among Female Probationers and Parolees," *Race and Justice* 4, no. 1 (2014).

9. Ariel L. Roddy and Merry Morash, "The Connections of Parole and Probation Agent Communication Patterns with Female Offenders' Job-Seeking Self-Efficacy," *International Journal of Offender Therapy and Comparative Criminology* 64, no. 8 (2020).

10. Joe Darden et al., "The Measurement of Neighborhood Socioeconomic Characteristics and Black and White Residential Segregation in Metropolitan Detroit: Implications for the Study of Social Disparities in Health," *Annals of the Association of American Geographers* 100, no. 1 (2010); Joe T. Darden and Sameh M. Kamel, "Black Residential Segregation in the City and Suburbs of Detroit: Does Socioeconomic Status Matter?," *Journal of Urban Affairs* 22, no. 1 (2000); Tracey Farrigan and Timothy Parker, *The Concentration of Poverty Is a Growing Rural Problem*, U.S. Department of Agriculture Economic Research Service, Washington, DC, 2012; and Douglas S. Massey, Jonathan Rothwell, and Thurston Domina, "The Changing Bases of Segregation in the United States," *Annals of the American Academy of Political and Social Science* 626, no. 1 (2009).

11. Farrigan and Parker, *Concentration of Poverty Is a Growing Rural Problem*; and Massey, Rothwell, and Domina, " Changing Bases of Segregation in the United States."

12. Deven Carlson et al., "Long-Term Earnings and Employment Effects of Housing Voucher Receipt," *Journal of Urban Economics* 71, no. 1 (2012); and DeLuca, Garboden, and Rosenblatt, "Segregating Shelter."

13. Committee on Examination of the Adequacy of Food Resources and SNAP Allotments, "History, Background, and Goals of the Supplemental Nutrition Assistance Program," in *Supplemental Nutrition Assistance Program: Examining the Evidence to Define Benefit Adequacy*, ed. J. A. Caswell and A. L. Yaktine (Washington, DC: National Academies Press, 2013); and Kranti Mulik and Lindsey Haynes-Maslow, "The Affordability of Myplate: An Analysis of SNAP Benefits and the Actual Cost of Eating According to the Dietary Guidelines," *Journal of Nutrition Education and Behavior* 49, no. 8 (2017).

14. Lois K. Lee et al., "Women's Coverage, Utilization, Affordability, and Health after the ACA: A Review of the Literature," *Health Affairs* 39, no. 3 (2020).

15. Plan First! was Michigan's Section 1115 Demonstration Waiver for family planning services. Plan First! covered women of childbearing age (19 through 44) who are not eligible for Medicaid, whose other insurance does not cover family planning services, and whose income level is at or below 185 percent of the federal poverty level.

16. Jamie R. Daw et al., "Women in the United States Experience High Rates of Coverage 'Churn' in Months before and after Childbirth," *Health Affairs* 36, no. 4 (2017); and Stacey McMorrow et al., *Uninsured New Mothers' Health and Health Care Challenges Highlight the Benefits of Increasing Postpartum Medicaid Coverage* (Washington, DC: Urban Institute, 2020).

17. DeLuca, Garboden, and Rosenblatt, "Segregating Shelter."

18. Barry C. Feld, "Justice by Geography: Urban, Suburban, and Rural Variations in Juvenile Justice Administration," *Journal of Criminal Law and Criminology* 82, no. 1 (1991).

19. Sandra K. Danziger, Jessica Wiederspan, and Jonah A. Douglas-Siegel, "We're Not All Deadbeat Parents: Welfare Recipient Voices on Unmet Service Needs," *Journal of Poverty* 17, no. 3 (2013); Rebecca Joyce Kissane, "They Never Did Me Any Good: Welfare to Work Programs from the Vantage Point of Poor Women," *Humanity and Society* 32, no. 4 (2008); and Sandra Morgen, Joan Acker, and Jill Weight, *Stretched Thin: Poor Families Welfare Work, and Welfare Reform* (Ithaca, New York: Cornell University Press, 2010).

20. Liz Schott and LaDonna Pavetti, *Changes in TANF Work Requirements Could Make Them More Effective in Promoting Employment*, Center on Budget and Policy Priorities, Washington, DC, 2013, www.cbpp.org/research/family -income-support/changes-in-tanf-work-requirements-could-make-them-more -effective-in.

21. For evidence that a cut in access to food assistance was associated with an increase in economic-motivated crimes, see Nicholas Lovett, "Food Stamps, Income Shocks, and Crime: Evidence from California," *B.E. Journal of Economic Analysis and Policy* 18, no. 4 (2018).

7. ENDPOINTS

1. Kate C. McLean et al., "Redemptive Stories and Those Who Tell Them Are Preferred in the U.S," *Collabra: Psychology* 6, no. 1 (2020).

2. Shadd Maruna, *Making Good: How Ex-Convicts Reform and Rebuild Their Lives* (Washington, DC: American Psychological Association Books, 2001).

3. Rebecca Stone et al., "Women on Parole, Identity Processes, and Primary Desistance," *Feminist Criminology* 13, no. 4 (2018).

4. Jefferson A. Singer, "Narrative Identity and Meaning Making across the Adult Lifespan: An Introduction," *Journal of Personality* 72, no. 3 (2004).

5. Elizabeth Karyn Allen, "Justice-Involved Women: Narratives, Marginalization, Identity and Community Reintegration," *Affilia: Journal of Women and Social Work* 33, no. 3 (2018); and Dan P. McAdams, "Narrative Identity," in *Handbook of Identity Theory and Research*, ed. Seth J. Schwartz, Koen Luyckx, and Vivian L. Vignoles (New York: Springer, 2011).

6. Jennifer L. Pals, "Constructing the 'Springboard Effect': Causal Connections, Self-Making, and Growth within the Life Story," in *Identity and Story: Creating Self in Narrative*, ed. Dan P. McAdams, Ruthellen Josselson, and Amia Lieblich (Washington, DC: American Psychological Association, 2006); and Monisha Pasupathi, Emma Mansour, and Jed R. Brubaker, "Developing a Life Story: Constructing Relations between Self and Experience in Autobiographical Narratives," *Human Development* 50, nos. 2–3 (2007).

7. Merry Morash et al., "Women at the Nexus of Correctional and Social Policies: Implications for Recidivism Risk," *British Journal of Criminology* 57, no. 2 (2017).

8. Miriam Northcutt Bohmert and Alfred DeMaris, "Cumulative Disadvantage and the Role of Transportation in Community Supervision," *Crime and Delinquency* 64, no. 8 (2018); Felipe Estrada and Anders Nilsson, "Does It Cost More to Be a Female Offender? A Life-Course Study of Childhood Circumstances, Crime, Drug Abuse, and Living Conditions," *Feminist Criminology* 7, no. 3 (2012).

9. Nancy Chodorow, *The Reproduction of Mothering* (Berkeley: University of California Press, 1978); Julia McQuillan et al., "The Importance of Motherhood among Women in the Contemporary United States," *Gender and Society* 22, no. 4 (2008); Celia L. Ridgeway and Shelley J. Correll, "Motherhood as a Status Characteristic," *Journal of Social Issues* 60, no. 4 (2004); and Miriam Ulrich and Ann Weatherall, "Motherhood and Infertility: Viewing Motherhood through the Lens of Infertility," *Feminism and Psychology* 10, no. 3 (2000).

10. Kate C. McLean and Moin Syed, "Personal, Master, and Alternative Narratives: An Integrative Framework for Understanding Identity Development in Context," *Human Development* 58, no. 6 (2015); and Merry Morash et al., "Narrative Identity Development and Desistance from Illegal Behavior among Substance-Using Female Offenders: Implications for Narrative Therapy and Creating Opportunity," *Sex Roles* 83, nos. 1–2 (2020).

11. Carol Gilligan, *In a Different Voice: Psychological Theory and Women's Development* (Cambridge, Massachusetts: Harvard University Press, 1982); Judith V. Jordan, ed., *The Power of Connection: Recent Developments in Relational-Cultural Theory* (New York: Routledge, 2013); and Jean Baker Miller, *Toward a New Psychology of Women* (Boston: Beacon Press, 1976).

12. Jody Miller and Kristin Carbone-Lopez, "Beyond 'Doing Gender': Incorporating Race, Class, Place, and Life Transitions into Feminist Drug Research,"

Substance Use and Misuse 50, no. 6 (2015); and Morash et al., "Narrative Identity Development and Desistance from Illegal Behavior among Substance-Using Female Offenders."

13. Thomas P. LeBel, Matt Richie, and Shadd Maruna, "Helping Others as a Response to Reconcile a Criminal Past: The Role of the Wounded Healer in Prisoner Reentry Programs," *Criminal Justice and Behavior* 42, no. 1 (2015); and Shadd Maruna et al., "Pygmalion in the Reintegration Process: Desistance from Crime through the Looking Glass," *Psychology, Crime and Law* 10, no. 3 (2004).

14. Morash et al., "Narrative Identity Development and Desistance from Illegal Behavior among Substance-using Female Offenders."

15. Jamie J. Fader, *Falling Back* (New Brunswick, New Jersey: Rutgers University Press, 2013); and Nikki Jones, *The Chosen Ones: Black Men and the Politics of Redemption* (Oakland: University of California Press, 2018).

16. Clarification added by Marva Goodson-Miller, who interviewed Mary six times over the course of the research.

17. Peggy C. Giordano, *Legacies of Crime: A Follow-Up of the Children of Highly Delinquent Girls and Boys* (New York: Cambridge University Press, 2010).

18. Kayla M. Hoskins, "'I'm Going to Be Successful Someday': Women's Personal Projects to Improve Their Lives, and Implications for Clarifying the Nature of Agency in Criminological Theories of Desistance," *Feminist Criminology* 17, no. 2 (2022).

8. REFORM

1. Matthew H. Morton, Amy Dworsky, and Gina M. Samuels, *Missed Opportunities: Youth Homelessness in America, National Estimates* (Chicago: University of Chicago Press, 2017).

2. Matthew H. Morton et al., "Prevalence and Correlates of Youth Homelessness in the United States," *Journal of Adolescent Health* 62, no. 1 (2018).

3. Amy Dworsky, Matthew H. Morton, and Gina M. Samuels, *Missed Opportunities: Pregnant and Parenting Youth Experiencing Homelessness in America* (Chicago: Chapin Hall at the University of Chicago, 2018).

4. Kimberly Bender et al., "Factors Associated with Trauma and Posttraumatic Stress Disorder Among Homeless Youth in Three U.S. Cities: The Importance of Transience," *Journal of Traumatic Stress* 23, no. 1 (2010); Chyna E. Hill et al., "An Examination of Housing Interventions among Youth Experiencing Homelessness: An Investigation into Racial/Ethnic and Sexual Minority Status," *Journal of Public Health* 44, no. 4 (2021); Matthew H. Morton et al., *Developing a Direct Cash Transfer Program for Youth Experiencing Homelessness: Results of a Mixed Methods, Multi-Stakeholder Design Process* (Chicago: Chapin Hall at the University of Chicago, 2020).

5. Joanne Belknap, *The Invisible Woman*, 5th ed. (Los Angeles: Sage, 2021), 70–74.

6. Ioana Marinescu, *No Strings Attached: The Behavioral Effects of U.S Unconditional Cash Transfer Programs*, National Bureau of Economic Research, Cambridge, Massachusetts, 2018, www.nber.org/papers/w24337.

7. Heather Hahn et al., *Young People's Lived Experiences with Safety Net Programs: Insights from Young People and Youth-Serving Organizations*, Urban Institute, Washington, DC, 2001, .

8. Hahn et al., *Young People's Lived Experiences with Safety Net Programs*.

9. Morton et al., *Developing a Direct Cash Transfer Program for Youth Experiencing Homelessness*, 17; and Matthew H. Morton et al., "Interventions for Youth Homelessness: A Systematic Review of Effectiveness Studies," *Children and Youth Services Review* 116 (September, 2020).

10. Morton et al., "Interventions for Youth Homelessness."

11. U.S. Department of Education Office of Civil Rights, *An Overview of Exclusionary Discipline Practices in Public Schools for the 2017–18 School Year*, U.S. Office of Education, Washington, DC, 2021, https://ocrdata.ed.gov/assets/downloads/crdc-exclusionary-school-discipline.pdf.

12. Kathryn C. Monahan et al., "From the School Yard to the Squad Car: School Discipline, Truancy, and Arrest," *Journal of Youth and Adolescence* 43, no. 7 (2014).

13. Rebecca Epstein, Jamilia J. Blake, and Thalia González, *Girlhood Interrupted: The Erasure of Black Girls' Childhood* (Washington, DC: Center on Poverty and Inequality, Georgetown Law, 2017); Monique W. Morris, *Pushout: The Criminalization of Black Girls in Schools* (New York: The New Press, 2016); and Initiative on Gender Justice and Opportunity, *The Innocence Initiative: Translating National Research into Local Action in Central Texas*, Washington, DC, 2021, https://genderjusticeandopportunity.georgetown.edu/wp-content/uploads/2021/06/The-Innocence-Initiative-Translating-National-Research-into-Local-Action-in-Central-Texas-FINAL.pdf.

14. Daniel A. Waschbusch, Rosanna P. Breaux, and Dara E. Babinski, "School-Based Interventions for Aggression and Definace in Youth: A Framework for Evidence-Based Practice," *School Mental Health* 11, no. 1 (2019).

15. Aaron Muttillo, Jennifer L. Murphy, and Anne Galletta, "A Decade of Trauma-Informed Care: An Organizational Case Study," *Journal of Aggression, Maltreatment and Trauma* 31, no. 8 (2022).

16. Substance Abuse and Mental Health Services Administration, *SAMSA's Concept of Trauma and Guidance for a Trauma-Informed Aproach*. Rockville, Maryland: Substance Abuse and Mental Health Services Administration, 2014.

17. Gabriela Kirk et al., "Justice by Geography: The Role of Monetary Sanctions Across Communities," *RSF: The Russell Sage Foundation Journal of the Social Sciences* 8, no. 1 (2022); and Tyler Smith, Kristina J. Thompson, and Michele Cadigon, "Sensemaking in the Legal System: A Comparative Case Study of Changes to Monetary Sanction Laws," *RSF: The Russell Sage Foundation Journal of the Social Sciences* 8, no. 1 (2022).

18. Beth M. Huebner and Andrea Giuffre, "Reinforcing the Web of Municipal Courts: Evidence and Implications Post Ferguson," *RSF: The Russell Sage Foundation Journal of the Social Sciences* 1, no. 1 (2022).

19. Alicia Bannon, Rebekah Diller, and Matali Nagrecha, *Criminal Justice Debt: A Barrier to Reentry*, Brennan Center for Justice, New York, 2010, www.brennancenter.org/our-work/research-reports/criminal-justice-debt-barrier

-reentry; Fines and Fees Justice Center and Reform Alliance, *50 State Survey: Probation and Parole Fees*, 2022, https://finesandfeesjusticecenter.org/; and Russell Sage Foundation, "State Monetary Sanctions and the Costs of the Criminal Legal System: The Consequences of Monetary Sanctions," *RSF: The Russell Sage Foundation Journal of the Social Sciences* 8, no. 2 (2022).

20. Jordan Zvonkovich, Stacy H. Haynes, and R. Barry Ruback, "A Continuum of Coercive Costs: A State-Level Analysis of the Imposition and Payment Enforcement of Statutory Fees," *Federal Sentencing Reporter* 34, nos. 2–3 (2022).

21. Criminal Justice Policy Program, "50-State Criminal Justice Debt Reform Builder," Cambridge, Massachusetts: Harvard Law School, June 5, 2022, https://cjdebtreform.org/.

22. Lisa Servon, Ava Esquier, and Gillian Tiley, "Gender and Financialization of the Criminal Justice System," *Social Sciences* 10, no. 11 (2021).

23. Bryan L. Sykes et al., "Robbing Peter to Pay Paul: Public Assistance, Monetary Sanctions, and Financial Double-Dealing in America," *RSF: The Russell Sage Foundation Journal of the Social Sciences* 8, no. 1 (2022).

24. Mary Pattillo et al., "Monetary Sanctions and Housing Instability," *RSF: The Russell Sage Foundation Journal of the Social Sciences* 8, no. 2 (2022): 89.

25. Pattillo et al., "Monetary Sanctions and Housing Instability."

26. Lindsay Bing, Becky Pettit, and Ilya Slavinski, "Incomparable Punishments: How Economic Inequality Contributes to the Disparate Impact of Legal Fines and Fees," *The Russell Sage Foundation Journal of the Social Sciences* 8, no. 2 (2022); Eduardo Bonilla-Silva, "The Structure of Racism in Color-Blind, 'Post-Racial' America," *American Behavioral Scientist* 59, no. 11 (2015); Victor Ray, "A Theory of Racialized Organizations," *American Sociological Review* 84, no. 1 (2019); and Sykes et al., "Robbing Peter to Pay Paul."

27. Michael F. Crowley, Matthew J. Menendez, and Eisen Lauren-Brooke, "If We Only Knew the Cost: Scratching the Surface on How Much It Costs to Assess and Collect Court Imposed Criminal Fees and Fines," *UCLA Criminal Justice Law Review* 4, no. 1 (2020); Marie Gottschalk, *Caught: The Prison State and the Lockdown of American Politics* (Princeton, New Jersey: Princeton University Press, 2015), 36; and Matthew Menendez and Lauren Brooke-Eisen, *The Steep Costs of Criminal Justice Fees and Fines*, The Brennan Center, New York, 2019, 5, www.brennancenter.org/our-work/research-reports/steep-costs-criminal-justice-fees-and-fines.

28. Meghan M. O'Neil and J. J. Prescott, "Targeting Poverty in the Courts: Improving the Measurement of Ability to Pay," *Law and Contemporary Problems* 82, no. 1 (2019); and Meghan M. O'Neil and Daniel Strellman, "The Hidden Cost of the Disease: Fines, Fees, and Costs Assessed on Persons with Alleged Substance Use Disorder," *UCLA Criminal Justice Law Review* 4, no. 1 (2000).

29. Fines and Fees Justice Center, *End Fees, Discharge Debt, Fairly Fund Government: FFJC Policy Guidance for Eliminating Criminal Legal System Fees and Discharging Debt*, 2022, https://finesandfeesjusticecenter.org/content/uploads/2022/01/FFJC-Policy-Guidance-Fee-Elimination-1.13.22.pdf.

30. Criminal Justice Policy Program, *Confronting Criminal Justice Debt: A Guide for Policy Reform*, Harvard Law School, Cambridge, Massachusetts, 2016, 7.

31. Beth A. Colgan, "Beyond Graduation: Economic Sanctions and Structural Reform," *Duke Law Journal* 69, no. 7 (2020).

32. Elena Kantorowicz-Reznichenko, "Day-Fines: Should the Rich Pay More?," *Review of Law and Economics* 11, no. 3 (2015); and Pew Charitable Trusts, *Policy Reforms Can Strengthen Community Supervision* (Philadelphia, Pennsylvania: Pew Charitable Trusts, 2020).

33. E. Ann Carson, *Prisoners in 2020: Statistical Tables* (Washington, DC: Bureau of Justice Statistics, 2021).

34. The Sentencing Project, *Incarcerated Women and Girls*, The Sentencing Project, Washington DC, 2022, www.sentencingproject.org/wp-content /uploads/2016/02/Incarcerated-Women-and-Girls.pdf.

35. Kristy Holtfreter and Katelyn A. Wattanaporn, "The Transition from Prison to Community Initiative," *Criminal Justice and Behavior* 41, no. 1 (2014).

36. Shen Seng and Todd D. Minton, *Jail Inmates in 2019* (Washington, DC: U.S. Department of Justice, Bureau of Justice Statistics, 2021).

37. Aleks Kaistura, *Women's Mass Incarceration: The Whole Pie*, Prison Policy Initiative, Easthampton, Massachusetts, 2019, www.prisonpolicy.org /reports/pie2019women.html.

38. Tiana Herring, *Since You Asked: What Role Does Drug Enforcement Play in the Rising Incarceration of Women?*, Prison Policy Initiative, Easthampton, Massachusetts, 2020, www.prisonpolicy.org/blog/2020/11/10/women-drug -enforcement/.

39. Christian Henrichson, Joshua Rinaldi, and Ruth Delaney, *The Price of Jails: Measuring the Taxpayer Cost of Local Incarceration* (Brooklyn, New York: Vera Institute of Justice, 2015).

40. Alexi Jones and Wendy Sawyer, *Arrest, Release, Repeat: How Police and Jails are Misused to Respond to Social Problems*, Prison Policy Initiative, Easthampton, Massachusetts, 2019, www.prisonpolicy.org/reports/repeatarrests.html.

41. Henrichson, Rinaldi, and Delaney, *Price of Jails*; Ram Subramanian et al., *Incarceration's Front Door: The Misuse of Jails in America* (Brooklyn, New York: Vera Institute of Justice, 2015).

42. Katie Bailey et al., "Evaluation of a Police-Mental Health Co-response Team Relative to Traditional Police Response in Indianapolis," *Psychiatric Services* 73, no. 4 (2022); Chunghyeon Seo, Bitna Kim, and Nathan E. Kruis, "Variation across Police Response Models for Handling Encounters with People with Mental Illness: A Systematic Review and Meta-Analysis," *Journal of Criminal Justice* 72, no. 1 (2021).

43. David Loveland and Michael Boyle, "Intensive Case Management as a Jail Diversion Program for People with a Serious Mental Illness: A Review of the Literature," *International Journal of Offender Therapy and Comparative Criminology* 51, no. 2 (2007).

44. Cheyney Cooper Dobson, "Merging Criminal Justice and Social Welfare in Mental Health Court: The Disparate Impacts and Outcomes of Coercive Aid in the Era of Mass Incarceration" (PhD diss., University of Michigan, 2019).

45. Erika Parks and Sarah Godfrey, *Michigan Enacts Landmark Jail Reforms: Historic Legislation Aims to Reduce Incarcerated Populations, Improve Public Safety*, Pew Charitable Trusts, Philadelphia, Pennsylvania, 2021, www.pewtrusts.org/en/research-and-analysis/issue-briefs/2021/09/michigan-enacts-landmark-jail-reforms.

46. Danielle Kaeble, *Probation and Parole in the United States, 2020* (Washington, DC: U.S. Department of Justice, Bureau of Justice Statistics, 2021).

47. Jennifer E. Cobbina, "From Prison to Home: Women's Pathways in and out of Crime" (PhD diss., University of Missouri–St. Louis, 2009).

48. Pew Charitable Trusts, *Policy Reforms Can Strengthen Community Supervision.*

49. Pew Charitable Trusts, *Policy Reforms Can Strengthen Community Supervision*; and Michelle S. Phelps, "The Paradox of Probation: Community Supervision in the Age of Mass Incarceration," *Law and Policy* 35, nos. 1–2 (2013).

50. Amanda J. Holmstrom et al., "Supportive Messages Female Offenders Receive from Probation and Parole Officers about Substance Avoidance: Message Perceptions and Effects," *Criminal Justice and Behavior* 44, no. 11 (2017); and Ariel L. Roddy et al., "The Nature and Effects of Messages that Women Receive from Probation and Parole Agents in Conversations about Employment," *Criminal Justice and Behavior* 46, no. 4 (2019).

51. Marva V. Goodson-Miller, "A First Look at Justice-Involved Women's Egocentric Social Networks," *Social Networks* 70, no. 10 (July 2022).

52. Marva V. Goodson, "Help or Hindrance: Female Probationers' Navigation of Supervision Requirements through Personal Support Networks," *Criminal Justice and Behavior* 45, no. 10 (2018); and Michael D. Reisig, Kristy Holtfreter, and Merry Morash, "Social Capital among Women Offenders: Examining the Distribution of Social Networks and Resources," *Journal of Contemporary Criminal Justice* 18, no. 2 (2002).

53. Michael D. Clark, Todd A. Roberts, and Teresa Chandler, "Motivational Interviewing for Community Corrections: Expanding a Relationship-Based Approach with Exemplar Implementation," *Federal Probation* 84, no. 2 (2020).

54. Amber Wilson, Brandon K. Applegate, and Riane M. Bolin, "Evidence-Based Practices in Community Corrections: Officers' Perceptions of Professional Relevance and Personal Competence," *American Journal of Criminal Justice* 47 (2022).

55. Jill Viglione, Danielle S. Rudes, and Faye S. Taxman, "Probation Officer Use of Client-Centered Communication Strategies in Adult Probation Settings " *Journal of Offender Rehabilitation* 56, no. 1 (2017).

56. Rachel Goldhill, "Probation Policy and Practice with Vulnerable Women: A Focus on the Challenges of Organisational and Personal Change for Women Workers and Women Service Users" (PhD diss., University of Portsmouth, 2018).

57. Clark, Roberts, and Chandler, "Motivational Interviewing for Community Corrections."

58. Bandy L. Blasko et al., "Sorting through the Evidence: A Step Toward Prioritization of Evidence-Based Community Supervision Practices " *Criminal Justice and Behavior* 49, no. 6 (2022); Sara Debus-Sherrill, Alex Breno, and Faye S.

Taxman, "What Makes or Breaks Evidence-Based Supervision? Staff and Orga-
nizational Predictors of Evidence-Based Practice in Probation," *International
Journal of Offender Therapy and Comparative Criminology* 67, nos. 6–7 (2023);
and Jill Viglione, Brandy L. Blasko, and Faye S. Taxman, "Organizational
Factors and Probation Officer Use of Evidence-Based Practices: A Multilevel
Examination "*International Journal of Offender Therapy and Comparative
Criminology* 62, no. 6 (2018).

59. Erin Jacobs Valentine and Cindy Redcross, "Transitional Jobs after
Release from Prison: Effects on Employment and Recidivism," *IZA Journal of
Labor Policy* 4, no. 16 (2015).

60. J. J. Prescott and Sonja B. Starr, "Expungement of Criminal Convictions:
An Empirical Study," *Harvard Law Review* 133, no. 8 (2020).

61. Criminal Justice Policy Program, "50-State Comparison: Expungement, Sealing and Other Record Relief," Collateral Consequences Resource
Center, 2021, https://ccresourcecenter.org/state-restoration-profiles/50–state
-comparisonjudicial-expungement-sealing-and-set-aside/.

62. National Conference of State Legislatures, *The Evolving State of Occupational Licensing: Research, State Policies and Trends* (Washington, DC:
National Conference of State Legislatures, 2019).

63. Dick M. Carpenter et al., *License to Work: A National Study of Burdens
from Occupational Licensing* (Arlington, Virginia: Institute for Justice, 2017).

64. Bradley D. Custer, "The History of Denying Federal Financial Aid to
System-Impacted Students," *Journal of Student Financial Aid* 50, no. 1 (2021).

65. Ashley Burnside, *No More Double Punishments: Lifting the Ban on
SNAP and TANF for People with Prior Felony Drug Convictions* (Washington,
DC: Center for Law and Social Policy, 2022).

66. Robert Bozick et al., "Does Providing Inmates with Education Improve
Postrelease Outcomes? A Meta-Analysis of Correctional Education Programs in
the United States," *Journal of Experimental Criminology* 14, no. 3 (2018); and
Amanda Pompoco et al., "Reducing Inmate Misconduct and Prison Returns with
Facility Education Programs," *Criminology and Public Policy* 16, no. 2 (2017).

67. Tracy Sohoni and Sylwia Piatkowska, "Begging for Crime? The Effect of
State Laws Restricting Access to Temporary Assistance for Needy Families on
Unsuccessful Completion of Parole," *Crime and Delinquency* 68, no. 11 (2022);
and Crystal S. Yang, "American Economic Review: Papers and Proceedings,"
107, no. 5 (2017).

68. Ife Floyd et al., *TANF Policies Reflect Racist Legacy of Cash Assistance:
Reimagined Program Should Center Black Mothers*, Center on Budget and Policy Priorities, Washington DC, 2021, 5, www.cbpp.org/research/family-income
-support/tanf-policies-reflect-racist-legacy-of-cash-assistance.

69. Aditi Shrivasta and Gina Azito Thompon, *TANF Cash Assistance Should
Reach Millions More Families to Lessen Hardship*, Center on Budget and Policy Priorities, Washington, DC, 2022, www.cbpp.org/research/family-income
-support/tanf-cash-assistance-should-reach-millions-more-families-to-lessen.

70. Katie Shantz et al., *Welfare Rules Databook: State TANF Policies as
of July 2019* (Washington, DC: Office of Planning, Research, and Evaluation,

Administration for Children and Families, U.S. Department of Health and Human Services, 2020).

71. Floyd et al., *TANF Policies Reflect Racist Legacy of Cash Assistance*, 5; Rebecca McColl and Letita Logan Passarella, *Life after Welfare: 2019 Annual Update*, Ruth H. Young Center for Families and Children, University of Maryland School of Social Work, Baltimore, Maryland, 2019, www.ssw.umaryland .edu/media/ssw/fwrtg/welfare-research/life-after-welfare/life2019.pdf; and Ali Safawi and LaDonna Pavetti, *Most Parents Leaving TANF Work, but in Low-Paying, Unstable Jobs, Recent Studies Find*, Center on Budget and Policy Priorities, Washington, DC, 2020, www.cbpp.org/research/family-income-support /most-parents-leaving-tanf-work-but-in-low-paying-unstable-jobs.

72. Jacqueline Kauff et al., *Using Work-Oriented Sanctions to Increase TANF Program Participation: Final Report*, Mathematica Policy Research, Inc., Washington, DC, 2007, www.acf.hhs.gov/opre/report/using-work-oriented -sanctions-increase-tanf-program-participation-final-report; and Dezara Ware and Deborah Dennis, *Best Practices for Increasing Access to SSI/SSDI upon Exiting Criminal Justice Settings*, Substance Abuse and Mental Health Services Administration, Rockville, Maryland, 2013, https://nicic.gov/best-practices -increasing-access-ssissdi-upon-exiting-criminal-justice-settings.

73. Diana Azevedo-McCaffrey and Ali Safawi, *To Promote Equity, States Should Invest More TANF Dollars in Basic Assistance*, Center on Budget and Policy Priorities, Washington, DC, 2022, www.cbpp.org/research/family -income-support/to-promote-equity-states-should-invest-more-tanf-dollars-in -basic. For recommendations for reform by an advocacy organization, see Children's Defense Fund, *TANF at 25: A Reflection and Reckoning* (Washington, DC: Children's Defense Fund, 2021).

74. Vincent A. Fusaro, "State Politics, Race, and 'Welfare' as a Funding Stream: Cash Assistance Spending under Temporary Assistance for Needy Families," *Policy Studies Journal* 49, no. 3 (2021); and Zachary Parolin, "Temporary Assistance for Needy Families and the Black-White Child Poverty Gap in the United States," *Socio-Economic Review* 19, no. 3 (2021).

75. Liana E. Fox and Kalee Burns, *The Supplemental Poverty Measure: 2020* (Washington, DC: U.S. Department of Commerce, U.S. Census Bureau, September 2021).

76. Elliot Currie, *A Peculiar Indifference: The Neglected Toll of Violence on Black America* (New York: Metropolitan Books, 2020).

77. Debra L. Brucker, "Social Construction of Disability and Substance Abuse within Public Disability Benefit Systems," *International Journal of Drug Policy* 20, no. 5 (2009).

78. For similar findings, see Lynne Haney, "Introduction: Gender, Welfare, and States of Punishment," *Social Politics* 11, no. 3 (2004); and Smita Vir Tyagi, "Victimization, Adversity and Survival in the Lives of Women Offenders: Implications for Social Policy and Correctional Practice," *Canadian Woman Studies* 25, nos. 1–2 (2006).

79. Devika Hazra and Jose Aranzazu, "Crime, Correction, Education and Welfare in the U.S.—What Role Does the Government Play?," *Journal of Policy Modeling* 44 (2022).

APPENDIX: METHOD AND SAMPLE CHARACTERISTICS

1. For more detailed information on sampling bias, see Merry Morash and Deborah A. Kashy, "The Relevance of Women's Economic Marginalization to Recidivism," *Criminal Justice and Behavior* 49, no. 3 (2022).

2. Much of this descriptive information replicates material in Merry Morash et al., "Narrative Identity Development and Desistance from Illegal Behavior among Substance-using Female Offenders: Implications for Narrative Therapy and Creating Opportunity," *Sex Roles* 83, nos. 1–2 (2020).

Bibliography

Allard, Patricia. *Life Sentences: Denying Welfare Benefits to Women Convicted of Drug Offenses*. The Sentencing Project. Washington, DC, 2002. www.opensocietyfoundations.org/publications/life-sentences-denying-welfare-benefits-women-convicted-drug-offenses.

Allard, Scott W. *Out of Reach: Place, Poverty, and the New American Welfare State*. New Haven, Connecticut: Yale University Press, 2009.

Allen, Elizabeth Karyn. "Justice-Involved Women: Narratives, Marginalization, Identity and Community Reintegration." *Affilia: Journal of Women and Social Work* 33, no. 3 (2018): 346–62.

American Civil Liberties Union. *In for a Penny: The Rise of America's New Debtors' Prison*. New York: American Civil Liberties Union, 2010.

Anda, Robert F., V. J. Felitti, Douglas Bremner, John D. Walker, Charles Whitfield, Bruce D. Perry, Shanta R. Dube, and Wayne H. Giles. "The Enduring Effects of Abuse and Related Adverse Experiences in Childhood: A Convergence of Evidence from Neurobiology and Epidemiology." *European Archives of Psychiatry and Clinical Neuroscience* 256, no. 3 (2006): 174–86.

Andrews, D. A. "Reintroducing Rehabilitation to Corrections." In *Applying Social Science to Reduce Violent Offending*, edited by Joel A. Dvoskin, Jennifer L. Skeem, Raymond W. Novaco, and Kevin S. Douglas, 127–56. New York: Oxford University Press, 2011.

Andrews, D. A., and James Bonta. *Psychology of Criminal Conduct*. 5th ed. Newark, New Jersey: LexisNexis, 2010.

Arnold, Regina A. "Processes of Victimization and Criminalization of Black Women." *Social Justice* 17, no. 3 (1990): 153–66.

Azevedo-McCaffrey, Diana, and Ali Safawi. *To Promote Equity, States Should Invest More TANF Dollars in Basic Assistance*. Center on Budget and Policy Priorities. Washington, DC, 2022. www.cbpp.org/research/family-income -support/to-promote-equity-states-should-invest-more-tanf-dollars-in-basic.

Bailey, Katie, Evan M. Lowder, Eric Grommon, Staci Rising, and Bradley R. Ray. "Evaluation of a Police-Mental Health Co-Response Team Relative to Traditional Police Response in Indianapolis." *Psychiatric Services* 73, no. 4 (2022): 366–73.

Bakken, Nicholas W., and Christy A. Visher. "Successful Reintegration and Mental Health." *Criminal Justice and Behavior* 45, no. 8 (2018): 1121–35.

Bannon, Alicia, Rebekah Diller, and Matali Nagrecha. *Criminal Justice Debt: A Barrier to Reentry*. Brennan Center for Justice. New York, 2010. www.brennan center.org/our-work/research-reports/criminal-justice-debt-barrier-reentry.

Beichner, Dawn, and Cara Rabe-Hemp. "'I Don't Want to Go Back to That Town': Incarcerated Mothers and Their Return Home to Rural Communities." *Critical Criminology* 22, no. 4 (2014): 527–43.

Belknap, Joanne. *The Invisible Woman*. 5th ed. Los Angeles: Sage, 2021.

Bell, Hannah S., Anna C. Martinez-Hume, Allison M. Baker, Kristan Elwell, Isabel Montemayor, and Linda M. Hunt. "Medicaid Reform, Responsiblization Policies, and the Synergism of Barriers to Low-Income Health Seeking." *Human Organization* 76, no. 3 (2017): 275–86.

Bender, Kimberly, Kristin Ferguson, Sanna Thompson, Chelsea Kolo, and David Pollio. "Factors Associated with Trauma and Posttraumatic Stress Disorder among Homeless Youth in Three U.S. Cities: The Importance of Transience." *Journal of Traumatic Stress* 23, no. 1 (2010): 161–68.

Berman, Judith. *Women Offender Transition and Reentry: Gender Responsive Approaches to Transitioning Women Offenders from Prison to the Community*. Washington, DC: U.S. Department of Justice, National Institute of Corrections, 2005.

Bing, Lindsay, Becky Pettit, and Ilya Slavinski. "Incomparable Punishments: How Economic Inequality Contributes to the Disparate Impact of Legal Fines and Fees." *Russell Sage Foundation Journal of the Social Sciences* 8, no. 2 (2022): 118–36.

Blank, Rebecca M. *It Takes a Nation: A New Agenda for Fighting Poverty*. Princeton, New Jersey: Princeton University Press, 1997.

Blasko, Bandy L., Jill Viglione, Liana R. Taylor, and Faye S. Taxman. "Sorting through the Evidence: A Step toward Prioritization of Evidence-Based Community Supervision Practices." *Criminal Justice and Behavior* 49, no. 6 (2022): 817–37.

Bloom, Barbara, Barbara Owen, Stephanie S. Covington, and Myrna S. Raeder. *Gender-Responsive Strategies: Research, Practice, and Guiding Principles for Women Offenders*. Washington, DC: National Institute of Corrections, 2003.

Bonilla-Silva, Eduardo. "The Structure of Racism in Color-Blind, 'Post-Racial' America." *American Behavioral Scientist* 59, no. 11 (2015): 1358–76.

Bosworth, Mary. "Resistance and Compliance in Women's Prisons: Towards a Critique of Legitimacy." *Critical Criminology* 7, no. 2 (1996): 5–19.

Bozick, Robert, Jennifer Steele, Lois Davis, and Susan Turner. "Does Providing Inmates with Education Improve Postrelease Outcomes? A Meta-Analysis of Correctional Education Programs in the United States." *Journal of Experimental Criminology* 14, no. 3 (2018): 379–428.

Brennan, Tim, Markus Breitenbach, William Dieterich, Emily J. Salisbury, and Patricia Van Voorhis. "Women's Pathways to Serious and Habitual Crime: A Person-Centered Analysis Incorporating Gender Responsive Factors." *Criminal Justice and Behavior* 39, no. 11 (2012): 1481–508.

Brucker, Debra L. "Social Construction of Disability and Substance Abuse within Public Disability Benefit Systems." *International Journal of Drug Policy* 20, no. 5 (2009): 418–23.

Buchanan, Erin, and Margaret Ann Keaton. "Anticipated Stereotypes of Female Convicted Felons." *American Journal of Forensic Psychology* 32, no. 4 (2014): 43–55.

Burnside, Ashley. *No More Double Punishments: Lifting the Ban on SNAP and TANF for People with Prior Felony Drug Convictions.* Washington, DC: Center for Law and Social Policy, 2022.

Bush-Baskette, Stephanie. "Is Meth the New Crack for Women in the War on Drugs? Factors Affecting Sentencing Outcomes for Women and Parallels between Meth and Crack." *Feminist Criminology* 7, no. 1 (2012): 46–69.

———. "The War on Drugs and the Incarceration of Mothers." *Journal of Drug Issues* 30, no. 4 (2000): 919–28.

Cadigan, Michele, and Gabriela Kirk. "On Thin Ice: Bureaucratic Processes of Monetary Sanctions and Job Insecurity." *RSF: The Russell Sage Foundation Journal of the Social Sciences* 6, no. 1 (2020): 113–31.

Cameron, Sarah Kate, Jacquia Rodgers, and Dave Dagnan. "The Relationship between the Therapeutic Alliance and Clinical Outcomes in Cognitive Behaviour Therapy for Adults with Depression: A Meta-Analytic Review." *Clinical Psychology and Psychotherapy* 25, no. 3 (2018): 446–56.

Cantora, Andrea. "Navigating the Job Search after Incarceration: The Experiences of Work-Release Participants." *Criminal Justice Studies* 28, no. 2 (2015): 141–60.

Carlen, Pat. *Women, Crime and Poverty.* Milton Keynes, England: Open University Press, 1988.

Carlen, Pat, and Jacqueline Tombs. "Reconfigurations of Penalty: The Ongoing Case of the Women's Imprisonment and Reintegration Industries." *Theoretical Criminology* 10, no. 3 (2006): 337–60.

Carlson, Deven, Robert Haverman, Tom Kaplan, and Barbara Wolfe. "Long-Term Earnings and Employment Effects of Housing Voucher Receipt." *Journal of Urban Economics* 71, no. 1 (2012): 128–50.

Carpenter, Dick M., Lisa Knepper, Kyle Sweetland, and Jennifer McDonald. *License to Work: A National Study of Burdens from Occupational Licensing.* Arlington, Virginia: Institute for Justice, 2017.

Carr, Alan, Hollie Duff, and Fiona Craddock. "A Systematic Review of Reviews of the Outcome of Noninstitutional Child Maltreatment." *Trauma, Violence, and Abuse* 21, no. 4 (2020): 828–43.

Carson, E. Ann. *Prisoners in 2020: Statistical Tables*. Washington, DC: Bureau of Justice Statistics, 2021.

Carson, E. Ann, and Rich Kluckow. *Correctional Populations in the United States, 2021—Statistical Tables, 2021*. Washington, DC: U.S. Department of Justice, Bureau of Justice Statistics, 2023.

Charles, Kerwin K., and Ming Ching Luoh. "Male Incarceration, the Marriage Market, and Female Outcomes." *Review of Economics and Statistics* 92, no. 3 (2010): 614–27.

Cherney, Adrian, and Robin Fitzgerald. "Efforts by Offenders to Manage and Overcome Stigma: The Case of Employment." *Current Issues in Criminal Justice* 28, no. 1 (2016): 17–31.

Chesney-Lind, Meda, and Lisa J. Pasko. *The Female Offender: Girls, Women, and Crime*. 3d ed. Los Angeles: Sage, 2013.

Chesney-Lind, Meda, and Noelie Rodriguez. *Women under Lock and Key: A View from the Inside*. Manoa: Youth Development and Research Center, School of Social Work, University of Hawaii, 1983.

Chesney-Lind, Meda, and Randall G. Sheldon. *Girls, Delinquency and Juvenile Justice*. 3d ed. Belmont, California: Wadsworth/Thompson Learning, 2004.

Chetty, Raj, Nathaniel Hendren, Maggie R. Jones, and Sonya R. Porter. "Race and Economic Opportunity in the United States: An Intergenerational Perspective." *Quarterly Journal of Economics* 135, no. 2 (2020): 711–83.

Children's Defense Fund. *TANF at 25: A Reflection and Reckoning*. Washington, DC: Children's Defense Fund, 2021.

Chodorow, Nancy. *The Reproduction of Mothering*. Berkeley: University of California Press, 1978.

Clark, Michael D., Todd A. Roberts, and Teresa Chandler. "Motivational Interviewing for Community Corrections: Expanding a Relationship-Based Approach with Exemplar Implementation." *Federal Probation* 84, no. 2 (2020): 35–43.

Clear, Todd R. *Imprisoning Communities: How Mass Incarceration Makes Disadvantaged Neighborhoods Worse*. New York: Oxford University Press, 2007.

Cobbina, Jennifer E. "From Prison to Home: Women's Pathways in and out of Crime." PhD diss., University of Missouri–St. Louis, 2009.

Cobbina, Jennifer E., Merry Morash, Deborah A. Kashy, and Sandi W. Smith. "Race, Neighborhood Danger, and Coping Strategies among Female Probationers and Parolees." *Race and Justice* 4, no. 1 (2014): 3–28.

Colgan, Beth A. "Beyond Graduation: Economic Sanctions and Structural Reform." *Duke Law Journal* 69, no. 7 (2020): 1529–83.

Collins, Patricia Hill. *Black Feminist Thought: Knowledge, Consciousness, and the Politics of Empowerment*. Boston: Unwin Hyman, 1990.

Coltrane, Scott. "Research on Household Labor: Modeling and Measuring the Social Embeddedness of Routine Family Work." *Journal of Marriage and the Family* 62, no. 4 (2000): 1208–33.

Committee on Examination of the Adequacy of Food Resources and SNAP Allotments. "History, Background, and Goals of the Supplemental Nutrition Assistance Program." In *Supplemental Nutrition Assistance Program:*

Examining the Evidence to Define Benefit Adequacy, edited by J. A. Caswell and A. L. Yaktine. Washington, DC: National Academies Press, 2013.

Community Mental Health Association of Michigan. *Addressing the Systemic Underfunding of Michigan's Public Mental Health System*. 2019. https://cmham.org/wp-content/uploads/2019/03/Systemic-underfunding-of -Michigans-public-mental-health-system-rev.pdf.

Cornacchione, Jennifer, and Sandi W. Smith. "Female Offenders' Multiple Goals for Engaging in Desired Communication with Their Probation/Parole Officers." *Communication Quarterly* 65, no. 1 (2017): 1–19.

Cornacchione, Jennifer, Sandi W. Smith, Merry Morash, Miriam Northcutt Bohmert, Jennifer Cobbina, and Deborah A. Kashy. "An Exploration of Female Offenders' Memorable Messages from Probation and Parole Officers on the Self-Assessment of Behavior from a Control Theory Perspective." *Journal of Applied Communication Research* 4, no. 1 (2016): 60–77.

Costello, Margaret. "Fulfilling the Unfulfilled Promise of Gideon: Litigation as a Viable Strategic Tool." *Iowa Law Review* 99 (2014): 1951–78.

Couloute, Lucius, and Daniel Kopf. *Out of Prison and Out of Work: Unemployment among Formerly Incarcerated People*. Prison Policy Initiative. Northampton, Massachusetts, 2018. www.prisonpolicy.org/reports/outofwork.html.

Cournoyer, Louis-Georges, Serge Brochu, Michel Landry, and Jacques Bergeron. "Therapeutic Alliance, Patient Behaviour and Dropout in a Drug Rehabilitation Programme: The Moderating Effect of Clinical Subpopulations." *Addiction* 102, no. 12 (2007): 397–410.

Covington, Stephanie. *Helping Women Recover*. San Francisco: Jossey-Bass, 2019.

Covington, Stephanie, and Barbara Bloom. "Gendered Justice: Addressing Female Offenders." In *Gendered Justice: Women in the Criminal Justice System*, 1–20. Durham, North Carolina: Center for Gender and Justice, 2003.

Covington, Stephanie S., and Barbara E. Bloom. "Gender Responsive Treatment and Services in Correctional Settings." *Women and Therapy* 29, nos. 3–4 (2007): 9–33.

Crenshaw, Kimberlé. "Demarginalizing the Intersection of Race and Sex: A Black Feminist Critique of Antidiscrimination Doctrine, Feminist Theory and Antiracist Politics." *University of Chicago Legal Forum* 14 (1989): 139–67.

———. "Mapping the Margins: Intersectionality, Identity Politics, and Violence against Women of Color." *Stanford Law Review* 43, no. 6 (1991): 1241–99.

Criminal Justice Policy Program. "50-State Comparison: Expungement, Sealing and Other Record Relief." Collateral Consequences Resource Center, 2021. https://ccresourcecenter.org/state-restoration-profiles/50–state-comparison judicial-expungement-sealing-and-set-aside/.

———. "50-State Criminal Justice Debt Reform Builder." Cambridge, Massachusetts: Harvard Law School, June 5, 2022. https://cjdebtreform.org/.

———. *Confronting Criminal Justice Debt: A Guide for Policy Reform*. Harvard Law School. Cambridge, Massachusetts, 2016. www.nclc.org/issues /confronting-criminal-justice-debt.html.

Crone, Eveline A. *The Adolescent Brain: Changes in Learning, Decision-Making and Social Relations*. New York: Routledge, 2017.

Crowley, Michael F., Matthew J. Menendez, and Eisen Lauren-Brooke. "If We Only Knew the Cost: Scratching the Surface on How Much It Costs to Assess and Collect Court Imposed Criminal Fees and Fines." *UCLA Criminal Justice Law Review* 4, no. 1 (2020): 165–76.

Currie, Elliot. *A Peculiar Indifference: The Neglected Toll of Violence on Black America*. New York: Metropolitan Books, 2020.

Custer, Bradley D. "The History of Denying Federal Financial Aid to System-Impacted Students." *Journal of Student Financial Aid* 50, no. 1 (2021): 1–16.

Daly, Kathleen. "Women's Pathways to Felony Court: Feminist Theories of Lawbreaking and Problems of Representation." *Southern California Review of Law and Women's Studies* 2, no. 1 (1992): 11–52.

Danziger, Sandra K., Jessica Wiederspan, and Jonah A. Douglas-Siegel. "We're Not All Deadbeat Parents: Welfare Recipient Voices on Unmet Service Needs." *Journal of Poverty* 17, no. 3 (2013): 305–30.

Danziger, Sheldon, Matthew M. Davis, Sean Orzol, and Harold A. Pollack. "Health Insurance and Access to Care among Welfare Leavers." *Inquiry* 45, no. 2 (2008): 184–97.

Darden, Joe T., and Sameh M. Kamel. "Black Residential Segregation in the City and Suburbs of Detroit: Does Socioeconomic Status Matter?" *Journal of Urban Affairs* 22, no. 1 (2000): 1–14.

Darden, Joe T., Mohammad Rahbar, Mouise Jezierski, Min Li, and Ellen Velie. "The Measurement of Neighborhood Socioeconomic Characteristics and Black and White Residential Segregation in Metropolitan Detroit: Implications for the Study of Social Disparities in Health." *Annals of the Association of American Geographers* 100, no. 1 (2010): 137–58.

Davis, Jordan P., Joan S. Tucker, Bradley D. Stein, and Elizabeth J. D'Amico. "Longitudinal Effects of Adverse Childhood Experiences on Substance Use Transition Patterns During Young Adulthood." *Child Abuse and Neglect* 120 (October 2021): 105201.

Daw, Jamie R., Laura A. Hatfield, Katherine Swartz, and Benjamin D. Sommers. "Women in the United States Experience High Rates of Coverage 'Churn' in Months before and after Childbirth." *Health Affairs* 36, no. 4 (2017): 598–606.

Debus-Sherrill, Sara, Alex Breno, and Faye S. Taxman. "What Makes or Breaks Evidence-Based Supervision? Staff and Organizational Predictors of Evidence-Based Practice in Probation." *International Journal of Offender Therapy and Comparative Criminology* 67, nos. 6–7 (2023): 662–86.

Decker, Scott H., Natalie Ortiz, Cassia Spohn, and Eric Hedberg. "Criminal Stigma, Race, and Ethnicity: The Consequences of Imprisonment for Employment." *Journal of Criminal Justice* 43, no. 2 (2015): 108–21.

DeCou, Christopher R., Shannon M. Lynch, Dana D. DeHart, and Joanne Belknap. "Evaluating the Association between Childhood Sexual Abuse and Attempted Suicide across the Lifespan: Findings from a Nationwide Study of Women in Jail." *Psychological Services* 13, no. 2 (2016): 254–60.

DeHart, Dana, Shannon Lynch, Joanne Belknap, Pricilla Dass-Brailsford, and Bonnie Green. "Life History Models of Female Offending: The Roles of

Serious Mental Illness and Trauma in Women's Pathways to Jail." *Psychology of Women Quarterly* 38, no. 1 (2014): 138–51.

DeLuca, Stephanie, Phillp M. E. Garboden, and Peter Rosenblatt. "Segregating Shelter: How Housing Policies Shape the Residential Locations of Low-Income Minority Families." *Annals of the American Academy of Political and Social Sciences* 647, no. 1 (2013): 268–99.

DeMichele, Matthew. "Studying the Community Corrections Field: Applying Neo-Institutional Theories to a Hidden Element of Mass Social Control." *Theoretical Criminology* 18, no. 4 (2014): 546–64.

Department of Health and Human Services. *National Survey of Substance Abuse Treatment Services (N-SSATS): 2011 Data on Substance Abuse Treatment Facilities*. Substance Abuse and Mental Health Services Administration. Rockville, Maryland, 2012. https://mhanational.org/issues/2017-state -mental-health-america-ranking-states.

Dewey, Susan, Bonnie Zare, Catherine Connolly, Rhett Epler, and Rosemary Bratton. *Outlaw Women: Prison, Rural Violence, and Poverty in the American West*. New York: New York University Press, 2019.

Dobson, Cheyney Cooper. "Merging Criminal Justice and Social Welfare in Mental Health Court: The Disparate Impacts and Outcomes of Coercive Aid in the Era of Mass Incarceration." PhD diss., University of Michigan, 2019.

Domhardt, Matthias, Annika Münzer, Jörg M. Fegert, and Lutz Goldbeck. "Resilience in Survivors of Child Sexual Abuse: A Systematic Review of the Literature." *Trauma, Violence, and Abuse* 18, no. 4 (2015): 476–93.

Downing, Nancy R., Marvellous Akinlotan, and Carly W. Thornhill. "The Impact of Childhood Sexual Abuse and Adverse Childhood Experiences on Adult Health Related Quality of Life." *Child Abuse and Neglect* 120 (October 2021).

Dube, Shanta R., Jacqueline W. Miller, David W. Brown, Wayne H. Giles, Vincent J. Felitti, Maxia Dong, and Robert F. Anda. "Adverse Childhood Experiences and the Association with Ever Using Alcohol and Initiating Alcohol Use During Adolescence." *Journal of Adolescent Health* 38, no. 4 (2006): 1–10.

Dworsky, Amy, Matthews H. Morton, and Gina M. Samuels. *Missed Opportunities: Pregnant and Parenting Youth Experiencing Homelessness in America*. Chicago: Chapin Hall at the University of Chicago, 2018.

Economic Innovation Group. *The 2016 Distressed Communities Index*. Washington, DC. https://eig.org/wp-content/uploads/2016/02/2016-Distressed -Communities-Index-Report.pdf.

Edin, Kathryn, and Maria Kefala. *Promises I Can Keep: Why Poor Women Put Motherhood before Marriage*. Berkeley: University of California Press, 2005.

Edin, Kathryn, and Laura Lein. *Making Ends Meet: How Single Mothers Survive Welfare and Low-Wage Work*. New York: Russell Sage Foundation, 1997.

Epstein, Rebecca, Jamilia J. Blake, and Thalia González. *Girlhood Interrupted: The Erasure of Black Girls' Childhood*. Washington, DC: Center on Poverty and Inequality, Georgetown Law, 2017.

Estrada, Felipe, and Anders Nilsson. "Does It Cost More to Be a Female Offender? A Life-Course Study of Childhood Circumstances, Crime, Drug Abuse, and Living Conditions." *Feminist Criminology* 7, no. 3 (2012): 196–219.

Fader, Jamie J. *Falling Back: Incarceration and Transitions to Adulthood among Urban Youth.* New Brunswick, New Jersey: Rutgers University Press, 2013.

Farrigan, Tracey, and Timothy Parker. *The Concentration of Poverty Is a Growing Rural Problem.* U.S. Department of Agriculture Economic Research Service. Washington, DC, 2012. www.ers.usda.gov/topics/rural-economy -population/rural-poverty-well-being.aspx#.UdWj_qzWOSo.

Fazel, Seena, Isabel A. Yoon, and Adrian J. Hayes. "Substance Use Disorders in Prisoners: An Updated Systematic Review and Meta-Regression Analysis in Recently Incarcerated Men and Women." *Addiction* 112, no. 10 (2017): 1725–39.

Fearn, Noelle E., Michael G. Vaughn, Erik J. Nelson, Christopher P. Salas-Wright, Matt DeLisi, and Zhengmin Qian. "Trends and Correlates of Substance Use Disorders among Probationers and Parolees in the United States 2002–2014." *Drug and Alcohol Dependence* 167 (October 1, 2016): 128–39.

Feld, Barry C. "Justice by Geography: Urban, Suburban, and Rural Variations in Juvenile Justice Administration." *Journal of Criminal Law and Criminology* 82, no. 1 (1991): 156–210.

Fernandes, April D., Michelle Cadigan, Frank Edwards, and Alexes Harris. "Monetary Sanctions: A Review of Revenue Generation, Legal Challenges, and Reform." *Annual Review of Law and Social Science* 15, no. 1 (2019): 397–413.

Fines and Fees Justice Center. *End Fees, Discharge Debt, Fairly Fund Government: FFJC Policy Guidance for Eliminating Criminal Legal System Fees and Discharging Debt.* 2022. https://finesandfeesjusticecenter.org/content/uploads /2022/01/FFJC-Policy-Guidance-Fee-Elimination-1.13.22.pdf.

Fines and Fees Justice Center and Reform Alliance. *50-State Survey: Probation and Parole Fees.* 2022. https://finesandfeesjusticecenter.org/.

Fivush, Robyn, Melissa A. Brotman, Janine P. Buckner, and Sherryl H. Goodman. "Gender Differences in Parent-Child Emotion Narratives." *Sex Roles* 42, nos. 3–4 (2000): 233–53.

Fivush, Robyn, and Kelly Marin. "Development of a Gendered Narrative Identity." In *APA Handbook of the Psychology of Women: History, Theory and Battlegrounds*, edited by Cheryl B. Travis, Jacquelyn W. White, Alexandra Rutherford, Wendi S. Williams, Sarah L. Cook, and Karen F. Wyche, 473–87. Washington, DC: American Psychological Association, 2018.

Floyd, Ife, LaDonna Pavetti, Laura Meyer, Ali Safawi, Liz Schott, Evelyn Bellew, and Abigail Magnus. *TANF Policies Reflect Racist Legacy of Cash Assistance: Reimagined Program Should Center Black Mothers.* Center on Budget and Policy Priorities. Washington DC, 2021. www.cbpp.org/research/family -income-support/tanf-policies-reflect-racist-legacy-of-cash-assistance.

Fox, Liana E., and Kalee Burns. *The Supplemental Poverty Measure: 2020.* Washington, DC: U.S. Department of Commerce, U.S. Census Bureau, September 2021.

Fusaro, Vincent A. "State Politics, Race, and 'Welfare' as a Funding Stream: Cash Assistance Spending under Temporary Assistance for Needy Families." *Policy Studies Journal* 49, no. 3 (2021): 811–34.

Gaardner, Emily, and Joanne Belknap. "Tenuous Borders: Girls Transferred to Adult Court." *Criminology* 40 (2002): 481–517.

Gido, Rosemary L., and Lanette Dalley. *Women's Mental Health Issues across the Criminal Justice System.* Upper Saddle River, New Jersey: Prentice Hall, 2009.

Gilligan, Carol. *In a Different Voice: Psychological Theory and Women's Development.* Cambridge, Massachusetts: Harvard University Press, 1982.

Giordano, Peggy C. *Legacies of Crime: A Follow-up of the Children of Highly Delinquent Girls and Boys.* New York: Cambridge University Press, 2010.

Giordano, Peggy C., Stephen A. Cernkovich, and Jennifer L. Rudolph. "Gender, Crime, and Desistance: Toward a Theory of Cognitive Transformation." *American Journal of Sociology* 107, no. 4 (2002): 990–1064.

Gleicher, Lily, and Caitlin DeLong. *The Cost of Justice: The Impact of Criminal Justice Financial Obligations on Individuals and Families.* Illinois Criminal Justice Authority. 2018. https://icjia.illinois.gov/researchhub/articles/the-cost-of-justice-the-impact-of-criminal-justice-financial-obligations-on-individuals-and-families.

Goldhill, Rachel. "Probation Policy and Practice with Vulnerable Women: A Focus on the Challenges of Organisational and Personal Change for Women Workers and Women Service Users." PhD diss., University of Portsmouth, 2018.

Goodson, Marva V. "Help or Hindrance: Female Probationers' Navigation of Supervision Requirements through Personal Support Networks." *Criminal Justice and Behavior* 45, no. 10 (2018): 1483–506.

Goodson-Miller, Marva V. "A First Look at Justice-Involved Women's Egocentric Social Networks." *Social Networks* 70 (July, 2022): 152–65.

Gottschalk, Marie. *Caught: The Prison State and the Lockdown of American Politics.* Princeton, New Jersey: Princeton University Press, 2015.

Gramm, Phil, and Mike Solon. "If You Like Michigan's Economy, You'll Love Obama's." *Wall Street Journal Eastern Edition*, September 13, 2008, A13.

Gruhn, Meredith A., and Bruce E. Compas. "Effects of Maltreatment on Coping and Emotional Regulation in Childhood and Adolescence: A Meta-Analytic Review." *Child Abuse and Neglect* 103 (2020).

Gustafson, Kaaryn S. *Cheating Welfare: Public Assistance and the Criminalization of Poverty.* New York: New York University Press, 2012.

Hahn, Heather, Lauren Farrell, Amelia Coffey, and Gina Adams. *Young People's Lived Experiences with Safety Net Programs: Insights from Young People and Youth-Serving Organizations.* Urban Institute. Washington, DC, 2001. www.urban.org/research/publication/young-peoples-lived-experiences-safety-net-programs-insights-young-people-and-youth-serving-organizations.

Halpern-Meekin, Sarah, Kathryn Edin, Laura Tach, and Jennifer Sykes. *It's Not Like I'm Poor: How Working Families Make Ends Meet in a Post-Welfare World.* Oakland: University of California Press, 2015.

Hampton, Robert, William Oliver, and Lucia Magarian. "Domestic Violence in the African American Community: An Analysis of Social and Structural Factors." *Violence Against Women* 9, no. 5 (2003): 533–57.

Haney, Lynne. "Introduction: Gender, Welfare, and States of Punishment." *Social Politics* 11, no. 3 (2004): 333–62.

———. *Offending Women: Power, Punishment, and the Regulation of Desire.* Berkeley: University of California Press, 2010.

Harris, Alexes. *A Pound of Flesh: Monetary Sanctions as Punishment for the Poor.* New York: Russell Sage Foundation, 2016.

Harris, Alexes, Mary Pattillo, and Bryan L. Sykes. "Studying the System of Monetary Sanctions." *RSF: The Russell Sage Foundation Journal of the Social Sciences* 8, no. 1 (2022): 1–33.

Harris, Alexes, and Tyler Smith. "Monetary Sanctions as Chronic and Acute Health Stressors: The Emotional Strain of People Who Owe Court Fines and Fees." *RSF: The Russell Sage Foundation Journal of the Social Sciences* 8, no. 2 (2022): 36–56.

Hatton, Erin. "Mechanisms of Invisibility: Rethinking the Concept of Invisible Work." *Work, Employment and Society* 31, no. 2 (2017).

Hazra, Devika, and Jose Aranzazu. "Crime, Correction, Education and Welfare in the U.S.—What Role Does the Government Play?" *Journal of Policy Modeling* 44 (2022): 474–91.

Heimer, Karen. "Changes in the Gender Gap in Crime and Women's Economic Marginalization." In *From the Nature of Crime: Continuity and Change; Criminal Justice 2000*, edited by Gary LaFree, 427–83. Washington, DC: National Institute of Justice, 2000.

Heiner, Brady T., and Sarah K. Tyson. "Feminism and the Carceral State: Gender Responsive Justice, Community Accountability, and the Epistemology of Antiviolence." *Feminist Philosophy Quarterly* 3, no. 1 (2017): 1–36.

Henrichson, Christian, Joshua Rinaldi, and Ruth Delaney. *The Price of Jails: Measuring the Taxpayer Cost of Local Incarceration.* Brooklyn, New York: Vera Institute of Justice, 2015.

Herring, Tiana. *Since You Asked: What Role Does Drug Enforcement Play in the Rising Incarceration of Women?* Easthampton, Massachusetts: Prison Policy Initiative, 2020. www.prisonpolicy.org/blog/2020/11/10/women-drug -enforcement/.

Hill, Chyna E., Hsu-Ta Hsu, Monique Holguin, Matthew H. Morton, Hailey Winetrobe, and Eric Rice. "An Examination of Housing Interventions among Youth Experiencing Homelessness: An Investigation into Racial/Ethnic and Sexual Minority Status." *Journal of Public Health* 44, no. 4 (2021): 834–43.

Hogan, Sean R., George J. Unick, Richard Speiglman, and Jean C. Norris. "Social Welfare Policy and Public Assistance for Low-Income Substance Abusers: The Impact of 1996 Welfare Reform Legislation on the Economic Security of Former Supplemental Security Income Drug Addiction and Alcoholism Beneficiaries." *Journal of Sociology and Social Welfare* 35, no. 1 (2008): 221–46.

Holmstrom, Amanda J., Elizabeth A. Adams, Merry Morash, Sandi W. Smith, and Jennifer E. Cobbina. "Supportive Messages Female Offenders Receive from Probation and Parole Officers about Substance Avoidance: Message Perceptions and Effects." *Criminal Justice and Behavior* 44, no. 11 (2017): 1496–517.

Holtfreter, Kristy, Michael D. Reisig, and Merry Morash. "Poverty, State Capital, and Recidivism among Women Offenders." *Criminology and Public Policy* 3, no. 2 (2004): 185–208.

Holtfreter, Kristy, and Katelyn A. Wattanaporn. "The Transition from Prison to Community Initiative." *Criminal Justice and Behavior* 41, no. 1 (2014): 41–57.

Holzer, Harry. "The Spatial Mismatch Hypothesis: What Has the Evidence Shown?" *Urban Studies* 28, no. 1 (1991): 105–22.

Hook, Jennifer L. "Gender Inequality in the Welfare State: Sex Segregation in Housework: 1965–2003." *American Journal of Sociology* 115, no. 5 (2010): 1480–523.

hooks, bell. *Ain't I a Woman: Black Women and Feminism.* Boston: South End Press, 1981.

Hoskins, Kayla M. "'I'm Going to Be Successful Someday': Women's Personal Projects to Improve Their Lives, and Implications for Clarifying the Nature of Agency in Criminological Theories of Desistance." *Feminist Criminology* 17, no. 2 (2022): 185–205.

Hoskins, Kayla M., and Merry Morash. "How Women on Probation and Parole Incorporate Trauma into Their Identities." *Journal of Interpersonal Violence* 36, nos. 23–24 (2021): NP12807–NP12830.

Howard, Ruth, Katherine Berry, and Gillian Haddock. "Therapeutic Alliance in Psychological Therapy for Posttraumatic Stress Disorder: A Systematic Review and Meta-Analysis." *Clinical Psychology and Psychotherapy* 29, no. 2 (2021): 373–99.

Huebner, Beth M., Christina DeJong, and Jennifer E. Cobbina. "Women Coming Home: Long-Term Patterns of Recidivism." *Justice Quarterly* 27, no. 2 (2010): 225–54.

Huebner, Beth M., and Andrea Giuffre. "Reinforcing the Web of Municipal Courts: Evidence and Implications Post Ferguson." *RSF: The Russell Sage Foundation Journal of the Social Sciences* 1, no. 1 (2022): 108–27.

Initiative on Gender Justice and Opportunity. *The Innocence Initiative: Translating National Research into Local Action in Central Texas.* Georgetown Law Center on Poverty and Inequality. Washington, DC, 2021. https://gender justiceandopportunity.georgetown.edu/wp-content/uploads/2021/06/The -Innocence-Initiative-Translating-National-Research-into-Local-Action-in -Central-Texas-FINAL.pdf.

Irwin, Katherine, Lisa Pasko, and Janet T. Davidson. "Girls and Women in Conflict with the Law." In *Routledge Handbook of Critical Criminology*, edited by Walter S. DeKeseredy and Molly Dragiewicz, 358–68. New York: Routledge, 2018.

Jenkins, Esther J. "Community Insights on Domestic Violence among African Americans." *Journal of Aggression, Maltreatment and Trauma* 30, no. 6 (2021): 714–30.

Jimroglou, Krissi. *U.S. Prison Count Continues to Drop.* Pew Charitable Trusts. Washington, DC, 2013. www.pewtrusts.org/en/about/news-room /press-releases-and-statements/2013/03/08/us-prison-count-continues -to-drop.

Jones, Alexi, and Wendy Sawyer. *Arrest, Release, Repeat: How Police and Jails Are Misused to Respond to Social Problems.* Prison Policy Initiative. Easthampton, Massachusetts, 2019. www.prisonpolicy.org/reports/repeatarrests.html.

Jones, Nikki. *The Chosen Ones: Black Men and the Politics of Redemption.* Oakland: University of California Press, 2018.

Jordan, Judith V., ed. *The Power of Connection: Recent Developments in Relational-Cultural Theory.* New York: Routledge, 2013.

Jurkovic, Gregor J. *Lost Childhoods: The Plight of the Parentified Child.* New York: Routledge, 2014.

Kaeble, Danielle. *Probation and Parole in the United States, 2020.* Washington, DC: U.S. Department of Justice, Bureau of Justice Statistics, 2021.

Kaistura, Aleks. *Women's Mass Incarceration: The Whole Pie.* Prison Policy Initiative. Easthampton, Massachusetts, 2019. www.prisonpolicy.org/reports/pie2019women.html.

Kantorowicz-Reznichenko, Elena. "Day-Fines: Should the Rich Pay More?" *Review of Law and Economics* 11, no. 3 (2015): 481–501.

Kauff, Jacqueline, Michelle K. Derr, LaDonna Pavetti, and Emily Sama Martin. *Using Work-Oriented Sanctions to Increase TANF Program Participation: Final Report.* Mathematica Policy Research, Inc. Washington, DC, 2007. www.acf.hhs.gov/opre/report/using-work-oriented-sanctions-increase-tanf-program-participation-final-report.

Kennealy, Patrick. J., Jennifer L. Skeem, Sarah M. Manchak, and Jennifer Eno Louden. "Firm, Fair, and Caring Officer-Offender Relationships Protect against Supervision Failure." *Law and Human Behavior* 36, no. 6 (2012): 496–505.

Kerig, Patricia K. "Polyvictimization and Girls' Involvement in the Juvenile Justice System: Investigating Gender-Differentiated Patterns of Risk, Recidivism, and Resilience." *Journal of Interpersonal Violence* 33, no. 5 (2018): 789–809.

Kilgore, James. "Repackaging Mass Incarceration." *Counterpunch*, June 6 2014. www.counterpunch.org/2014/06/06/repackaging-mass-incarceration/.

Kirk, Gabriela, Kristina J. Thompson, Beth M. Huebner, Christopher Uggen, and Sarah K. S. Shannon. "Justice by Geography: The Role of Monetary Sanctions across Communities." *RSF: The Russell Sage Foundation Journal of the Social Sciences* 8, no. 1 (2022): 200–20.

Kissane, Rebecca Joyce. "They Never Did Me Any Good: Welfare to Work Programs from the Vantage Point of Poor Women." *Humanity and Society* 32, no. 4 (2008): 336–60.

Kleit, Rachel Garshick, Seugbeom Kang, and Corianne Payton Scally. "Why Do Housing Mobility Programs Fail in Moving Households to Better Neighborhoods?" *Housing Policy Debate* 26, no. 1 (2016): 188–209.

Kubiak, Sheryl Pimlott, Woo Jong Kim, Gina Fedock, and Deborah Bybee. "Differences among Incarcerated Women with Assaultive Offenses: Isolated Versus Patterned Use of Violence." *Journal of Interpersonal Violence* 28, no. 12 (2013): 2462–90.

Kubrin, Charis E., and Eric A. Stewart. "Predicting Who Reoffends: The Neglected Role of Neighborhood Context in Recidivism Studies." *Criminology* 44, no. 1 (2006): 165–97.

Kushel, Margot, Judith A. Hahn, Jennifer L. Evans, David R. Bangsberg, and Andrew R. Moss. "Revolving Doors: Imprisonment Amongst the Homeless and Marginally Housed Population." *American Journal of Public Health* 95 (2005): 1747–52.

Lalor, Kevin, and Rosaleen McElvaney. "Child Sexual Abuse, Links to Later Sexual Exploitation/High-Risk Sexual Behavior, and Prevention/Treatment Programs." *Trauma, Violence, and Abuse* 11, no. 4 (2010): 159–77.

LeBel, Thomas P., Matt Richie, and Shadd Maruna. "Helping Others as a Response to Reconcile a Criminal Past: The Role of the Wounded Healer in Prisoner Reentry Programs." *Criminal Justice and Behavior* 42, no. 1 (2015): 108–20.

Lee, Lois K., Alyna Chien, Amanda Stewart, Larissa Truschel, Jennifer Hoffmann, Elyse Portillo, Lydia E. Pace, Mark Clapp, and Alison A. Galbraith. "Women's Coverage, Utilization, Affordability, and Health after the ACA: A Review of the Literature." *Health Affairs* 39, no. 3 (2020): 387–94.

Lee, Rebekah, and Chris Brown. "The Relations among Career-Related Self-Efficacy, Perceived Career Barriers, and Stigma Consciousness in Men with Felony Convictions." *Psychological Services*. forthcoming.

"The Life Story Interview." The Foley Center. 2008. https://sites.northwestern .edu/thestudyoflivesresearchgroup/instruments/.

Lindhorst, Taryn, and Ronald J. Mancoske. "The Social and Economic Impact of Sanctions and Time Limits on Recipients of Temporary Assistance to Needy Families." *Journal of Sociology and Social Welfare* 33, no. 1 (2006): 93–114.

Lindsey, Treva B. *America, Goddam: Violence, Black Women, and the Struggle for Justice*. Oakland: University of California Press, 2021.

Lopez, Vera. *Complicated Lives: Girls, Parents, Drugs, and Juvenile Justice*. New Brunswick, New Jersey: Rutgers University Press, 2017.

Loprest, Pamela. *How Are Families That Left Welfare Doing? A Comparison of Early and Recent Welfare Leavers*. 2001. www.urban.org/sites/default/files /publication/61306/310282-How-Are-Families-That-Left-Welfare-Doing -.PDF.

Loudermilk, Elaine, Kevin Loudermilk, Julie Obenauer, and Megan A. Quinn. "Impact of Adverse Childhood Experiences (Aces) on Adult Alcohol Consumption Behavior." *Child Abuse and Neglect* 86 (2018): 368–74.

Loveland, David, and Michael Boyle. "Intensive Case Management as a Jail Diversion Program for People with a Serious Mental Illness: A Review of the Literature." *International Journal of Offender Therapy and Comparative Criminology* 51, no. 2 (2007): 130–50.

Lovett, Nicholas. "Food Stamps, Income Shocks, and Crime: Evidence from California." *B.E. Journal of Economic Analysis and Policy* 18, no. 4 (2018): 1–19.

Lovins, Lori Brusman, Frank T. Cullen, Edward J. Latessa, and Cheryl Lero Jonson. "Probation Officer as a Coach: Building a New Professional Identity." *Federal Probation* 82, no. 1 (2018): 13–19.

Lynch, Shannon M., Dana D. DeHart, Joanne Belknap, and Bonnie L. Green. *Women's Pathways to Jail: Examining Mental Health, Trauma, and Substance Use*. Washington, DC: U.S. Department of Justice, 2013.

Lynch, Shannon M., Dana D. Dehart, Joanne E. Belknap, Bonnie L. Green, Pricilla Dass-Brailsford, Kristine A. Johnson, and Elizabeth Whalley. "A Multisite Study of the Prevalence of Serious Mental Illness, PTSD, and Substance Use Disorders of Women in Jail." *Psychiatric Services* 65, no. 5 (2014): 670–74.

MacKenzie, Doris L. "First Do No Harm: A Look at Correctional Policies and Programs Today." *Journal of Experimental Criminology* 9, no. 1 (2013): 1–17.

Maher, Lisa, and Kathleen Daly. "Women in the Street-Level Drug Economy: Continuity or Change?" *Criminology* 3, no. 4 (1996): 465–91.

Mai, Chris, and Maria Katarina E. Rafael. "User Funded? Using Budgets to Examine the Scope and Revenue Impact of Fines and Fees in the Criminal Justice System." *Sociological Perspectives* 63, no. 6 (2020): 1002–14.

Mallach, Alan. *The Divided City: Poverty and Prosperity in Urban America.* Washington, DC: Island Press, 2018.

Marinescu, Ioana. *No Strings Attached: The Behavioral Effects of U.S Unconditional Cash Transfer Programs.* National Bureau of Economic Research. Cambridge, Massachusetts: 2018. www.nber.org/papers/w24337.

Maruna, Shadd. *Making Good: How Ex-Convicts Reform and Rebuild Their Lives.* Washington, DC: American Psychological Association Books, 2001.

Maruna, Shadd, Thomas P. LeBel, Nick Mitchell, and Michelle Naples. "Pygmalion in the Reintegration Process: Desistance from Crime through the Looking Glass." *Psychology, Crime and Law* 10, no. 3 (2004): 271–81.

Massey, Douglas S., and Mary J. Fisher. "How Segregation Concentrated Poverty." *Ethnic and Racial Studies* 23 (2010): 670–91.

Massey, Douglas S., Jonathan Rothwell, and Thurston Domina. "The Changing Bases of Segregation in the United States." *Annals of the American Academy of Political and Social Science* 626, no. 1 (2009): 74–90.

McAdams, Dan P. *Coding Autobiographical Episodes for Themes of Agency and Communion.* Evanston, Illinois: Foley Center for the Study of Lives, Northwestern University, 1992.

———. "Coding Systems for Themes of Agency and Communion." 2002. https://sites.northwestern.edu/thestudyoflivesresearchgroup/instruments/.

———. "Narrative Identity." In *Handbook of Identity Theory and Research*, edited by Seth J. Schwartz, Koen Luyckx, and Vivian L. Vignoles, 99–116. New York: Springer, 2011.

———. *The Redemptive Self: Stories Americans Live By.* New York: Oxford University Press, 2013.

McClure, Kirk. "Deconcentrating Poverty with Housing Programs." *Journal of the American Planning Association* 74, no. 1 (2008): 90–99.

McColl, Rebecca, and Letita Logan Passarella. *Life after Welfare: 2019 Annual Update.* Ruth H. Young Center for Families and Children, University of Maryland School of Social Work. Baltimore, Maryland, 2019. www.ssw.umaryland.edu/media/ssw/fwrtg/welfare-research/life-after-welfare/life2019.pdf.

McCorkel, Jill A. *Breaking Women: Gender, Race, and the New Politics of Imprisonment.* New York: New York University Press, 2013.

———. "Criminally Dependent? Gender, Punishment, and the Rhetoric of Welfare Reform." *Social Politics* 11, no. 3 (2004): 386–410.

McLean, Kate C., Brianna C. Delker, William L. Dunlop, Rowan Salton, and Moin Syed. "Redemptive Stories and Those Who Tell Them Are Preferred in the U.S." *Collabra: Psychology* 6, no. 1 (2020): 1–20.

McLean, Kate C., and Moin Syed. "Personal, Master, and Alternative Narratives: An Integrative Framework for Understanding Identity Development in Context." *Human Development* 58, no. 6 (2015): 318–49.

McMorrow, Stacey, Lisa Dubay, Genevieve M. Kenney, Emily M. Johnston, and Clara Alvarez Caraveo. *Uninsured New Mothers' Health and Health Care Challenges Highlight the Benefits of Increasing Postpartum Medicaid Coverage.* Urban Institute. Washington, DC, 2020. www.urban.org/research /publication/uninsured-new-mothers-health-and-health-care-challenges -highlight-benefits-increasing-postpartum-medicaid-coverage.

McNichol, Elizabeth, Douglas Hall, David Cooper, and Vincent Palacios. *Pulling Apart: A State-by-State Analysis of Income Trends.* Center on Budget and Policy Priorities. Washington, DC, 2012. www.cbpp.org/research/poverty -and-inequality/pulling-apart-a-state-by-state-analysis-of-income-trends.

McQuillan, Julia, Arthur L. Greil, Karina M. Scheffler, and Veronica Tichenor. "The Importance of Motherhood among Women in the Contemporary United States." *Gender and Society* 22, no. 4 (2008): 477–96.

Menendez, Matthew, and Lauren Brooke-Eisen. *The Steep Costs of Criminal Justice Fees and Fines.* The Brennan Center. New York, 2019. www .brennancenter.org/our-work/research-reports/steep-costs-criminal-justice -fees-and-fines.

Messina, Nena, Jeremy Braithwaite, Stacy Calhoun, and Sheryl Kubiak. "Examination of a Violence Prevention Program for Female Offenders." *Violence and Gender* 3, no. 3 (2016): 143–49.

Messina, Nena, Stacy Calhoun, and Umme Warda. "Gender-Responsive Drug Court Treatment: A Randomized Controlled Trial." *Criminal Justice and Behavior* 39, no. 12 (2012): 1539–58.

Messina, Nena, Christine E. Grella, Jerry Cartier, and Stephanie Torres. "A Randomized Experimental Study of Gender-Responsive Substance Abuse Treatment for Women in Prison." *Journal of Substance Abuse Treatment* 38, no. 2 (2010): 97–107.

Meyers, Marcia K., Shannon Harper, Maria Klawitter, and Taryn Lindhorst. *Review of Research on TANF Sanctions: Report to Washington State Workfirst Subcabinet.* Seattle, WA: West Coast Poverty Center, 2006.

Michigan Department of Corrections. *Michigan Department of Corrections: Field Operations Administration, Community Alternatives (Annual Report).* Lansing: Michigan Department of Corrections, 2012.

Michigan Department of Health and Human Services. *Person-Centered Planning Pratice Guideline.* Lansing, 2021. www.michigan.gov/documents /mdhhs/Person-Centered_Planning_Practice_Guideline_702780_7.pdf.

Miller, Jean Baker. *Toward a New Psychology of Women.* Boston: Beacon Press, 1976.

Miller, Jody, and Kristin Carbone-Lopez. "Beyond 'Doing Gender': Incorporating Race, Class, Place, and Life Transitions into Feminist Drug Research." *Substance Use and Misuse* 50, no. 6 (2015): 693–707.

Monahan, Kathryn C., Susan Vanderhei, Jordan Baechtold, and Elizabeth Cauffman. "From the School Yard to the Squad Car: School Discipline, Truancy, and Arrest." *Journal of Youth and Adolescence* 43, no. 7 (2014): 1110–22.

Moore, Matthew D., and Anthony W. Tatman. "Adverse Childhood Experiences and Offender Risk to Re-Offend in the United States: A Quantitative Examination." *International Journal of Criminal Justice Sciences* 11, no. 2 (2016).

Moore, Quinn, Robert G. Wood, and Anu Rangarajan. "The Dynamics of Women Disconnected from Employment and Welfare." *Social Service Review* 86, no. 1 (2012): 93–118.

Morash, Merry. *Women on Probation and Parole: A Feminist Critique of Community Programs and Services.* Boston: Northeastern University Press, 2010.

Morash, Merry, and Deborah A. Kashy. "The Relevance of Women's Economic Marginalization to Recidivism." *Criminal Justice and Behavior* 49, no. 3 (2022): 330–49.

Morash, Merry, Deborah A. Kashy, Miriam Northcutt Bohmert, Jennifer E. Cobbina, and Sandi W. Smith. "Women at the Nexus of Correctional and Social Policies: Implications for Recidivism Risk." *British Journal of Criminology* 57, no. 2 (2017): 441–62.

Morash, Merry, Deborah A. Kashy, Jennifer E. Cobbina, and Sandi W. Smith. "Characteristics and Context of Women Probationers and Parolees Who Engage in Violence." *Criminal Justice and Behavior* 45, no. 3 (2018): 381–401.

———. "Technical Violations, Treatment and Punishment Responses, and Subsequent Recidivism of Women on Probation and Parole." *Criminal Justice Policy Review* 30, no. 5 (2019): 788–810.

Morash, Merry, Deborah A. Kashy, Sandi W. Smith, and Jennifer E. Cobbina. "The Connection of Probation/Parole Officer Actions to Women Offenders' Recidivism." *Criminal Justice and Behavior* 43, no. 4 (2016): 506–24.

———. "The Effects of Probation or Parole Agent Relationship Style and Women Offenders' Criminogenic Needs on Offenders' Responses to Supervision Interactions." *Criminal Justice and Behavior* 42, no. 4 (2015): 412–34.

Morash, Merry, Rebecca Stone, Kayla Hoskins, Deborah A. Kashy, and Jennifer E. Cobbina. "Narrative Identity Development and Desistance from Illegal Behavior among Substance-Using Female Offenders: Implications for Narrative Therapy and Creating Opportunity." *Sex Roles* 83, no. 1–2 (2020): 64–84.

Morgen, Sandra, Joan Acker, and Jill Weight. *Stretched Thin: Poor Families Welfare Work, and Welfare Reform.* Ithaca, New York: Cornell University Press, 2010.

Morris, Monique W. *Pushout: The Criminalization of Black Girls in Schools.* New York: The New Press, 2016.

Morton, Matthew H., Raúl Chávez, Melissa A. Kull, Erin D. Carreon, Jha'asryel-Akquil Bishop, Simeon Daferede, Elijah Wood, Larry Cohen, and Pilar Barreyro. *Developing a Direct Cash Transfer Program for Youth Experiencing Homelessness: Results of a Mixed Methods, Multi-Stakeholder Design Process.* Chapin Hall at the University of Chicago. Chicago, 2020. www.chapinhall.org/research/direct-cash-transfers-program-can-help-youth-sustainably-exit-homelessness/.

Morton, Matthew H., Amy Dworsky, Jennifer L. Matjasko, Susanna R. Curry, David Schlueter, Raúl Chávez, and Anne F. Farrell. "Prevalence and Correlates of Youth Homelessness in the United States." *Journal of Adolescent Health* 62, no. 1 (2018): 14–21.

Morton, Matthew H., Amy Dworsky, and Gina M. Samuels. *Missed Opportunities: Youth Homelessness in America, National Estimates.* University of Chicago. 2017. https://voicesofyouthcount.org/brief/national-estimates-of-youth-homelessness/.

Morton, Matthew H., Shannon Kugley, Richard Epstein, and Anne F. Farrell. "Interventions for Youth Homelessness: A Systematic Review of Effectiveness Studies." *Children and Youth Services Review* 116 (September 2020).

Mulik, Kranti, and Lindsey Haynes-Maslow. "The Affordability of Myplate: An Analysis of SNAP Benefits and the Actual Cost of Eating According to the Dietary Guidelines." *Journal of Nutrition Education and Behavior* 49, no. 8 (2017): 623–31.

Muttillo, Aaron, Jennifer L. Murphy, and Anne Galletta. "A Decade of Trauma-Informed Care: An Organizational Case Study." *Journal of Aggression, Maltreatment and Trauma* 31, no. 8 (2022): 1033–51.

National Conference of State Legislatures. *The Evolving State of Occupational Licensing: Research, State Policies and Trends.* Washington, DC: National Conference of State Legislatures, 2019.

National Low Income Housing Coalition. "America's Affordable Housing Shortage, and How to End It." *Housing Spotlight* 3, no. 2 (2013): 1–6.

Norris, Jean C., Richard Scott, Richard Speiglman, and Rex Green. "Homelessness, Hunger, and Material Hardship among Those Who Lost SSI." *Contemporary Drug Problems* 30, nos. 1–2 (2003): 241–73.

Northcutt Bohmert, Miriam, and Alfred DeMaris. "Cumulative Disadvantage and the Role of Transportation in Community Supervision." *Crime and Delinquency* 64, no. 8 (2018).

O'Brien, Patricia, and Diane S. Young. "Challenges for Formerly Incarcerated Women: A Holistic Approach to Assessment." *Families in Society: The Journal of Contemporary Social Services* 87, no. 3 (2006): 359–66.

O'Neil, Meghan M., and J. J. Prescott. "Targeting Poverty in the Courts: Improving the Measurement of Ability to Pay." *Law and Contemporary Problems* 82, no. 1 (2019): 199–226.

O'Neil, Meghan M., and Daniel Strellman. "The Hidden Cost of the Disease: Fines, Fees, and Costs Assessed on Persons with Alleged Substance Use Disorder." *UCLA Criminal Justice Law Review* 4, no. 1 (2000): 235–46.

Ortiz, Natalie. "The Gendering of Criminal Stigma: An Experiment Testing the Effects of Race/Ethnicity and Incarceration on Women's Entry-Level Job Prospects." PhD diss., Arizona State University, 2014.

Orwin, Robert G., Bernadette Campbell, Kevin Campbell, and Antoinette Krupski. "Welfare Reform and Addiction: A Priori Hypothesis, Post Hoc Explorations, and Assisted Sensemaking in Evaluating the Effects of Terminating Benefits for Chronic Substance Abusers." *American Journal of Evaluation* 25, no. 4 (2004): 409–41.

Pager, Devah, Bruce Western, and Naomi Sugie. "Sequencing Disadvantage: Barriers to Employment Facing Young Black and White Men with Criminal Records." *Annals of the American Academy of Political and Social Science* 623 (2009): 195–213.

Palmer, Emma J., Ruth M. Hatcher, James McGuire, and Clive R. Hollin. "Cognitive Skills Programs for Female Offenders in the Community." *Criminal Justice and Behavior* 42, no. 4 (2015): 345–60.

Pals, Jennifer L. "Constructing the 'Springboard Effect': Causal Connections, Self-Making, and Growth within the Life Story." In *Identity and Story: Creating Self in Narrative*, edited by Dan P. McAdams, Ruthellen Josselson, and Amia Lieblich, 175–99. Washington, DC: American Psychological Association, 2006.

Parks, Erika, and Sarah Godfrey. *Michigan Enacts Landmark Jail Reforms: Historic Legislation Aims to Reduce Incarcerated Populations, Improve Public Safety.* Pew Charitable Trusts. Philadelphia, Pennsylvania, 2021. www.pew trusts.org/en/research-and-analysis/issue-briefs/2021/09/michigan-enacts -landmark-jail-reforms.

Parolin, Zachary. "Temporary Assistance for Needy Families and the Black-White Child Poverty Gap in the United States." *Socio-Economic Review* 19, no. 3 (2021): 1005–35.

Pasupathi, Monisha, Emma Mansour, and Jed R. Brubaker. "Developing a Life Story: Constructing Relations between Self and Experience in Autobiographical Narratives." *Human Development* 50, nos. 2–3 (2007): 85–110.

Pattillo, Mary, Erica Banks, Brian Sargent, and Daniel J. Boches. "Monetary Sanctions and Housing Instability." *RSF: The Russell Sage Foundation Journal of the Social Sciences* 8, no. 2 (2022): 57–75.

Pattillo, Mary, and Gabriela Kirk. "Layaway Freedom: Coercive Financialization in the Criminal Legal System." *American Journal of Sociology* 126, no. 4 (2021): 889–930.

Pavetti, LaDonna. *Work Requirements Don't Cut Poverty, Evidence Shows.* Center on Budget and Policy Priorities. Washington, DC, 2016. www.cbpp .org/sites/default/files/atoms/files/6-6-16pov3.pdf.

Pemberton, Simon, Susie Balderston, and Jo Long. *Trauma, Harm and Offending Behaviour: What Works to Address Social Injury and Criminogenic Need with Criminal Justice Involved Women? Initial Findings.* Birmingham, England: University of Birmingham, 2019.

Peterson, Janice, Xue Song, and Avis Jones-DeWeever. *Life after Welfare Reform: Low-Income Single Parent Families, Pre- and Post-TANF.* Women's Policy Research. Washington, DC, 2002. https://iwpr.org/wp-content/uploads/2020 /12/d446.pdf.

Peterson, Ruth D., and Lauren J. Krivo. *Divergent Social Worlds: Neighborhood Crime and the Racial-Spatial Divide.* New York: Russell Sage Foundation, 2010.

Petrosky, Emiko, Janet M. Blair, Carter J. Betz, Katherine A. Fowler, Shane P. D. Jack, and Briget H. Lyons. "Racial and Ethnic Differences in Homicides of Adult Women and the Role of Intimate Partner Violence—United States,

2003–2014." *Morbidity and Mortality Weekly Report* 66, no. 28 (2017): 741–46.

Pew Charitable Trusts. *Policy Reforms Can Strengthen Community Supervision*. Philadelphia, Pennsylvania: Pew Charitable Trusts, 2020.

Phelps, Michelle S. "The Paradox of Probation: Community Supervision in the Age of Mass Incarceration." *Law and Policy* 35, nos. 1–2 (2013): 51–80.

Piven, Francis Fox. "Welfare Reform and the Cultural Reconstruction of Low-Wage Labor Markets." In *New Poverty Studies: The Ethnography of Power, Politics, and Impoverished People in the United States*, edited by Judith G. Goode and Jeff Maskovsky, 135–51. New York: New York University Press, 2001.

Platt, Tony. "The State of Welfare: United States 2003." *Monthly Review* 55, no. 5 (2003): 13–28.

Pleggenkuhle, Breanne. "The Financial Cost of a Criminal Conviction: Context and Consequences." *Criminal Justice and Behavior* 45, no. 1 (2018): 121–45.

Pollack, Harold A., and Peter Reuter. "Welfare Receipt and Substance-Abuse Treatment among Low-Income Mothers: The Impact of Welfare Reform." *American Journal of Public Health* 96, no. 11 (2006): 2024–31.

Pompoco, Amanda, John Wooldredge, Melissa Lugo, Carrie Sullivan, and Edward J. Latessa. "Reducing Inmate Misconduct and Prison Returns with Facility Education Programs." *Criminology and Public Policy* 16, no. 2 (2017): 515–47.

Prescott, J. J., and Sonja B. Starr. "Expungement of Criminal Convictions: An Empirical Study." *Harvard Law Review* 133, no. 8 (2020): 2460–555.

Radcliffe, Polly, and Alex Stevens. "Are Drug Treatment Services Only for 'Thieving Junkie Scumbags'? Drug Users and the Management of Stigmatised Identities." *Social Sciences and Medicine* 67, no. 7 (2008): 1065–73.

Ray, Victor. "A Theory of Racialized Organizations." *American Sociological Review* 84, no. 1 (2019): 26–53.

Reichman, Nancy E., Julien O. Teitler, and Marah A. Curtis. "TANF Sanctioning and Hardship." *Social Service Review* 79, no. 2 (2005): 215–36.

Reisig, Michael D., Kristy Holtfreter, and Merry Morash. "Social Capital among Women Offenders: Examining the Distribution of Social Networks and Resources." *Journal of Contemporary Criminal Justice* 18, no. 2 (2002): 167–87.

Richie, Beth E. *Compelled to Crime: The Gender Entrapment of Battered Black Women*. New York: Routledge, 1996.

Richie, Beth E., and Kayla M. Martensen. "Resisting Carcerality, Embracing Abolition: Implications for Feminist Social Work Practice." *Affilia: Journal of Women and Social Work* 35, no. 1 (2020): 12–16.

Ridgeway, Celia L., and Shelley J. Correll. "Motherhood as a Status Characteristic." *Journal of Social Issues* 60, no. 4 (2004): 683–700.

Roddy, Ariel L., and Merry Morash. "The Connections of Parole and Probation Agent Communication Patterns with Female Offenders' Job-Seeking Self-Efficacy." *International Journal of Offender Therapy and Comparative Criminology* 64, no. 8 (2020): 774–90.

Roddy, Ariel L., Merry Morash, Elizabeth A. Adams, Amanda J. Holmstrom, Sandi W. Smith, and Jennifer E. Cobbina. "The Nature and Effects of Messages That Women Receive from Probation and Parole Agents in Conversations about Employment." *Criminal Justice and Behavior* 46, no. 4 (2019): 550–67.

Roddy, Ariel L., Merry Morash, and Miriam Northcutt Bohmert. "Spatial Mismatch, Race and Ethnicity, and Unemployment: Implications for Interventions with Women on Probation and Parole." *Crime and Delinquency* 68, no. 12 (2022): 2175–99.

Rose, Nancy E. "Scapegoating Poor Women: An Analysis of Welfare Reform." *Journal of Economic Issues* 35, no. 1 (2000): 143–57.

Rosen, Eva, Philip M. E. Garboden, and Jennifer E. Cossyleon. "Racial Discrimination in Housing: How Landlords Use Algorithms and Home Visits to Screen Tenants." *American Sociological Review* 86, no. 5 (2021).

Ross, Lauren. M., Anne B. Shlay, and Mario G. Picon. "You Can't Always Get What You Want: The Role of Public Housing and Vouchers in Achieving Residential Satisfaction." *Cityscape: A Journal of Policy Development and Research* 4, no. 1 (2009): 35–53.

Ruhland, Ebony L., Amber A. Petkus, Nathan W. Link, Jordan M. Hyatt, Bryan Holmes, and Symone Pate. "Monetary Sanctions in Community Corrections: Law, Policy, and Their Alignment with Correctional Goals." *Journal of Contemporary Criminal Justice* 37, no. 1 (2021): 108–27.

Russell Sage Foundation. "State Monetary Sanctions and the Costs of the Criminal Legal System: The Consequences of Monetary Sanctions." *RSF: The Russell Sage Foundation Journal of the Social Sciences* 8, no. 2 (2022): 1–243.

Saar, Malika Saada, Rebecca Epstein, Lindsay Rosenthal, and Yasmin Vafa. *The Sexual Abuse to Prison Pipeline: The Girls' Story.* Human Rights Project for Girls, Center on Poverty and Inequality at Georgetown Law, and Ms. Foundation for Women. Washington, DC, 2015. https://rights4girls.org/wp-content/uploads/r4g/2015/02/2015_COP_sexual-abuse_layout_web-1.pdf.

Safawi, Ali, and LaDonna Pavetti. *Most Parents Leaving TANF Work, but in Low-Paying, Unstable Jobs, Recent Studies Find.* Center on Budget and Policy Priorities. Washington, DC, 2020. www.cbpp.org/research/family-income-support/most-parents-leaving-tanf-work-but-in-low-paying-unstable-jobs.

Salas, Mario, and Angela Ciolfi. *Driven by Dollars: A State-by-State Analysis of Driver's License Suspension Laws for Failure to Pay Court Debt.* Charlottesville, Virginia: Legal Aid Justice Center, 2017.

Salisbury, Emily J., Breanna Boppre, and Bridget Kelly. "Gender-Responsive Risk and Need Assessment: Implications for the Treatment of Justice-Involved Women." In *Handbook on Risk and Need Assessment: Theory and Practice*, edited by Faye S. Taxman, 220–43. New York: Routledge, 2017.

Sampson, Robert J. *Great American City: Chicago and the Enduring Neighborhood Effect.* Chicago: University of Chicago Press, 2012.

Sampson, Robert J., Jeffrey D. Morenoff, and Thomas Gannon-Rowley. "Assessing 'Neighborhood Effects': Social Processes and New Directions in Research." *Annual Review of Sociology* 28 (2002): 443–78.

Schaffner, Laurie. *Girls in Trouble with the Law.* New Brunswick, New Jersey: Rutgers University Press, 2006.

Schott, Liz, and LaDonna Pavetti. *Changes in TANF Work Requirements Could Make Them More Effective in Promoting Employment.* Center on Budget and Policy Priorities. Washington, DC, 2013. www.cbpp.org/research/family -income-support/changes-in-tanf-work-requirements-could-make-them -more-effective-in.

———. *Many States Cutting TANF Benefits Harshly Despite High Unemployment and Unprecedented Need.* Center on Budget and Policy Priorities. Washington, DC, 2011. www.cbpp.org/research/many-states-cutting-tanf -benefits-harshly-despite-high-unemployment-and-unprecedented-need.

Schott, Liz, Ladonna Pavetti, and Ife Finch. *How States Have Spent Federal and State Funds under the TANF Block Grant.* Center on Budget and Policy Priorities. Washington, DC, 2012. https://www.cbpp.org/research/how-states-have -spent-federal-and-state-funds-under-the-tanf-block-grant.

Schrantz, Dennis, Stephen DeBor, and Marc Mauer. *Decarceration Strategies: How 5 States Achieved Substantial Prison Population Reductions.* Washington, DC: The Sentencing Project, 2018.

Scott, Christy K., Christine E. Grella, Michael L. Dennis, and Rodney R. Funk. "Predictors of Recidivism over 3 Years among Substance-Using Women Released from Jail." *Criminal Justice and Behavior* 41, no. 11 (2014): 1257–89.

Seng, Shen, and Todd D. Minton. *Jail Inmates in 2019.* Washington, DC: U.S. Department of Justice, Bureau of Justice Statistics, 2021.

The Sentencing Project. *Incarcerated Women and Girls.* Washington, DC, 2022. www.sentencingproject.org/wp-content/uploads/2016/02/Incarcerated -Women-and-Girls.pdf.

Seo, Chunghyeon, Bitna Kim, and Nathan E. Kruis. "Variation across Police Response Models for Handling Encounters with People with Mental Illness: A Systematic Review and Meta-Analysis." *Journal of Criminal Justice* 72, no. 1 (2021).

Sered, Susan Starr, and Maureen Norton-Hawk. *Can't Catch a Break: Gender, Jail, Drugs and the Limits of Personal Responsibility.* Oakland: University of California Press, 2014.

Servon, Lisa, Ava Esquier, and Gillian Tiley. "Gender and Financialization of the Criminal Justice System." *Social Sciences* 10, no. 11 (2021): 1–14.

Shantz, Katie, Ilham Dehry, Sarah Knowles, Sarah Minton, and Linda Giannarelli. *Welfare Rules Databook: State TANF Policies as of July 2019.* Washington, DC: U.S. Department of Health and Human Services, Office of Planning, Research, and Evaluation, Administration for Children and Families, 2020.

Shrivasta, Aditi, and Gina Azito Thompon. *TANF Cash Assistance Should Reach Millions More Families to Lessen Hardship.* Center on Budget and Policy Priorities. Washington, DC, 2022. www.cbpp.org/research/family -income-support/tanf-cash-assistance-should-reach-millions-more-families -to-lessen.

Simkins, Sandra B., Amy E. Hirsch, Erin McNamara Horvat, and Marjorie B. Moss. "The School to Prison Pipeline for Girls: The Role of Physical and Sexual Abuse." *Harvard Civil Rights Journal* 24, no. 4 (2004): 56–72.

Singer, Jefferson A. "Narrative Identity and Meaning Making across the Adult Lifespan: An Introduction." *Journal of Personality* 72, no. 3 (2004): 437–59.

Sirdifield, Coral. "The Prevalence of Mental Health Disorders Amongst Offenders on Probation: A Literature Review." *Journal of Mental Health* 21, no. 5 (2012): 485–98.

Skeem, Jennifer L., John Encandela, and Jennifer Eno Louden. "Perspectives on Probation and Mandated Mental Health Treatment in Specialized and Traditional Probation Departments." *Behavioral Sciences and the Law* 21 (2003): 429–58.

Skeem, Jennifer L., Jennifer Eno Louden, Devon L. L. Polaschek, and Jacqueline Camp. "Assessing Relationship Quality in Mandated Community Treatment: Blending Care with Control." *Psychological Assessment* 19, no. 4 (2007): 397–410.

Smith, Anna Marie. "Neoliberalism, Welfare Policy, and Feminist Theories of Social Justice." In "Feminist Theory and Welfare," special issue of *Feminist Theory* 9, no. 2 (2008): 131–44.

Smith, Sandi W., Jennifer J. Cornacchione, Merry Morash, Deborah A. Kashy, and Jennifer E. Cobbina. "Communication Style as an Antecedent to Reactance, Self-Efficacy, and Restoration of Freedom for Drug- and Alcohol-Involved Women on Probation and Parole." *Journal of Health Communication* 21, no. 5 (2016): 504–11.

Smith, Sharon G., Jieru Chen, Kathleen C. Basile, Leah K. Gilbert, Melissa T. Merrick, Nimesh Patel, Margie Walling, and Anurag Jain. *The National Intimate Partner and Sexual Violence Survey (NISVS): 2010–2012.* Atlanta, Georgia: Centers for Disease Control and Prevention, 2017.

Smith, Tyler, Kristina J. Thompson, and Michele Cadigon. "Sensemaking in the Legal System: A Comparative Case Study of Changes to Monetary Sanction Laws." *RSF: The Russell Sage Foundation Journal of the Social Sciences* 8, no. 1 (2022): 63–81.

Sohoni, Tracy, and Sylwia Piatkowska. "Begging for Crime? The Effect of State Laws Restricting Access to Temporary Assistance for Needy Families on Unsuccessful Completion of Parole." *Crime and Delinquency* 68, no. 11 (2022): 2115–45.

Spjeldnes, Solveig, and Sara Goodkind. "Gender Differences and Offender Reentry: A Review of the Literature." *Journal of Offender Rehabilitation* 48, no. 4 (May 1, 2009): 314–35.

Sprague, Joey. *Feminist Methods for Critical Researchers: Bridging Differences.* Walnut Creek, California: Altamira Press, 2005.

"State of Mental Health in America—Ranking the States." Mental Health America. 2017. www.mhanational.org/issues/2017–state-mental-health-america-ranking-states.

Steffensmeier, Darrell, Jennifer Schwartz, Hua Zhong, and Jeff Ackerman. "An Assessment of Recent Trends in Girls' Violence Using Diverse Sources: Is the Gender Gap Closing?" *Criminology* 43, no. 2 (2005): 355–406.

Steiner, Benjamin, James Wada, Craig Hemmens, and Velmer S. Burton. "The Correctional Orientation of Community Corrections: Legislative Changes in the Legally Prescribed Functions of Community Corrections 1992–2002." *American Journal of Criminal Justice* 29, no. 2 (2005): 141–59.

Stevens, Tia, Merry Morash, and Meda Chesney-Lind. "Are Girls Getting Tougher, or Are We Tougher on Girls? Probability of Arrest and Juvenile Court Oversight in 1980 and 2000." *Justice Quarterly* 28, no. 5 (2011): 719–44.

Stone, Rebecca, Merry Morash, Marva Goodson, Sandi W. Smith, and Jennifer E. Cobbina. "Women on Parole, Identity Processes, and Primary Desistance." *Feminist Criminology* 13, no. 4 (2018): 382–403.

Subramanian, Ram, Ruth Delaney, Stephen Roberts, and Nancy Fishman. *Incarceration's Front Door: The Misuse of Jails in America*. Brooklyn New York: Vera Institute of Justice, 2015.

Substance Abuse and Mental Health Services Administration. *SAMSA's Concept of Trauma and Guidance for a Trauma-Informed Approach*. Substance Abuse and Mental Health Services Administration. Rockville, Maryland, 2014. https://store.samhsa.gov/product/TIP-57-Trauma-Informed-Care-in -Behavioral-Health-Services/SMA14-4816.

Sykes, Bryan L., Meghan Ballard, Adrea Giuffre, Rebecca Goodsell, Daniela Kaiser, Vincente Clestino Mata, and Justin Sola. "Robbing Peter to Pay Paul: Public Assistance, Monetary Sanctions, and Financial Double-Dealing in America." *RSF: The Russell Sage Foundation Journal of the Social Sciences* 8, no. 1 (2022): 148–78.

Taxman, Faye S. "Community Supervision in the Post Mass Incarceration Era." *Federal Probation* 79, no. 2 (2015): 41–45.

Terry, April N., and L. Susan Williams. "On the Outside Looking In: Rural Girls, Trauma, and Involvement in the Criminal Justice System." *Journal of Aggression, Maltreatment and Trauma* 30, no. 3 (2021): 368–88.

Theimer, Kate, and David J. Hansen. "Attributions of Blame in a Hypothetical Child Sexual Abuse Case: Roles of Behavior Problems and Frequency of Abuse." *Journal of Interpersonal Violence* 35, nos. 11–12 (2020): 2142–63.

Trisi, Danilo, and LaDonna Pavetti. *TANF Weakening as a Safety Net for Poor Families*. Center on Budget and Policy Priorities. Washington, DC, 2012. www.cbpp.org/research/tanf-weakening-as-a-safety-net-for-poor-families.

Tyagi, Smita Vir. "Victimization, Adversity and Survival in the Lives of Women Offenders: Implications for Social Policy and Correctional Practice." *Canadian Woman Studies* 25, nos. 1–2 (2006): 133–38.

Uggen, Christopher, and Robert Stewart. "Piling On: Collateral Consequences and Community Supervision." *Minnesota Law Review* 99 (2015): 1871–910.

Ullman, Sarah E., Cynthia J. Najdowski, and Erika B. Adams. "Women, Alcoholics Anonymous, and Related Mutual Aid Groups: Review and Recommendations for Research." *Alcoholism Treatment Quarterly* 30 (2012): 443–86.

Ulrich, Miriam, and Ann Weatherall. "Motherhood and Infertility: Viewing Motherhood through the Lens of Infertility." *Feminism and Psychology* 10, no. 3 (2000): 323–36.

UNICEF. *Committing to Child Survival: A Promise Renewed*. New York: UNICEF's Division of Policy and Strategy, 2012.

———. *Ending Child Marriage: Progress and Prospects*. New York: United Nations Children's Fund, 2014.

U.S. Department of Education Office of Civil Rights. *An Overview of Exclusionary Discipline Practices in Public Schools for the 2017–18 School Year.* U.S. Office of Education. Washington, DC, 2021. https://ocrdata.ed.gov /assets/downloads/crdc-exclusionary-school-discipline.pdf/offices/list/ocr /data.html.

Valentine, Erin Jacobs, and Cindy Redcross. "Transitional Jobs after Release from Prison: Effects on Employment and Recidivism." *IZA Journal of Labor Policy* 4, no. 16 (2015): 1–17.

Van Voorhis, Patricia. "On Behalf of Women Offenders: Women's Place in the Science of Evidence-Based Practice." *Criminology and Public Policy* 11, no. 2 (2012): 111–45.

Viglione, Jill, Brandy L. Blasko, and Faye S. Taxman. "Organizational Factors and Probation Officer Use of Evidence-Based Practices: A Multilevel Examination." *International Journal of Offender Therapy and Comparative Criminology* 62, no. 6 (2018): 1648–67.

Viglione, Jill, Danielle S. Rudes, and Faye S. Taxman. "Probation Officer Use of Client-Centered Communication Strategies in Adult Probation Settings ". *Journal of Offender Rehabilitation* 56, no. 1 (2017): 38–60.

Ware, Dezara, and Deborah Dennis. *Best Practices for Increasing Access to SSI/ SSDI upon Exiting Criminal Justice Settings.* Substance Abuse and Mental Health Services Administration. Rockville, Maryland, 2013. https://nicic .gov/best-practices-increasing-access-ssissdi-upon-exiting-criminal-justice -settings.

Waschbusch, Daniel A., Rosanna P. Breaux, and Dara E. Babinski. "School-Based Interventions for Aggression and Defiance in Youth: A Framework for Evidence-Based Practice." *School Mental Health* 11, no. 1 (2019): 92–105.

Western, Bruce, and Christopher Wildeman. "The Black Family and Mass Incarceration." *Annals of the American Academy of Political and Social Science* 621, no. 1 (2009): 221–42.

Wilson, Amber, Brandon K. Applegate, and Riane M. Bolin. "Evidence-Based Practices in Community Corrections: Officers' Perceptions of Professional Relevance and Personal Competence." *American Journal of Criminal Justice* 47 (2022): 117–39.

Yang, Crystal S. "American Economic Review: Papers and Proceedings." 107, no. 5 (2017): 551–55.

Young, Amy M., and Hannah d'Arcy. "Older Boyfriends of Adolescent Girls: The Cause or a Sign of the Problem?" *Journal of Adolescent Health* 36, no. 5 (2005): 410–19.

Zvonkovich, Jordan, Stacy H. Haynes, and R. Barry Ruback. "A Continuum of Coercive Costs: A State-Level Analysis of the Imposition and Payment Enforcement of Statutory Fees." *Federal Sentencing Reporter* 34, nos. 2–3 (2022): 113–18.

Index

174–76, 179; resource diversion, 112;
trauma-informed, 102–3
messages affecting behavior: from agents,
59–61, 69–70, 76, 86, 123; from
treatment providers, 97, 113
methodology, 2–3, 6–9; analysis, 191; data
collection procedure, 190–91; data
sources, 24, 50, 68–69, 97–98, 118, 145,
190–91; research team, 4; sample
characteristics for agents, 189–90;
sample characteristics for supervised
women, 1–2, 51, 190
motherhood. *See* family making; gendered
expectations
motivational interviewing, 20, 68, 100;
reform needed, 179–81, 186

Narcotics Anonymous (NA). *See* Alcoholics
Anonymous (AA) and Narcotics
Anonymous (NA)
narrative identity theory, 5, 144–46; identity
and desistance, 5, 120; making good
from past difficulties, 129, 1x56–58;
religious redemption, 158–59;
stagnation, 5, 144–45
neoliberal policies, 9, 127; and marginalization, 117; in Michigan, 15–17; ideology,
127; safety-net programs, 14–15. *See
also* safety-net benefits

participants in the larger group (in multiple
chapters): Anna, 12, 42; Ariana, 7, 62;
Carley, 111–12, 137; Eddie, 11, 109–10;
Elsie, 57, 79–80, 177; Fiona, 8, 59–61,
105–6, 153–54, 159, 170; Francesca, 10,
33–35, 59, 91–92, 161; Grace, 110–11,
141; Hope, 7–8, 13, 103–5, 126,
158–59; Jasmine, 82–84, 107; Jolene,
33, 35, 113–16, 140, 152–53, 174,
179–80; Kiara, 102–3, 126; Kirsten, 86,
131–32, 158; Lana, 13, 103, 128–30,
174; Latrelle, 45–46, 129–30; Lena, 11,
132, 154–55, 177–78; Lily, 12, 61–62,
175, 177–78; Linsey, 65–66, 89–90,
107–9, 142, 157–58; Louisa, 125–26,
181–82; Lydia, 46, 87–88, 137, 159–60;
Lynette, 12, 37–38, 48, 89–90, 161–62;
Marie, 88–89, 130, 138; Mary, 33–34,
133–36, 163–64; Maya, 41–42, 44, 142;
Molly, 7, 58–59, 67, 83–85, 137,
157–58, 183–84; Pamela, 12, 92–93,
129, 179; Renee, 46, 57; Sally, 40, 46,
169; Shannon, 60–61, 135, 162–64,

178; Sugar, 45, 62, 85–86; Tina, 3–4,
125, 138, 155–58, 178; Tova, 11, 133,
139, 155; Vivian, 44–45, 137, 168
participants with touchstone stories: Bree,
27, 54, 56, 76–77, 100–101, 119,
124–26, 139, 146–47, 152, 168, 170;
Carla, 30, 54–55, 72–74, 98–99,
119–20, 149–50, 152, 170; Carmen,
24–27, 52–54, 70–72, 100, 118–19,
145–46, 152; Mallory, 28–30, 55, 77,
101, 123, 150–52, 168, 170, 176–78;
Marion, 30–31, 55–56, 77–78, 99,
123–24, 150–52; Raven, 31–32, 56–57,
74–76, 99, 121–23, 147–49, 152
Personal Protection and Affordable Care
Act (PPACA), 139, 186, 150. *See also*
safety-net benefits, medical care and
insurance
poverty causes: costs of conviction, 51–52;
interdependent benefits, 140–43;
neoliberal policies, 9, 14–17, 147; reform
needed, 168–69, 170–73, 181–84
probation and parole in Michigan, 18–19,
179–81; structure, 17, 68; treatment
resources, 18–19, 199n56, 204n5. *See
also* agent advocacy; agent communication pattern; agent referrals; agent
relationship style; agent variation;
collaborative case management;
motivational interviewing

race effects: adultification and school push
out, 169; childhood bullying, 45–46,
129; conviction costs, 172; employment
opportunity, 117, 127–29, 133, 136;
housing, 117, 137; intimate partner
violence, 75; juvenile court criminalization, 26; men's mass incarceration, 75;
neighborhood and residential mobility,
9–13, 117, 120, 122–23, 127, 118,
134–36; racial segregation, 136;
safety-net benefits, 183–85; trauma, 102
reform needed: drop licensing restrictions,
182; end school to prison pipeline,
169–70; expunge criminal history, 182;
improve community supervision, 178–81;
reduce conviction costs, 170–73; reduce
incarceration, 174–76; reform in a box,
186–87; structural change, 185–86;
trauma-informed practice, 170, 179
relapse: after benefits cut, 57, 79, 114–15,
139; agent response, 82, 84, 92–94;
recovery, 109, 115, 153, 179–80

Founded in 1893,
UNIVERSITY OF CALIFORNIA PRESS
publishes bold, progressive books and journals
on topics in the arts, humanities, social sciences,
and natural sciences—with a focus on social
justice issues—that inspire thought and action
among readers worldwide.

The UC PRESS FOUNDATION
raises funds to uphold the press's vital role
as an independent, nonprofit publisher, and
receives philanthropic support from a wide
range of individuals and institutions—and from
committed readers like you. To learn more, visit
ucpress.edu/supportus.

www.ingramcontent.com/pod-product-compliance
Lightning Source LLC
Chambersburg PA
CBHW020851270326
41928CB00006B/650